DATE DUE FOR RETURN

LAW AND THE WEAKER PARTY

An Anglo-Swedish Comparative Study

LAW AND THE WEAKER PARTY

An Anglo-Swedish Comparative Study

General Editors

Steve Anderman
Alan C. Neal
Tore Sigeman
Anders Victorin

VOLUME II

THE ENGLISH EXPERIENCE

Edited by

STEVE ANDERMAN

PROFESSIONAL BOOKS LTD

Printed and published
in Great Britain in 1982 by
Professional Books Ltd.
Milton Trading Estate, Abingdon
Oxfordshire

ISBN 0-86205.044.8

FOREWORD

Law and the Weaker Party is the result of a partnership, initially forged between the Schools of Law in the Universities of Stockholm, Sweden and Warwick, England, which has developed during the past five years. Building upon previous collaboration in the area of industrial relations law, the Editors have sought to explore, through comparative study, some of the problems encountered by the legal systems in England and Sweden when regulating relationships in the areas of housing, consumer, and employment and labour relations law.

The selection for the material for the second volume, as in the case of the first volume, was prompted by a desire to investigate aspects of the relationship between law and the weaker party at three distinct levels. First there was the question of how statute law was used directly to offset differences in bargaining power in individual contractual relationships. For this we looked to consumer protection law, landlord and tenant law and individual employment law. Secondly, there was the issue of how the law responded to collective organisations formed autonomously by individuals to provide a private counterweight to overwhelming bargaining power wielded by other individuals, organisations or groups. The law of collective labour relations was the obvious starting point. However, elements of collective bargaining organisations were also to be found on the Swedish housing market. Finally, there was the question of protection offered by the law of social welfare, social security and its inter-relationship with the institutions of the labour market.

The difference between the two volumes is that whereas Volume I concentrated upon the Swedish experience, Volume II takes as its starting point the English experience.

In Part I of this volume David Yates outlines the major rules relating to security of tenure in rented residential property under English law, so as to provide a basis for comparative study. The paper concludes with an examination and an evaluation of the various arguments that have been raised both in favour of and against security of tenure as an aim of housing law.

In his response, Anders Victorin shows that although security of tenure in the Swedish rental market does not possess the elaborate formal categories of the English system there are great similarities in the substantive content of the rules. In other words, it is clear that the legislators have addressed themselves to the same problems and the same situations.

Tim Murphy's contribution consists of a comprehensive examination of the law of home ownership. He attempts to show how, within the field of home ownership, English courts and Parliament have come to designate particular social/economic relationships as appropriate for intervention. He also highlights the *ad hoc* and largely reactive way in which this has occurred, in contrast with the more comprehensive manner in which this has proceeded in other jurisdictions.

Carl Hemström's response contains a description of current Swedish law relevant to the right of spouses and co-habitants to the common home when their relationship ends. He also provides a brief summary of the rules in the Swedish Housing Acts for the protection of the weaker party.

In Part II, in his paper on the "Applicability of general rules of private law to consumer disputes" Francis Reynolds puts forward the view that it is inappropriate to amend the law by introducing special rules for consumer disputes, and that law reform should rather aim at modifying the general rules of law so that they may more readily take in the special consumer problems which have been identified in recent years. He suggests that the special rules suggested for consumers would often be equally appropriate to commercial disputes, and that it may be only considerations of practical politics which have led to the introduction of rules covering consumer cases only.

Jan Hellner argues in his contribution that distinguishing between consumer and commercial sales is less important than the need to give due allowance to the differences between various kinds of goods and the requirements of various buyers. There is a problem of how far freedom of contract should be restricted in both types of sales.

In his paper surveying English law, John Miller contrasts the advances in substantive law enacted for the benefit of consumers with the relative lack of progress in improving procedures for individual and collective consumer redress. He notes the recent developments in small claims and arbitration procedures, and considers the possibility of collective redress through class actions and a wider role for consumer organisations and public agencies.

Lars Heuman's paper deals with the practice and procedure of the Swedish general advertising board, and looks at the possibilities of limiting legal support in pursuit of similar objectives to an experimental case.

In Part III, Steve Anderman provides a survey of the current British law of labour relations. He describes the way in which the system of collective bargaining grew autonomously with little support from the law, drawing attention to the way in which the right to strike was defined in terms of negative immunities rather than positive rights. He also discusses the consequences that the earlier autonomous development has entailed for the more recent attempts to provide legal support for trade unions and to apply legal restrictions to strike action and the closed shop.

Tore Sigeman compares the law of industrial conflict in Gt. Britain and Sweden. He explains why, unlike Gt. Britain, there has been no need in Sweden for trade union immunities, and how collective agreements in Sweden are legally enforcible. He suggests that a system of binding collective agreements in conjunction with a broad right to take sympathetic action might contribute to a more centralised trade union movement and a better economic performance in the labour market.

Håkan Göransson draws a distinction between the right to strike and the freedom to strike, and suggests that the British system of immunities satisfactorily establishes only a freedom to strike and not an adequate right to strike.

Finally, Laurence Lustgarten describes the evolution of unemployment compensation in Britain since the War, emphasising the influence work incentive considerations have had on the manner in which compensation has been designed and administered. Statutory schemes outside as well as within the social security system are considered, as is the impact of provisions of revenue law. He concludes that the compensation now caters inadequately for the great majority of the unemployed, largely because it has become increasingly dominated by a simplistic view of economic deprivation as a goad to re-entry into the labour market.

EDITOR'S FOREWORD

This volume contains revised papers from the second Anglo-Swedish Comparative Law Seminar, held at the University of Stockholm in September 1981. The situation described here therefore represents the state of the law at that time. Where developments have taken place between September 1981 and the completion of this volume, these have been mentioned by way of additional footnotes. The task of editing was completed in August 1982.

We would like to thank the Social Science Research Council for their financial support to the Seminar and the Humanistisk-samhällsvetenskapliga forskningsrådet for their financial support of the Seminar and this publication

A debt of gratitude is also owed to Sally Venebles and the secretarial staff of the University of Warwick Law Faculty, without whose support and assistance the task of producing this volume would have been considerably more difficult.

Williamscot   Steve Anderman
August 1982

TABLE OF CONTENTS

PART I

HOUSING LAW

SECURITY OF TENURE IN THE ENGLISH RENTAL MARKET

by

David Yates

In this paper I propose to select what are the principal features of the law governing security of tenure in English property law. The first thing that will no doubt strike a foreign lawyer is the tremendous complexity of the English law. This is in part due to the rather piecemeal growth of the residential tenancy code, in part due to the desire on the part of landlords to find avoidance devices (and the consequent need for the legislature and the judiciary to "plug" gaps), but mainly due to the intensely "political" nature of housing law legislation in England. The desire of the two major political parties to repeal the "undesirable" parts of each other's legislative activities, while at the same time preserving the uncontroversial parts and adding to them new provisions, has resulted in a steady growth of laws of ever-increasing complexity. It is not my aim to set these out *in extenso* here. There are many English texts on the law of landlord and tenant to which the dedicated reader may refer. My purpose is to isolate, and to some extent simplify (though I hope not at the expense of accuracy) those features of landlord and tenant law that relate to security of tenure (omitting, through lack of time and space, those provisions protecting the "long" leaseholder and the business tenant), with a view to providing a basis for comparative study. I trust that I have said enough about the English system for the Swedish lawyer to be able to discern what the English "way of doing things" is, at what points the English and Swedish systems proceed on common assumptions, and at what points they depart. I conclude with some remarks upon what I see as the justification for embodying a principle of security of tenure in landlord and tenant law. These, I hope, will have validity both for English and Swedish housing law and, indeed, for all housing systems operating within capitalist economies.

A. The Private Rented Sector

Before the Second World War the private rented sector provided housing for the majority of the population. By 1947 the percentage had fallen to 61 per cent and the decline was thereafter rapid. By 1980 the proportion of housing provided by the private rented sector was a little under 12 per cent. Since the end of the First World War, the place of the private landlord had increasingly been taken by local authorities and by the growth in ownerьccupation. For over 150 years the privately rented sector dominated the British housing scene, but its recent decline has been very rapid. Unlike the situation in Sweden and North America, virtually no new housing has been built for short-term private letting since before the Second World War, and even between the wars the numbers built were very small indeed.[1] The reasons for this dramatic decline have been most ably described elsewhere[2] and it is beyond the scope of this paper to re-examine that ground.

The private rental sector, then, plays a continuously decreasing role in the United Kingdom's recent past and future housing policy. Demolition of slum and unfit properties removes more dwellings each year from the private rental market. Eighty per cent of those that remain were constructed prior to the First World War and are either small houses lacking the amenities now considered essential, or are larger houses once occupied by a single family but now in multiple occupation, frequently without the necessary modifications called for by this intensification of user. Despite the impact of improvement grants introduced by the Housing Act, 1969, a great many of these houses are still unfit. The private landlord has been, for many years, subject to restrictions and disincentives (some of which were rendered most necessary by the social evils and abuses that some notorious landlords visited upon their tenants), while other forms of tenure prospered. Britain has yet to resolve the great housing dilemma of whether it really wants a privately rented sector or not, but at present the law bolsters up this crumbling private sector with a vast array of procedures and controls, many statutory in origin such as the public health legislation, the Rent Acts and the rent allowance system, and some judicial, such as the common law rules of landlord and tenant. In contrast the public sector, whose numerical and social importance is paramount, received, until the Housing Act 1980, scant attention from the legislature and even less from the courts. The proliferation of statutory rules and regulations governing the private sector makes it difficult for those not intimately acquainted with the English system to discern upon what principles the statutory code operates. It is paradoxical that government intervention, through housing standards and rent control, coupled with changing economic circumstances, slum clearance and redevelopment, and the growth of alternative forms of tenure, has resulted in a vast and complex body of law regulating an ever-decreasing share of the housing market.

[1] For a concise and useful account see Murie, Niner & Watson, *Housing Policy and the Housing System*, Chapter 6.
[2] *Ibid.*, pp. 174-189; see also Berry, *Housing: The Great British Failure, passim.*

B. Protected Tenancies
The bulk of the current legislation regulating private sector tenancies (called regulated tenancies) is to be found in the Rent Act 1977. Before a tenancy can be regarded as "protected" within the meaning given to that term by the legislation, three distinct requirements must be fulfilled.

1. There must be a tenancy under which a dwelling house is let as a separate dwelling: Rent Act 1977, s.1.

Protection is only conferred where the relationship of landlord and tenant exists between the parties. This will depend upon the essential requirements of a lease being present, including either the formal creation of a lease or an enforceable agreement for a lease. The Rent Act 1977 does not, however, accord the status of "protected tenancy" to an occupation of premises governed by a mere licence or permission, as opposed to a letting or tenancy.[3] This is a rule developed by the courts to deal with a variety of situations where no true tenancy could be said to exist and where the existing presumptions which gave rise to a tenancy at common law had to be reconsidered in the light of the judiciary's view of the purposes of the Rent Act. It has unfortunately produced a morass of litigation, the main result of which has been to point the way to landlords to indulge in wholesale avoidance of considerable portions of the Rent Act 1977, to the detriment of some residential occupants.

The Rent Act 1977, s.1, provides that a protected tenancy is restricted to the letting of a dwelling-house which may be a house or part of a house. These words are not defined in the statute, but in most cases their meaning is obvious. However, they are wider than simply the normal house or flat residence. Two separate flats, if let together as a dwelling, may constitute a house[4], as may a house and adjacent cottage similarly let[5]. Part of a house may also be a dwelling, and this may be a single room, provided it contains essential living accommodation. A single house, therefore, in the popular sense, may contain several dwelling-houses for the purposes of the Rent Act 1977[6].

The word "let", in addition to indicating the need for a tenancy, also qualifies the words "as a separate dwelling", which means that if the premises are let for some other purpose, the fact that there is a tenancy will not

---

[3] Although residential licensees within R.A. 1977, Pt. V, may not now be evicted without a court order: H.A. 1980, s. 69, amending the Protection from Eviction Act 1977, s. 3(2A); *cf.* H.A. 1980, s. 48(1), which affords the same protection to licensees as is granted to "secure" tenants in the public sector.
[4] *Langford Property Co Ltd* v *Goldrich* [1949] 1 K.B. 511
[5] *Whitty* v *Scott-Russell* [1950] 2 K.B. 32
[6] *Abraham* v *Webster* [1925] 1 K.B. 563

result in protection. The premises must be let for residential purposes, such purposes to be expressly or impliedly stated in the lease or tenancy agreement[7].

2. The dwelling-house must have a rateable value which does not exceed prescribed limits on particular dates: Rent Act, 1977,s.4.

These provisions are exceedingly complex and turn, in part, upon when the premises first appeared in the local authority's valuation list for rating (local taxation) purposes. The general flavour of the provision will be clear if I confine myself to properties that first appeared in the local authority's valuation list on or after April 1, 1973. In these cases the tenancy will be protected (provided it satisfies the other conditions) if its premises have a rateable value which is equal to or less than £1,500 in Greater London, and £750 elsewhere. A dwelling is deemed to be within the prescribed rateable value limits unless the contrary is shown. The statutory presumption so raised can be rebuted by obtaining a certificate from the clerk to the rating authority showing that the rateable value is outside the statutory limits[8].

3. The tenancy must not come within any of the various categories of exempt agreements.

Even where a dwelling is within the prescribed rateable value limits, and is let as a separate dwelling, the tenancy is not protected unless it falls outside the various categories of tenancies excepted from the application of the Rent Act 1977. These are:

(a) Tenancies exempt by virtue of the nature of the premises
     i Tenancies of houses let with a substantial quantity of other land[9].
     ii Mixed business and residential tenancies. Where the premises are used by the tenant partly for residence and partly for business use, the tenancy is not protected under the Rent Act but is protected under the business tenancy code contained in the Landlord and Tenant Act 1954, Pt. II[10].
     iii Agricultural holdings occupied by the farmer[11].
     iv Public houses[12].
     v. Parsonage houses[13].

---

[7] *Wolfe* v *Hogan* [1949] 2 K.B. 194
[8] See *R* v *City of Westminster London Borough Rent Officer, ex parte Rendall* [1973] 3 All E.R. 119.
[9] See R.A. 1977, ss. 6, 26.
[10] R.A. 1977, s. 24(3).
[11] R.A. 1977, ss. 10, 137. See *Sherwood* v *Moody* [1952] 1 All E.R. 389; *Maunsell* v *Olins* [1975] 1 All E.R. 16.
[12] R.A. 1977, s. 11.
[13] *Bishop of Gloucester* v *Cunningham* [1943] 1 K.B. 101.

vi. Overcrowded or insanitary dwellings[14].

This is a curious head of exemption, since it results in tenants occupying overcrowded or unfit houses remaining unprotected by the Rent Act. No doubt the public interest in preventing the use of such property as residential accommodation outweighed any particular interest an individual tenant may have in resisting a possession action or seeking a fair rent. Nevertheless, it has the curious result that landlords who neglect their properties or over-crowd, while suffering minor criminal law penalties, may be assisted in preserving their perceived freedom to deal with their properties as they wish by avoiding the fair rent and security of tenure provisions of the Rent Act.

(b) Tenancies exempt by virtue of the status of the landlord

    i. Crown property, other than property vested in the Crown Estate Commissioners[15].

    ii. Houses let by an exempt body[16].

Tenancies granted by a number of public and quasi-public bodies are not protected tenancies. The most important of these are tenancies granted by local authorities and housing associations. These now have their own code of protection under the Housing Act 1980 and are discussed later.

    iii. Dwellings let by a resident landlord[17].

A tenancy will not be a protected tenancy if it was granted on or after August 14, 1974, by a landlord who is resident in the premises. For the exemption to operate the dwelling-house must form part only of a building and, except where the dwelling itself also forms part of a flat, the building must not be a purpose-built block of flats. A "purpose-built" block is defined as a building which, as constructed, contained and still contains two or more flats. A flat is a dwelling-house which forms part only of a building and is separated horizontally from another dwelling-house which forms part of the same building[18]. The circumstances normally covered by the exemp-tion are where a two or three storey dwelling-house constructed as a single dwelling, is divided into two or more flats and the landlord lives in one flat [19]. There are complex rules covering the need for *personal* residence by the landlord in another dwelling-house in the same building or flat, both at the time the tenancy was granted, and throughout the duration of the tenancy. There are also provisions allowing for certain gaps in the landlord's resi-dence without depriving the tenancy of its exempt status.[20]

[14] R.A. 1977 s. 101(1).
[15] R.A. 1977, s. 13, as amended by H.A. 1980, s. 73.
[16] R.A. 1977, ss. 14-16.
[17] R.A. 1977, s. 12 as amended by H.A. 1980, s. 63.
[18] R.A. 1977, Sched. 2, para. 4.
[19] *Cf. Bardrick* v *Haycock* [1976] 31 P & C.R. 420.
[20] See R.A. 1977, Sched. 2.

So long as the tenancy is precluded from being a protected tenancy by virtue of the resident landlord exception, the tenancy is treated as a "restricted contract". These tenancies constitute the major group subject to the jurisdiction of rent tribunals. Rent tribunals can fix "reasonable" rents (as opposed to the "fair" rents fixed by rent officers in respect of protected tenancies) but, as a result of the Housing Act 1980, they cannot grant security of tenure in respect of contracts made on or after November 28th 1980[21].

    iv. Tenancies granted by universities or colleges of further education to students[22].

    v. Tenants sharing with landlords[23].

Most cases of sharing with landlords will be covered by the rules governing resident landlords discussed in (iii) above. However, not all cases of sharing will fall within the rules of the resident landlord exception. If a tenant is in exclusive occupation of part of his accomodation and shares other living accomodation with his landlord, the tenancy will not be protected.

    vi. Assured tenancies.

During the debates on the Housing Bill 1980, the government expressed concern about the lack of incentive for persons wanting to invest new money in the provision of residential accommodation for private letting. The lack of incentive, it was argued, arose from the status of irremovability of the protected tenant, and the inability of an investor relying on "fair rents" to obtain the same return on his capital as he could hope to obtain in other markets. Many informed commentators, however, see the problem as too deep seated and too long standing to be cured by the simple expedient of providing exemption from some of the most recent landlord and tenant legislation, and the government's hope that the present trend can be reversed by creating assured tenancies must be misconceived. Nevertheless, in a vain attempt to encourage new building, the government devised the assured tenancy as a much publicised feature of the 1980 housing legislation[24]. In appearance, it will be an ordinary protected or housing association tenancy. In practice, it will be free from the Rent Act security and rent controls, but subject to the regime set out in the Landlord and Tenant Act 1954, Pt. II, governing *business* tenancies. There is no control over the level of initial rents. The provisions for statutory continuation of the tenancy, formal notices to terminate or request renewal of the lease, the right to *apply* for a *new* lease with the court settling both terms and rent, the grounds for landlord opposition to a new lease, and the compensation provisions which apply to business tenancies, apply with only minor modifications to the new

[21] H.A. 1980, s. 69
[22] R.A. 1977, s. 8
[23] R.A. 1977, s. 21
[24] H.A. 1980, s. 56

assured tenancies (see Housing Act 1980, Schedule 5). Aside from the absence of rent control, therefore, the assured tenancy provides a security of tenure rather similar to that provided by the Swedish Rent Act.

However, before an assured tenancy can be granted, three important conditions must be satisfied. First, since the creation of the tenancy, the landlord's interest must have belonged to an "approved body" There is considerable doubt about the nature and identity of these approved bodies who will responsibly manage assured tenancies free of the usual statutory restraints. Lord Bellwin, speaking for the government when pressed on the matter in the House of Lords (see H.L. Deb. July 2, 1980, Co. 432), spoke of encouraging into private renting, as landlords, building societies, pension funds, insurance companies or housing associations backed by such bodies. But, to ensure that *new* money is introduced, the second condition is that construction work must first have begun on the premises after the passing of the Housing Act on August 8, 1980. The third condition is that, before the tenant first occupied, no part of the premises may be let to anyone other than under an assured tenancy.

It seems highly unlikely that bodies such as building societies and pension funds are going to invest their money by building new property for renting in the residential market. Only a handful of bodies have so far applied for and been granted the status of an "approved body". The practical significance of these assured tenancy provisions is therefore slight.

(c) Tenancies exempt by virtue of the terms of the tenancy

    i. Tenancies at a low rent.

A tenancy is not a protected tenancy if no rent is payable under the tenancy at all or the rent payable is less than two-thirds of the rateable value[25].

    ii. Lettings with board or attendance.

The Rent Act 1977, s. 7(1) provides that a tenancy is not protected if the dwelling is let, bona fide, at a rent which includes a payment in respect of board or attendance. Section 7(2) enacts that this requirement cannot be met unless the amount of rent fairly attributable to attendance (though not to board, which is not mentioned in the sub-section) forms a substantial part of the whole rent, having regard to the value of the attendance to the tenant. The dwelling must be "bona fide" let, which means that sham transactions (for example, where the tenancy makes reference to board and attendance which is not, in fact, provided) are excluded.

"Attendance" means service personal to the tenant (such as flat cleaning or porterage). "Board" means the provision of sufficient food to exclude the

---

[25] R.A. 1977, s. 5(1). See *Barnes* v *Barratt* [1970] 2 All E.R. 483.

"de minimis" principle or to avoid the allegation that the transaction is a sham. It does not necessarily involve the provision of full meals[26].

iii. Holiday homes.

The Rent Act 1977, s. 9, exempts from protected tenancy status a dwelling let for the purpose of a holiday occupation. This provision has undoubtedly encouraged landlords to let premises, ostensibly for a holiday, in some unlikely locations, simply to avoid the protection of the Act. The courts are then faced with the difficult task of deciding whether the arrangement is a genuine holiday let, entitled to the exemption, or a sham, when it is not[27].

iv. Shorthold lettings.

Shorthold lettings are creatures both of the Housing Act 1980 and of the government's view, already commented upon, that a considerable amount of property is lost to the residential market because landlords cannot be sure of recovering possession unless they can bring themselves within one of the mandatory grounds for possession under the Rent Act 1977 (discussed below). As a result, it is argued, landlords will tend to sell houses when they become vacant. When vacant houses form part of deceased persons' estates, the new owners will, it is alleged, be inclined to leave them empty with a view to sale with vacant possession. Perhaps, with slightly more force, it is argued that much flat property is left vacant when it is over lock-up business accomodation, as the landlord does not want to find himself in the position where he can dispose of the vacant business premises only subject to an existing residential tenant of the flat above.

Much interest and not a little heat was generated by the suggestion of legislation enabling the creation of short term lets free from statutory security of tenure and rent control. In the event, the Housing Act 1980 provides for lettings free from the normal security of tenure provisions, when the short term has expired, (the term has to be for not less than one year nor more than five), but as originally devised, still subject to the usual "fair" rent regulation. The Labour Party have stated their intention to repeal the relevant legislation. Whether that intention is carried out will depend not only on the exigencies of the polling booth, but also on whether it can be established that the existence of shortholds has led to a general reduction in the number of protected tenancies, in no way compensated by the increase of additional property brought onto the letting market.

The new legal provisions are to be found in the Housing Act 1980, ss. 52-55. They are extremely complex, obscure and, in places ambiguous. A

[26] See *Palser* v *Grinling* [1948] A.C.291; *Woodward* v *Docherty* [1974] 2 All E.R. 844; *Mann* v *Cornella* [1980] 254 E.G. 403.
[27] See *Kemp* v *Cunningham* [1975] L.A.G. Bull. 192; *Buchmann* v *May* [1978] 2 All E.R. 993. *R* v *Camden London Borough Rent Officer, ex p. Plant* [1980] 257 E.G. 713.
[28] Protected Shorthold Tenancies (Rent Registration) Order 1981, S. I. 1578.

detailed discussion of these statutory rules is beyond the scope of this paper but it is inevitable that, if much used, the provisions are bound to generate much litigation. It may be the very obscurity and complexity of the law that discourages its use by landlords but, that notwithstanding, the legislation as originally drafted did contain one extra-ordinary contradiction in that, in order to qualify for the exempt shorthold status, a prospective landlord had to apply for and obtain a certificate of fair rent from a rent officer *before* the grant of the tenancy, and make an application for the registration of the rent within 28 days of the grant. A failure to observe the rent provision could only be waived in possession proceedings if the court thought it just and equitable to make a possession order. On the government's assumption that it is the statutory framework of protection in the Rent Act 1977 that is causing so much loss of residential property to the rental market, the fact that there had to be a registered rent for the premises or that the landlord must apply for one, before the letting can qualify for exempt shorthold status was likely to discourage landlords from utilising the shorthold provisions in the first place. As a result of landlord and "back-bench" pressure, therefore, a hasty amendment to the 1980 Act was made in 1981, exempting shorthold lettings from the fair rent provisions[28], (except in London).

C. Statutory Security of Tenure

1. The Statutory Tenancy

(a) Nature

A statutory tenancy is not an interest in property, but a "status of irremovability", or a personal right, conferred by the Rent Act 1977 to enable a tenant, whose tenancy has expired, to remain in possession of his dwelling[29]. The statutory tenancy cannot be assigned or transferred, except under the limited provisions of the Rent Act 1977, Schedule 1, para. 13[30]. A statutory tenancy cannot be disposed of by will and does not vest in the tenant's personal representatives[31] unlike the contractual tenancy, on the termination of which the statutory tenancy arises. Similarly, a statutory tenancy cannot vest in a trustee in bankruptcy[32]. It cannot be sub-let as a whole, because the tenant has no estate out of which to create such an interest[33], and because retention of possession of at least part of the dwelling is, as we shall

---

[29] See *Keeves v Dean* [1924] 1 K.B. 685; *Thompson v Ward* [1953] 2 Q.B. 153; *Atyoe v Fardoe* [1978] 37 P. & C.R. 494. See also *Gofor Investments Ltd v Roberts* [1975] 29 P & C.R. 366, per Lawton L.J. at p. 374. *Cf.* Hand, [1980] Conv. 351.
[30] *Maxted v McAll* [1952] C.P.L. 185; *Atyoe v Fardoe* [1978] 37 P & C.R. 494.
[31] *Lovibond & Sons v Vincent* [1929] 1 K.B. 687.
[32] *Sutton v Dorf* [1932] 2 K.B. 304.
[33] *Solomon v Orwell* [1954] 1 W.L.R. 624.

see, essential to the maintenance by the tenant of his statutory tenancy. The mere sub-letting of part of the premises, however, does not necessarily remove protection from that part.

The emphasis on personal occupation by the tenant enables him to defend or assert this right of occupation against unlawful interference. A statutory tenant can obtain damages for trespass or unlawful re-entry by the landlord[34] and an injunction to restrain a trespass or a threatened trespass[35]. If he loses his status as a statutory tenant, however, his right to maintain an action for trespass is also lost[36]. A statutory tenant can recover damages for breach of the covenant for quiet enjoyment, and for unlawful eviction, together with an order restoring him to possession in such circumstances[37]. However, he will not be able to claim protection against a person claiming by title paramount, if the contractual tenancy out of which the statutory tenancy arose would not be a protected tenancy[38]. So, if a mortgagee holds a charge and there is a clause in it whereby there are to be no tenancies granted or surrendered except with the written consent of the mortgagee, any tenancy granted by the mortgagor without such consent will not be binding on the mortgagee, and is not capable of being a protected or statutory tenancy within the legal relationship of mortgagor and mortgagee and, should the mortgagee seek possession from the tenant, it will not be granted unless it is sought bona fide and reasonably for the purpose of enforcing the security. Possession will not be granted where the mortgagee is simply doing the landlord a favour to enable him to circumvent the Rent Act[40].

An important difference between a statutory tenancy and a contractual tenancy is that a statutory tenancy subsists only in relation to the dwelling-house, whereas a contractual tenancy of a house on land is a tenancy of the land to which the house is annexed. This means that if the house is destroyed, the statutory tenancy will come to an end[41]. A contractual tenancy, on the other hand, will continue until determined, regardless of the condition of the premises, unless the premises are flats[42]. The mere occurrence of damage rendering the house uninhabitable will not necessarily destroy the statutory tenancy unless the damage is so considerable that the house has substantially

---

[34] *Cruise* v *Terrell* [1922] 1 K.B. 664.
[35] *Maynard* v *Maynard* [1969] 1 All E.R. 1
[36] *Thompson* v *Ward* [1953] 1 W.L.R. 672; *Olidowura* v *Fulmuk* [1975] C.L.Y. 1929.
[37] *Dudley & District Benefit Building Society* v *Emerson* [1949]Ch. 707.
[38] *Ibid*., but *cf.* Smith [1977] 41 Conv. 197 and Yates & Hawkins, *Landlord and Tenant Law*, Chap. 3, Sect. II,D.
[39] *Quennell* v *Maltby* [1979] 1 All E.R. 568.
[40] *Morleys (Birmingham) Ltd* v *Slater* [1950] 1 K.B. 506.
[41] *Ellis & Sons Amalgamated Properties* v. *Sisman* [1948] 1 K.B. 653; *Hemns* v. *Wheeler* [1948] 2 K.B. 61.
[42] When the lease will probably be frustrated, at least if above the ground floor: see *National Carriers* v *Panalpina (Northern)* [1981] 2 W.L.R. 45; Yates & Hawkins, *Landlord and Tenant Law*, Chap. 5.

ceased to exist[43]. Presumably the statutory tenancy will also be lost, even when damage is not so substantial, if the tenant abandons the premises or fails to show the required *animus revertendi*.

The nature of the statutory tenancy must appear a curious animal to a Swedish lawyer. The reluctance of English law to go all the way and allow the tenant a new tenancy (save in the comparatively rare assured tenancy and in the case of the "long lease", i.e. for more than 21 years) is difficult to understand. No doubt it is tied up with rather quaint notions of freedom of property and contract and a reluctance to confer a "proprietary interest" on a tenant for a longer period than that for which he originally bargained.

(b) Commencement

When a protected tenancy has been brought to an end, either by the landlord of by effluxion of time, the person who, immediately before the termination, was the protected tenant, becomes the statutory tenant if and so long as he occupies the house as his residence[44]. Where a protected tenancy is granted to joint tenants and one of them leaves the premises before the expiry of the contractual term, the tenant remaining on the premises is entitled to become a statutory tenant of the premises at the end of the contractual term[45]. So, a statutory tenancy comes into existence only if three conditions are satisfied: the tenant is holding over from a contractual tenancy which has terminated; the contractual tenancy was a protected tenancy when it terminated; and the tenant continues to occupy the house or flat as his residence.

No statutory tenancy can arise while a contractual tenancy remains in existence. While the contractual tenancy continues, the rights and duties of the parties are governed by the terms and conditions of their agreement or by terms implied in their agreement by law, except in so far as such rights are affected by the tenant's status as a protected tenant. The statutory tenancy arises regardless of the consent of the landlord, whose common law rights are curtailed by the Rent Act 1977. This has affected the attitude taken by the courts to the relationship between contractual and statutory tenancies, and has led to tight control of the circumstances in which a holding over will give rise to a new contractual tenancy.

Apart from certain very limited circumstances[46], the mode by which a contractual tenancy comes to an end is immaterial, since the purpose of the Rent Act 1977, s. 2, is to confer a statutory tenancy on a contractual tenant whose tenancy has determined. So, for example, a tenant whose contractual tenancy has terminated by forfeiture for breach of an obligation, will

[43] *Morleys (Birmingham) Ltd* v *Slater* [1950] 1 K.B. 506.
[44] R.A. 1977, s. 2(1) (a).
[45] *Lloyd* v *Sadler* [1978] 2 W.L.R. 721.
[46] *E.g.* surrender, disclaimer and merger.

become a statutory tenant, even though the breach may give the landlord a ground for possession under the Rent Act[47]. The object of the Act is to ensure that possession will be granted only to a landlord who satisfies the conditions for recovery of possession.

The requirement of continued occupation is essentially a question of fact, although the courts have attempted to formulate some rules of guidance as to how the evidence should be assessed. Since a statutory tenancy is a personal right conferred by the Rent Act to enable a tenant to remain in his dwelling, it can be enjoyed only by a tenant who continues to *reside* there from the moment his contractual tenancy ends and who, should he go away for a period of temporary absence, intends to return[48].

The legal personality of some tenants may render them incapable of residing and thus of becoming statutory tenants. This is especially true of limited liability companies, who cannot plead vicarious residence for this purpose[49]. The question may also arise whether the premises themselves have retained their residential character, or still come within the requirements of being let as a separate dwelling. This is particularly a problem with premises let for mixed user; if the residential user has ceased by the time the contractual tenancy determines, no statutory tenancy arises.

Ceasing to reside in the premises because of their bad condition will not, of itself, justify a claim to be a statutory tenant, but absence due to a sudden calamity (such as burst waterpipes) will not result in a loss of the statutory tenancy, so long as the intention to return as soon as possible can be shown[51]. A statutory tenancy can still arise even if the tenant is deprived of his security of tenure by reason of overcrowding or a closing order[52].

(c) Terms and Conditions

The general provisions governing the terms and conditions of statutory tenancies are contained in the Rent Act 1977, s. 3(1), which states that so long as the statutory tenant retains possession, he is to observe and be entitled to the benefit of all terms and conditions of the original contract of tenancy, so far as they are consistent with the provisions of the Rent Act 1977. The main types of inconsistent terms and conditions are those which relate to rent, recovery of possession and covenants against assignment and sub-letting. A statutory tenant is liable to pay only the rent provided by the

---

[47] *Tideway Investment & Property Holdings Ltd* v *Wellwood* [1952] Ch. 791 at p. 818.
[48] *Skinner* v *Geary* [1931] 2 K.B. 546; *Brown* v *Brash* [1948] 2 K.B. 247, per Asquith L.J. at pp. 254-255; *Roland House Gardens Ltd* v *Cravitz* [1975] 29 P & C.R. 432; *Gofor Investments Ltd* v *Roberts* [1975] 23 P & C.R. 366; *Tickner* v *Hearn* [1960] 1 W.L.R. 1406.
[49] *Hiller* v *United Dairies (London) Ltd* [1934] 1 K.B. 57.
[50] *John M Brown Ltd* v *Bestwick* [1951] 1 K.B. 21.
[51] *Tickner* v *Hearn* [1960] 1 W.L.R. 1406; *cf. Hoggett* v *Hoggett* [1979] 39 P & C.R. 121
[52] *Bushford* v *Falco* [1954] 1 W.L.R. 672.

Rent Act 1977 and it is under the Act, rather than under a covenant in the lease, that a statutory tenant pays his rent. Terms requiring the tenant to give up possession at the end of his tenancy are clearly inconsistent with the Rent Act protection and, since the statutory tenancy cannot be assigned or sub-let as a whole, provisions in the contract which deal with this are excluded. Options for purchase or for a further lease are likewise inconsistent.

(d) Determination

A statutory tenancy terminates if the court makes an order for possession[53]. Also, any unequivocal act by which the statutory tenant gives up possession to his landlord will bring the tenancy to an end. The tenant must here, however, comply with the Rent Act 1977, s. 3(3), which provides that a statutory tenant is entitled to give up possession if, and only if, he gives such notice to the landlord as would have been required under the original contract or, if no notice was required, on giving not less than three months notice.

Special provision is made by the Rent Act 1977, Sched. I, para. 12, for payments demanded by statutory tenants either as a condition of giving up possession, or in payment for furniture or other articles. A statutory tenant who, as a condition of giving up possession, asks for or receives payment from anyone other than the landlord, is guilty of an offence and may be made to pay the money back. If the statutory tenant demands that furniture or effects be purchased as a condition of giving up possession, the person on whom the demand is made can request that the price be quoted in writing and, if it exceeds a reasonable price, the excess is treated in the same way as payments for giving up possession with the same penalties.

2. The Main Provisions

The Rent Act 1977 and the Rent (Agriculture) Act 1976 contain restrictions on the landlord's normal rights to recover possession where a dwelling is let on a protected tenancy, or is subject to a statutory tenancy, or is a protected occupancy or statutory tenancy under the Rent (Agriculture) Act 1976. Certain of these restrictions allow the court a discretion to award the landlord possession if he can make out the necessary statutory grounds; certain of them are mandatory, in that if the landlord makes out the appropriate statutory ground, then the court must grant him possession.

(a) Terminating the tenancy

While a contractual tenancy subsists, the rights and duties of the parties are governed by the terms of the contract. This is particularly important when the landlord seeks to recover possession from a contractual tenant. He will

---

[53]R.A. 1977, ss. 98,99.

be able to do so only if the terms of the tenancy provide a means of bringing it to an end, such as forfeiture for breach of terms or conditions, or notice to quit. Otherwise the tenancy will continue until it terminates by effluxion of time. If the tenancy provides for forfeiture upon breach of terms or conditions, the landlord must show that a breach exists within the manner specified and that the breach has not been waived. If the tenancy is determinable by notice to quit then the appropriate period of notice must be given. By the Protection from Eviction Act 1977, s. 5(1), no notice by a landlord or a tenant to quit any premises let as a dwelling is valid unless it is in writing, and is given not less than four weeks before the date on which it is to take effect. It must also contain certain information, prescribed by statutory instrument, designed to inform tenants of their rights to security under the Rent Act and Protection from Eviction Act 1977. Once the contractual tenancy has been duly determined, the landlord must then show that he has satisfied the grounds for possession under the Rent Act 1977, s. 98. In no circumstances can the landlord dispense with the need for a court order. By the Protection from Eviction Act 1977, s. 2, where any premises are let as a dwelling on a lease which is subject to a right of re-entry or forfeiture, it is illegal to enforce that right otherwise than by proceedings in court. Section 3 of that Act makes it unlawful to recover possession from a residential occupier otherwise than by court order.

Once the contractual tenancy has come to an end, the tenant's position changes. His right to remain in possession arises solely by virtue of his statutory tenancy under the Rent Act 1977, and accordingly he can retain possession for only so long as that Act operates to deprive the landlord of possession. If the statutory tenancy comes to an end for any reason, the landlord can commence proceedings for possession under the Rent Act 1977 immediately and is not required to give the statutory tenant any notice to quit[54].

(b) Discretionary grounds for possession

Certain of the grounds (here referred to as the "discretionary grounds") upon which the landlord can claim possession of a statutory tenancy are discretionary in that the court should not make the order for possession unless it "considers it reasonable to make such an order".[55]

   i. Suitable alternative accomodation.

The court may make an order for possession if it is satisfied that suitable alternative accommodation is available to the tenant, or will be available to him when the order for possession takes effect.

---

[54] R.A. 1977, s. 3(4).
[55] *Ibid.*, s. 98(1).
[56] *Ibid.*, s. 98 (1) (a); Sched. 16, Case 1, para. 1.

ii. Non-payment of rent or other breaches[57].

A landlord may claim possession on the ground of non-payment by the tenant of the lawfully due rent. In general, the discretion of the court under this head will be exercised so as to refuse the landlord possession where the tenant has paid off the arrears due either before the action or before the judgment. If the arrears are not paid off until later, the tenant's situation will fall within the case, but it may nevertheless be unreasonable for the court to make the possession order. In any event, the court has a discretion under the Rent Act 1977, s. 100, to suspend the operation of a possession order on conditions.

A landlord can also claim possession for other breaches of covenant, such as failure to allow the landlord access and reasonable facilities for carrying out repairs[58], failure to observe repairing covenants or covenants not to assign or sub-let.

iii. Nuisance, immoral or illegal use[59].

A court may award a landlord possession where the tenant or any person residing with him or any sub-tenant of his has been guilty of conduct which is a nuisance or annoyance to adjoining occupiers or, where he has been convicted of using the dwelling-house or allowing it to be used for immoral or illegal purposes. This ground for possession can cover an extensive range of conduct, and there is here clearly room for large differences of opinion between landlord, tenant and neighbours. The question of nuisance or annoyance is dependant essentially on the type of neighbourhood and the attitude of the people who live in it.

iv. Deterioration of dwelling-house[60]

If the condition of the property has, in the opinion of the court deteriorated owing to acts of waste by, or the neglect or default of, the tenant, the court may grant the landlord possession of the dwelling. Where the responsibility for the waste or neglect can be laid at the door of lodger or sub-tenant, the court may nevertheless grant possession if it is satisfied that the tenant has not taken such steps as he ought reasonably to have taken to get the lodger or sub-tenant out of the property.

v. Deterioration of furniture[61]

Where the condition of any furniture provided for use under the tenancy has, in the opinion of the court, deteriorated owing to ill-treatment by the tenant, it may order possession. Again, if the responsibility for the damage is that of a lodger or sub-tenant, the court may order possession unless the tenant takes all reasonable steps to remove the person responsible.

[57] *Ibid.*, Sched. 15, para. 4.
[58] *Ibid.*, ss 3(2), 148
[59] *Ibid.*, Sched. 15, Pt. 1, Case 2
[60] *Ibid.*, Sched. 15, Pt. 1, Case 3
[61] *Ibid.*, Sched. 15, Pt. 1, Case 4

   vi. Tenant's notice to quit[62]

The landlord may claim possession if the tenant has given notice to quit and, in consequence of that notice, the landlord has contracted to sell or let the dwelling-house or has taken other steps as a result of which he would, in the court's opinion, be seriously prejudiced if he could not obtain possession. This Case is designed to deal with a tenant who, having given his landlord a notice to quit, changes his mind and wishes to stay on in the property. If, in the meantime, the landlord, in reliance of the notice, has committed the property elsewhere, he may be able to secure possession of the property.

   vii. Assignment or sub-letting of whole without consent[63]

A landlord may claim possession where, without his consent, the tenant has assigned or sub-let the whole of the dwelling or sub-let part, the remainder being already sub-let.

   viii. Premises required for an employee[64]

This case (which does not apply to agricultural occupiers) enables a landlord to recover possession from a service tenant where the premises are required for a new employee. It applies only to service tenancies; service occupancies or licences are governed by the general law. To recover on this ground the landlord, apart from the general question of reasonableness, has to show that the dwelling is reasonably required as a residence for a person engaged in his whole-time employment, or in the whole-time employment of one of his tenants. Or he may show that the dwelling is required for a prospective employee with whom a contract has been made, conditional upon housing being provided. Apart from the question of the new employee, the landlord must also show that the existing tenant was in his employment or the employment of a former landlord, that the dwelling-house was let to him in consequence of that employment, and that he has ceased to be in that employment.

   ix. Premises required for landlord or family[65]

A landlord may recover possession of a dwelling-house let on a protected or statutory tenancy if he can show that it is reasonably required for occupation as a residence for:

(a) himself, or

(b) any son or daughter of his over 18, or

(c) his father or mother, or

(d) the father or mother of the landlord's spouse.

   Persons who have become landlords by recent purchase may not rely on

[62] *Ibid*., Sched. 15, Pt. 1, Case 5
[63] *Ibid*., Sched. 15, Pt. 1, Case 6
[64] *Ibid*., Sched. 15, Pt. 1, Case 8
[65] *Ibid*., Sched. 15, Pt. 1, Case 9

this ground. The object of excepting from the Case landlords by recent purchase, is to prevent people from buying houses over the heads of sitting tenants and then evicting them without giving them alternative accomodation. The limitation operates only where there is a protected tenant in occupation at the time of purchase. Consequently, if a person buys a house with vacant possession and then lets it to a tenant without first living in it himself, he will not be precluded from recovering possession by reason of this limitation[66].

The Rent Act 1977, Sched. 15, Pt. III, para. 1, states that a court shall not make an order for possession on this ground unless it is satisfied that, having regard to all the circumstances, including the question of whether other accommodation is available for the landlord or the tenant, greater hardship would be caused by refusing the order than granting it. The object of this "greater hardship" qualification is to give the judge discretion to consider all the circumstances of both the landlord and the tenant before making an order for possession. The onus is on the tenant to show greater hardship, but it is not clear how much this qualification adds to the general duty placed upon the court by the Rent Act 1977, s. 98(1), to be satisfied that it is reasonable to make the order for possession. The judge has a duty to consider greater hardship at the date of the hearing and not on the basis of prior admissions by the parties.

Where a landlord obtains an order for possession on this ground by means of misrepresentation or concealment of material facts, he may be ordered to compensate the tenant thus injured.

 x. Overcharging sub-tenants[67]

A court may grant the landlord possession if it is satisfied that the rent charged by the tenant is more than could be lawfully recovered by the landlord for the part sub-let.

(c) Mandatory grounds for possession

In the case of regulated tenancies, certain grounds upon which the landlord can obtain possession are set out in the Rent Act 1977, Sched. 15, Pt. II. These are mandatory grounds, in that if the landlord can make out any of the grounds detailed in Cases 11-15, the court is obliged to make the order without regard to the question of whether it is reasonable to do so.

 i. Dwelling-house let by an owner-occupier (Case 11)

There are complex conditions which must be met before this ground can be relied upon. They specify such things as the need for notices to be served on tenants by certain dates, and the need for possession that must be shown before the court may grant the order. In practice, this exemption is some-

[66] *Epps* v *Rothnie* [1945] K.B. 562
[67] R.A. 1977, Sched. 15, Pt. 1, Case 10.

times resorted to by landlords whose job takes them abroad for a short period.

ii. Landlord's retirement home (Case 12)

The court must grant the landlord possession if he can show that he intends to occupy the house as his residence at such time as he might retire from regular employment, and that he let it on a regulated tenancy before he retired. The landlord must also satisfy certain other conditions concerning the establishment of the need for possession and the service of appropriate notices on tenants.

iii. Out of season lettings (Case 13)

This ground enables a landlord to recover possession from a tenant, following the giving of appropriate notice, when the dwelling-house was previously occupied for holiday purposes. A court must order possession where the dwelling is let under a tenancy not exceeding eight months, and:

(1) not later than the commencement of the tenancy the landlord gave notice in writing to the tenant that possession might be recovered on this ground; and

(2) the dwelling was, at some time within the period of 12 months ending on the relevant date, occupied under the right to occupy it for a holiday.

This provision offers a corollary to the Rent Act 1977, s. 9, enabling a landlord to alternate holiday lettings with out-of-season lettings without conferring security of tenure on any of his tenants. Because, however, this ground of possession is not specifically related to section 9 at all, presumably holiday occupation by the landlord himself would be sufficient for the purposes of condition (2) above.

iv. Vacation lettings (Case 14)

This ground enables an institution of further or higher education to let dwellings for a period not exceeding 12 months, and to recover possession without the court being able to exercise any discretion in the tenant's favour, provided the tenant was informed by written notice before or at the time of the letting that possession might be recovered on this ground, and provided also that at some time within the 12 months before the letting, the dwelling was let to a student under the exemption in the Rent Act 1977, s. 8 (1). Technically, this ground of possession is not wholly confined to educational institutions, and may be used for example, where such an institution, which has been letting accomodation to students, sells a dwelling with vacant possession to a new landlord, who re-lets the property within 12 months.

v. Letting of dwellings for ministers of religion (Case 15)

vi. Lettings by Servicemen (Housing Act 1980, s. 67, introducing Rent Act 1977, Schedule 15, Case 20).

Possession of a dwelling-house can be recovered by a person who, both when he acquired the house and when he let it was a member of the armed forces and who is able to satisfy the conditions relating to need for possession and service of the appropriate notice on the tenant.

3. Orders and Suspended Orders

Once the court has concluded that the landlord is entitled to possession, it may make an order for possession forthwith. Alternatively, it may stay or suspend the execution of the order or postpone the date of possession for such period or periods as it thinks fit[68]. Where the court exercises this power, it must impose conditions with regard to payment of any arrears of rent, for payment of current rent or mesne profits, or any other conditions it thinks appropriate. If the imposition of conditions would cause the tenant exceptional hardship, or would otherwise be unreasonable, they may be dispensed with[69]. Where possession is sought on one of the mandatory grounds, any postponement of the effect of the order must normally be limited to 14 days[70]. The delay can be longer in the case of exceptional hardship, up to a maximum of six weeks.

4. Attempts to Avoid Rent Act Protection

The Rent Acts are designed to provide both some security of tenure and control over rents. Attempts are made to avoid one or other or, in some cases, both these forms of control. Sometimes the landlord's motive is simply exploitive, and he deliberately sets out to evade and to disregard the Rent Acts. In other cases, landlords may only be prepared to let their property if they can be sure of recovering possession. It remains to be seen how far the shorthold provisions in the Housing Act 1980 will result in the disappearance of some of the more blatant attempts to evade the Acts[71]. The principle means of avoidance, which are in any event more commonly found in "stress areas" are:

(a) Disregard of the registered rent
(b) The use of "Licence" agreements
(c) The unlawful sub-tenant or licensee

An intermediate stage to the direct granting of licences is for the landlord to grant a lease to a limited company whose members are the tenants. If the tenancy is of residential accommodation it will be within the rent control provisions of the Rent Acts. If the lease prohibits the creation of sub-tenancies and licences, the rights of the individual occupiers will not be protected on the termination of the grant.

[68] R.A. 1977, s. 100
[69] H.A. 1980, s. 75(2)
[70] *Ibid*., s. 89. *Quaere* an apparent inconsistency with the Protection from Eviction Act 1977, s. 4.
[71] A discussion of the various attempts at avoidance is to be found in Yates & Hawkins, *Landlord and Tenant Law*, Ch. 2 and pp. 350-353. See also Myers, [1979] S.L.T. 249

(d) The "holiday-let"

The exploitation of this form of avoidance has been the subject of considerable litigation and adverse comment. No steps have been taken in the Housing Act 1980 to curb some of the alleged abuses, although a number of suggestions for reform were made in the House of Lords[72].

(e) "Bed and Breakfast" lets

It has already been seen that lettings with attendance may fall outside the regulated sector, and lettings with board and attendance outside all protection. Again, this has led to exploitation by landlords prepared to provide little more than a continental breakfast, and possibly minimal cleaning services to the occupiers of single rooms. As in so many of these cases, the issue will be to determine whether the agreement is a sham with a common intention to deceive or a bona fide agreement providing some, albeit limited, board and attendance.

5. Restricted Contracts

(a) Introduction

For many years the tenants of furnished premises formed a legal category of their own. From 1920 to 1946 they benefited from some degree of rent control. After 1946 they enjoyed limited protection of tenure afforded by the rent tribunals. In the case of periodic furnished tenancies, the rent tribunal could theoretically postpone the effect of a notice to quit if an application was made to it every six months. In practice nine month's security of tenure was and is likely to be the maximum period of security of tenure given by rent tribunals, and often the period would be much reduced. The Protection from Eviction Act 1964 was designed to prevent landlords of furnished accommodation from evicting their tenants, whether they enjoyed fixed or periodic terms, without the benefit of a court order. The Rent Act 1974 converted most furnished tenancies into regulated tenancies, leaving a rump known as "restricted contracts" still receiving rent tribunal protection. Restricted contracts do not enjoy a common factor by which they can be readily identified. Tenancies where there is a resident landlord are the most significant group and it is immaterial whether the premises are furnished. But a large number of residential licences can also fall within the definition of a restricted contract. Restricted contracts entered into after the commencement of section 69 of the Housing Act 1980 on November 28 1980 enjoy only the rent control provisions and not the limited security afforded by the rent tribunal and enjoyed by holders of such contracts made before that date. Further, although court proceedings are necessary before recovery of possession of premises occupied under a restricted contract, the order

[72] H.L. Debates, July 3, 1980

for possession cannot be postponed or suspended for more than three months from its date[73].

(b) Restricted contracts defined

The statutory definition of a restricted contract is meagre – "a contract . . . whereby one person grants to another person, in consideration of a rent which includes payment for the use of furniture or for services, the right to occupy a dwelling as a residence." (Rent Act 1977, s. 19(2)). The definition covers not only lease but also licences, provided there is a monetary payment and the right given is to occupy a dwelling as a residence. Although a personal permissive right to occupy accomodation can be protected, it is not always easy in given circumstances to say with confidence that a case for protection is established. The hotel guest, lodger, occupant under a sharing-arrangement all may be able to point to a room they have the use of on a settled basis. Although unlikely, it is not impossible, for a single room to be a dwelling. In many cases, there is a sharing with others of part of the accomodation, *e.g.* bathroom or kitchen. To be able to claim a restricted contract, one must have "exclusive occupation" of at least part[74]. The fact that the landlady has rights of access is irrelevant, unless she has reserved either the right to share in the occupation herself, or more commonly, the right to put someone else in the room[75].

Any of three statutory factors may take the contract outside the restricted category:

i. Property exceeding rateable value

A contract relating to a dwelling will not be restricted if the rateable value for the dwelling exceeds a certain figure. The rating limits are not precisely the same as for protected tenancies, but, for the sake of simplicity, it can here be assumed that they are since the number of exceptional cases is not great[76].

ii. The nature of the agreement

Regulated tenancies[77], protected occupancies within Rent (Agriculture) Act 1976[78], and contracts to occupy dwellings for holidays[79] are all outside the restricted contract net. So also are contracts where the payment covers board, and payment for that item forms a substantial proportion of the whole rent. Section 7(2) of the Rent Act 1977 takes a contract out of the *protected* sector if a substantial part of the payment is attributable to atten-

---

[73] H.A. 1980, s. 69(2); R.A. 1977, s. 106A
[74] R.A. 1977, s. 19(6)
[75] *R v Battersea, Wandsworth, Mitcham & Wimbledon Rent Tribunal, ex parte Parikh* [1957] 1 W.L.R. 410
[76] R.A. 1977, ss. 19(4), 25.
[77] *Ibid.*, s. 19(5) (a)
[78] *Ibid.*, s. 19 (5) (d)
[79] *Ibid.*, s. 19(7)

dance. Section 19(5) (c) takes the contract out of the *restricted* sector if a substantial part of the payment is for board. This exception obviously encourages some landlords to indulge in sham bed and breakfast arrangements[80].

iii. The nature of the landlord

Contracts where the Crown[81] is the lessor are outside the restricted contract sector simply because of that fact. Similarly, contracts where the lessor is a local authority[82] are not restricted contracts[83]. The same applies where the lessor is a housing association, housing trust or the Housing Corporation[84].

(c) Principal contracts within the restricted are:
  i. Resident or sharing landlords, and
  ii. *Tenancies* with attendance, and *contracts* with furniture or services.

The fact that tenancies with attendance are not protected tenancies has already been considered. Services are statutorily defined to include "attendance, the provision of heating or lighting, the supply of hot water and any other privilege or facility connected with the occupancy of a dwelling, other than a privilege or facility requisite for the purpose of access, cold water supply or sanitary accommodation." Tenancies with attendance, and contractual licences with furniture or services are a very significant group of restricted contracts. It must be remembered that only those licences that grant "exclusive occupation" are in the restricted sector, and there must be a term requiring monetary payment for either furniture or services. Student lettings may well, therefore, come within the restricted sector where they are prevented by section 8 of the Rent Act 1977 from being a protected tenancy. But in many cases education institutions will grant non-exclusive licences, which take the arrangement outside the ambit of restricted contracts.

(d) Security provisions for restricted contracts

The tenants of restricted contracts are not afforded statutory security of tenure. There are, however, a number of restraints on the landlord attempting to recover possession, which are significantly reduced for contracts entered into after November 28th, 1980.

i. Contracts made prior to November 28, 1980

Since there are still a large number of restricted contracts in existence dating

---

[80] *Cf. Holiday Flat Co* v *Kuczera* [1978] S.L.T. (Sh. Ct.) 47, considering the adequacy of a continental breakfast since the entry of the U.K. into the E.E.C.

[81] *I.e.* where the interest belongs to the Queen in right of the Crown (unless it is under the management of the Crown Estates Commissioners), or a Government Department: R.A. 1977, s. 19 (5) (b), as amended by H.A. 1980, s. 73(2).

[82] As defined in R.A. 1977, s. 14

[83] R.A. 1977, s. 19(5) (a); H.A. 1980, Sched. 25, para. 36.

[84] *Ibid.*, s. 19(5) (e).

from a time prior to November 28th, 1980, the limited security of tenure that may be granted to this group of occupants (they may not all be tenants – an occupant under a restricted contract may be a licensee) by a rent tribunal is still of some practical significance. The details of the tribunals' powers in this regard are to be found in sections 103 and 104 of the Rent Act 1977.

If a tenant fears he is about to be evicted, or wishes to have a "reasonable" rent fixed for his contract[85], or both, he may apply to a rent tribunal. Should the landlord then serve a notice to quit, either before or in the six months following the rent tribunal's decision, that notice will be automatically suspended until six months after the rent tribunal's decision. The tribunal, having heard the case can, however, direct that the notice to quit be suspended for a shorter period.

If the tenant has already received a notice to quit from his landlord *before* he makes application to the rent tribunal, the effect of his subsequent application to the tribunal (provided it takes place before the notice to quit expires) will be to suspend the notice to quit until the rent tribunal has heard the case. The tribunal can then direct that the notice to quit shall have no effect apart from the direction they make. In theory, it is open to the tenant to make an infinite number of applications provided he does so before the notice takes effect and until the tribunal refuses to exercise its discretion to grant further periods of security. If the tribunal refuses to grant any security, the notice to quit will take effect, but not before the expiry of seven days from the determination of the application by the tribunal.

ii. Contracts made on or after November 28, 1980

The Housing Act 1980 makes a significant change in the limited security of tenure enjoyed by occupiers under restricted contracts. Section 69(3) provides that the tribunal has no discretion to grant security in respect of restricted contracts entered into after the commencement of the section. The only remaining rights of security such tenants have are those relating to notice and court proceedings, discussed below. The changes do not affect occupiers whose contracts antedate the commencement of the section on November 28th, 1980.

iv. Notices and court proceedings

Tenants properly so called of periodic restricted tenancies will need the usual four weeks' notice, together with the prescribed information[86]. But tenants and licensees under restricted contracts cannot in any event be

---

[85] Rent tribunals fix "reasonable" rents: R.A. 1977, s. 78. The rent officer, with jurisdiction over protected tenancies, fixes "fair rents": R.A. 1977, s. 70.
[86] Protection from Eviction Act 1977,s.5; *Crane* v *Morris* [1965] 1 W.L.R. 1104.

evicted without due process of law[87]. Proceedings are taken in the county court and execution can be stayed, or suspended, or the date of possession postponed. In the case of contracts made after November 28, 1980, unless exceptional hardship would be caused to the tenant, there must be an order for the payment of arrears or rent and for rent or mesne profits for the occupation until possession is obtained. Furthermore the order for possession cannot be postponed for longer than three months after the date of the making of the order[88].

D. The Public Sector
The lack of security of tenure in relation to council housing was for long a source of criticism and concern to lawyers and others concerned with housing matters. This became acute as a result of a series of decisions during the 1970's in the Court of Appeal which, while in principle asserting that certain rules of administrative law relating to *ultra vires* and abuse of power applied to local authorities in their attempts to evict tenants, made it quite impossible in practice for tenants to resist possession proceedings by placing upon them the burden of raising and then proving the issue of *vires* or abuse of power[89]. Central government had already accepted the need for security of tenure in the public sector in the Green Paper on *Housing Policy* (Cmnd. 6851) and the Housing Act 1980 has conferred such security on the majority of municipal tenants. It does this by setting up a broad group of tenants, called "secure tenants", who may be tenants either of a local authority or of a housing association, and then confers on them certain rights, including security of tenure and the right to buy their home from the landlord.

1. Secure tenancies
The Housing Act 1980 creates a new legal classification of public authority tenancies, embracing both council and housing association lettings, known as secure tenancies. A tenant can be a secure tenant even if his tenancy was granted before the commencement of Part I of the Housing Act 1980 on October 3, 1980[90]. Even a licensee is entitled to security provided that, had he been in occupation under a tenancy, he would have otherwise qualified[91]. The one exception is a licence granted as a temporary expedient to a squatter[92].

[87] Protection from Eviction Act 1977, s. 3. This section is extended to licences created after November 28th, 1980.
[88] R.A. 1977, s. 106A; H.A. 1980, s. 69(2).
[89] e.g.*Bristol District Council* v *Clark* [1975] 1 W.L.R. 1443; *Cannock Chase District Council* v *Kelly* [1978] 1 W.L.R. 1; *Sevenoaks District Council* v *Emmott* (1979) 39 P & C.R. 404
[90] H.A. 1980, s. 47
[91] *Ibid.*, s. 48(1)
[92] *Ibid.*, s. 48(2)

In order for a tenancy of a council or housing association property to be a secure tenancy, there must be a letting of a dwelling-house, let as a separate dwelling[93]. A dwelling-house may be a house or part of a house. Land let together with the dwelling is considered part of it, unless it is agricultural land exceeding two acres. The considerations applicable here are therefore the same as the requirements for protected tenancies under the Rent Act 1977, s. 1.

2. Exemption from Secure Tenancy Status

The Housing Act 1980, Sched. 3, contains a list of tenancies that cannot be secure. These provisions are summarised below.

(i) Long tenancies

Tenancies for fixed terms exceeding 21 years cannot be secure tenancies.

(ii) Service tenancies

If the tenant is an employee of the landlord or, if not an employee, is an employee of a local authority, development corporation, the Commission for New Towns, a county council or the Development Board for Rural Wales, and he is required by his contract of employment to occupy the house for the better performance of his duties[94], the tenancy cannot be secure.

(iii) Development land

Where the house is on land acquired for development and is being used by the landlord pending development, it cannot be let on a secure tenancy[95].

(iv) Homeless persons

A tenancy or licence granted under the Housing (Homeless Persons) Act 1977 as a temporary expedient while the local authority complete their enquiries concerning the applicant, or granted for a short time because the authority have no duty to house permanently, cannot be a secure tenancy.

(v) Tenancies granted to persons seeking employment

This exclusion is designed to cover people to whom temporary accommodation has been made available while moving jobs. A tenancy will not be secure until one year from the date of grant if the house is in a district or

---

[93] *Ibid.*, s. 28(1). Insofar as s. 48(1) applies the provisions of Pt. 1 of the Act to licences, the word "let" does not have the same significance as it does in relation to the R.A. 1977, s. 1.

[94] Even if occupation is not for the better performance of duties, if the dwelling is in a building actually held for certain specified educational or social service purposes, or within the curtilage of such a building, then secure status can be prevented by a provision in the tenancy that it shall determine at the end of the employment: H.A. 1980, Sched. 3, para. 3.

[95] On the meaning of "development" see: Town and Coutry Planning Act 1971, s. 22(1),(2).

London borough and is granted to a person who was not formerly resident in that district or borough but who has come there in order to work. The tenancy must therefore be granted to meet the tenant's needs for temporary accommodation, pending the securing of permanent accommodation, and the tenant must have secured employment, or the offer of it, in the district or borough before the grant of the tenancy in question. To fall within the exempt status the landlord must also have notified the tenant in writing of the provisions of this exception, and of their opinion that the tenancy will fall within it.

(vi) Short-term arrangements[96]

A house let to a council or housing association with vacant possession for use as temporary housing accommodation cannot be subject to a secure tenancy if, under the terms of that letting, the landlord may recover possession from the council or association either on expiry of a specified period or whenever he requires it back. The lessor to the council or association must not himself be a landlord bound by the secure tenancy provisions of the 1980 Act, and the council's or association's only interest in the property must be as the lessee under the superior tenancy. If these conditions are satisfied, the sub-tenancy from the council or association will not be secure. The purpose of providing that the lessor to the council must not himself be a landlord bound by the secure tenancy provisions of the 1980 Act is to prevent collusive arrange-ments between councils, or councils and housing associations, to defeat the security provision of the Act.

(vii) Temporary accommodation

A tenancy is not a secure tenancy if it was granted for occupation by a tenant, or the tenant's predecessor in title, while works are carried out to premises he previously occupied as a home, and neither he nor the predecessor in title was a secure tenant of that other home. This provision enables authorities or associations to house people while works, repairs, alterations or improve-ments are carried out, preventing the tenant from acquiring secure status in his temporary home.

(viii) Agricultural holdings

A tenancy is not a secure tenancy if the house is comprised in an agricultural holding as defined in the Agricultural Holdings Act 1948, and it is occupied by the person responsible for the control, either as tenant or as the agent or employee of the tenant, of the farming of the holding. Such tenancies will be rare in the public housing field, but are sometimes encountered, especially in the rural areas of East Anglia.

[96] See (1977) 127 New L.J. 667.

(ix) Licensed premises

A tenancy is not a secure tenancy if the house consists of or includes premises with an on-licence.

(x) Student lettings

A tenancy is not a secure tenancy until the expiry of six months from the date when the tenant ceases to attend a designated course at a university or further education college as specified in the landlord's notice to the tenant, if the tenancy has been granted to enable the tenant to attend a designated course at an educational establishment. The landlord must notify the tenant of the provisions of this exemption, and of their opinion that the tenancy would fall within it, before the tenancy is granted.

(xi) Tenancies within the Landlord and Tenant Act 1954, Pt. II

A tenancy is not a secure tenancy if it is one to which the Landlord and Tenant Act 1954, Pt. II applies, either because it is a business tenancy or because it is an assured tenancy. The Landlord and Tenant Act 1954, Pt. II contains the code for the protection of business tenants. It is applied to one group of residential tenants only (assured tenants) by the Housing Act 1980, section 56 and Schedule 5.

(xii) Almshouse licences

A licence granted by an almshouse charity, whose rules prevent it from granting tenancies, is not a secure tenancy. To qualify for the exemption, any sum payable by the occupier must not exceed the maximum contribution to the cost of maintenance and services from time to time authorised or approved by the Charity Commisioners.

(xiii) Tenancies and licences granted before May 8, 1980[97]

A tenancy is not a secure tenancy if it was granted before May 8, 1980, and under the tenancy the landlord is a charity within the meaning of the Charities Act 1960, and prior to the grant of the tenancy the tenant was told, in writing, that the landlord intended to carry out works on the building or part of it (including the house in question), and could not reasonably do so without obtaining possession.

3. Losing Secure Tenancy Status

(i) Exercise of right to buy

Any secure tenancy ends when, after the tenant has exercised the right to buy, conferred on public tenants by the Housing Act 1980, the freehold of his house or a long lease of his flat is transferred to him.

[97] H.A. 1980, Sched. 25, para. 73.

(ii) Effluxion of time

If the secure tenancy is a fixed-term tenancy which expires by effluxion of time, and the council do not grant the tenant a new secure tenancy, then his secure tenancy will expire. In its place a periodic tenancy arises automatically between the same parties and on the same terms as the former secure tenancy, for periods equivalent to the rental periods under the first tenancy. The only difference is that it will not be secure[98]. In practice this provides a local authority or housing association with the most obvious means of avoidance of the secure tenancy provisions. A tenant can be granted a fixed-term tenancy of very short duration (say one month), which the landlord will not renew. The fixed-term tenancy will be secure, but once this has determined by effluxion of time, the periodic tenancy that then arises under the Housing Act 1980, s. 29(1) (should the landlord not renew the

It is worthwhile explaining why the tenancy that arises automatically on the expiry of the fixed term is not secure, since all the British commentators on the 1980 Act have so far assumed that it is secure. Where a court orders the termination of fixed-term secure tenancy for reasons that, but for the 1980 Act, would have been grounds for the landlord exercising a right of re-entry or forfeiture, section 32(2) provides that the court cannot order possession but can, instead, only terminate the *secure* tenancy. Section 29(1) provides that "where a secure tenancy . . . is a tenancy for a term certain *and comes to an end by effluxion of time or by an order under section 32(2) . . .*a periodic tenancy of the same dwelling-house arises by virtue of this section . . ." Now, if the periodic tenancy which arises by virtue of section 29(1) were another secure tenancy, then section 32(2) becomes redundant and the court's exercise of its power under that section a nonsense. What is the point of the court solemnly terminating the secure tenancy under section 32(2), only to have it arise again automatically under section 29(1)? The obvious explanation is that the tenancy that arises automatically under section 29(1) is not a secure one. This argument is reinforced by the fact that wherever the phrase "fixed term" or "periodic" tenancy is used to denote a secure tenancy elsewhere in the Act (e.g. section 28(5), the opening words of section 29(1), section 30(1), 31(1), 32(1)) the words "secure tenancy" are coupled with it. The part of section 29(1) now under dispute refers simply to "a periodic tenancy of the same dwelling-house", not "a periodic tenancy which is a secure tenancy of the same dwelling-house".

(iii) Order of the court

A secure tenancy continues until such time as the court orders that possession must be given up on one of the statutory grounds set out in Part I of

[98] H.A. 1980, s. 29(1).

Schedule 4 to the 1980 Act[99]. In the case of fixed-term secure tenancies subject to a right of forfeiture or a proviso for re-entry, the court may order possession at the same time as the order ending the fixed term, provided one of the grounds for possession under the Act can be made out[100].

(iv) Subletting and assignment
If a tenant sublets the whole of the property (even with consent), or part of it where the remainder is sublet, the tenancy ceases to be secure[101]. Similarly, where a tenancy is assigned it ceases to be secure[102].

4. Security of Tenure

(i) Service of notice
A local authority or housing association landlord wishing to obtain possession of a house or flat let on a secure tenancy, or wanting an order ending the secure tenancy (which may or may not also involve possession) under a proviso for re-entry or forfeiture, must first serve a notice on the tenant giving particulars of the ground on which the landlord will apply to the court[103]. The court has no power to order possession unless this notice is served[104]. In the case of a periodic tenancy the notice must specify a date after which possession proceedings may be commenced[105]. That date cannot be earlier than the landlord could then have brought the tenancy to an end by notice to quit *i.e.* it must be at least four weeks or one rental period, whichever is longer, after service of the notice[106]. The notice expires 12 months after the date specified in it, and proceedings can only be validly brought under the notice during that year[107], after which the landlord must commence the whole procedure over again.

(ii) Grounds for possession
An order for possession of a house let on a secure tenancy can only be granted on one or more of the grounds set out in Schedule 4, Part I of the 1980 Act.

There are two possible overriding conditions to be satisfied before a possession order can be made, in addition to establishing one or more of the

[99] H.A. 1980, s. 32(1), 34(1).
[100] *Ibid.*, ss. 33(4). It should be remembered that if a public authority tenancy is not secure, or loses secure tenancy status, the tenant, in practice, enjoys no security of tenure.
[101] H.A. 1980, s. 37(2)
[102] *Ibid.*, s. 37(1)
[103] *Ibid.*, s. 33(2). See the Secure Tenancies (Notices) Regulations 1980 S.I. 1980 No. 1339
[104] H.A. 1980 s. 33(1)
[105] *Ibid.*, s. 33(3), (4)
[106] *Ibid.*, s. 33(3)
[107] *Ibid.*, s. 33(3) (b)

statutory grounds. One or both of these overriding conditions will apply[108]. The first is that the court considers it reasonable to make the order and the second is the availability of suitable alternative accommodation for the tenant when the order takes effect.

(iii) Grounds for possession where reasonableness is the overriding criterion
A court may (not must) order possession of a house, if the landlord persuades the court that it is reasonable so to do. Some of these grounds are almost identical in terms with those in the Rent Act 1977 for the private sector. The grounds are:
(1) Failure to pay rent or breach of any other obligation of the tenancy agreement.
(2) Conduct by the tenant, or anyone residing in the house, which causes a nuisance or annoyance to neighbours, or conviction of using the house for immoral or illegal purposes, or of allowing it to be so used.
(3) Neglect, default or acts of waste by the tenant or anyone living in the house, causing deterioration to it or to the common parts.
(4) Ill-treatment of any furniture provided by the landlord under the tenancy or in any common parts, causing its deterioration.
(5) The making of a false statement, knowingly or recklessly, which induced the landlord to grant the tenancy to the tenant, either alone or jointly with others.
(6) The house which the tenant, or a predecessor in title, occupied as a secure tenant (and which he vacated pending the carrying out of works there) is again available for the remainder of the period for which the current secure tenancy was granted, on completion of the works.

(iv) Grounds where alternative accommodation must be offered[110]
The landlord may obtain possession of a public sector house let on a secure tenancy on any one or more of the following grounds, provided they can persuade the court that suitable alternative accommodation is available or will be available when the order takes effect. The grounds are:
(7) The house is overcrowded in circumstances rendering the occupier guilty of an offence.
(8) The landlord intends to carry out, within a reasonable time of obtaining possession, demolition, reconstruction or other works on the building comprising the dwelling or on land treated as part of it, and cannot reasonably do so without obtaining possession.
(9) In the case of charitable housing trusts only, the landlord can show that

---

[108] *Ibid.*, s. 34(2), (3).
[109] *Ibid.*, Sched. 4, Pt. I
[110] *Ibid.*, s. 34(2) (b), Sched. 4, Pt. II.

the tenant's continued occupation of the property conflicts with the objects of the charity. Presumably the trustees would be bound to seek possession in such cases, but would be relieved of any liability for breach of trust if the court refused or suspended the order.

(v) Grounds where both reasonableness and the offer of alternative accommodation must be established

The landlord may be granted an order for possession (though again, the grounds are not mandatory) if it can be shown to the satisfaction of the court both that it is reasonable to grant the order and that suitable alternative accommodation will be available to the tenant when the order takes effect[111], and also make out one or more of the following grounds:

(10) The accommodation has special features making it suitable for occupation by a physically disabled person, no such person is still living there and the landlord requires it to house such a person, with or without his family.

(11) A housing association or housing trust which lets dwellings only for occupation by people whose circumstances (other than financial circumstances) make it difficult to satisfy their housing needs, may recover possession where it can be shown either that no such person is still resident, or that a local authority has offered the tenant a secure tenancy. The association or trust must also show that it needs possession of the dwelling so that it can be offered to another person who qualifies because of his or her personal circumstances.

(12) Where the house forms one of a group which the landlord lets to people with special needs, fulfilled by the provision in the area of some social service or special facility (such as special medical care or educational facilities), and where it is established that there is no longer a person with those special needs residing there, possession may be obtained so that someone with that special need may be accommodated there.

(13) If the landlord can show that the accommodation is more extensive than is reasonably required by the present tenant, to whom the tenancy was statutorily transmitted under the 1980 Act on the death of the former tenant, they may recover possession from that successor tenant, provided he or she is not the spouse of the deceased tenant[112].

(viii) Postponing or suspending possession orders

Under the Housing Act 1980, s.87(1) the court has wide powers to adjourn proceedings for possession of a dwelling-house let on a secure tenancy. Under section 87(2) it may also postpone the date of possession, or stay or

[111] *Ibid.*, s. 34(2) (c)
[112] For an explanation of the statutory transmission procedure for secure tenancies see Hughes, *Public Sector Housing Law*, pp. 101-102.

suspend the execution of the possession order. The only circumstances in which, it appears, the court does not have this discretion is when possession is ordered on one of those grounds which are subject to the overall requirement of the availability of suitable alternative accommodation.

E. The Need for Security

Most of the security of tenure schemes in the common law world (Newfoundland, Quebec, British Columbia in Canada, New South Wales and Victoria in Australia, Massachusetts in the U.S.A., as well as the British scheme) have formed part of a larger plan of rent control[113]. Rent control was first introduced in Great Britain in 1915 as a response to the housing shortage of World War I. It both froze rents and granted security from eviction. Various attempts have been made over the years to free large numbers of dwellings from its application. In the 1950's there was a noticeable trend towards relaxing control, partly because this represented a manifestation of some rather confused notions of freedom of property, allowing a landlord to do what he wished with his own house, and partly because of the belief that the lifting of restrictions would result in more properties being made available on the private rental market in a better state of repair. As will be demonstrated later, the first of these rationales was misconceived and the second a total failure. The de-controlling Rent Act of 1957, which lifted both rent and security controls, did not result in more houses for rent or in significantly better maintenance. Indeed, the post-war accelerated decline continued much as before but, in addition, the country was treated to the horror of some notorious scandals involving landlords abusing and terrorising their tenants. The most famous being that characterised as "the Rachman affair".

At first, the 1957 Rent Act had little public impact (apart from among people experiencing the attentions of harassing landlords). Its broad objectives were not being met, but neither were they causing much comment. In 1961, in their evaluation of *Housing Since the Rent Act*, Donnison, Cockburn and Corlett concluded that the whole measure had little effect, particularly concerning repairs. They found that it was in the North of England, where rents were lowest, that landlords were the most reluctant to repair.

It was in the South of England, particularly London, where rents were higher (but so too were opportunity costs) that the 1957 Rent Act had most effect. There the consequences of the Act became more and more notice-

---

[113] Useful summaries of the security provisions in many jurisdictions are to be found in Sinclair, *Survey of Landlord and Tenant Law*, a working paper prepared for the Law Reform Division of the New Brunswick Department of Justice, 1973. See also the *Report on Landlord and Tenant Relationships*, Law Reform Commission of British Columbia, Project No. 12, 1973.

able, and housing – or at least those aspects of housing shortage manifested by harassment, eviction and homelessness – became a political issue. By 1964 the pressure on private rented tenants in London was so great that the Milner Holland Committee found that, in London alone, there were 750 cases of reported physical ill-treatment by landlords of tenants, as well as much general evidence of persuasion by means other than assault. Security of tenure became an election issue and the newly elected Labour government in 1964 hurriedly passed the Protection from Eviction Act while promising a fuller measure in due course.

The subsequent legislation – the Rent Act 1965 – formulated the principles which are still the basis of the current legislation – the Rent Act 1977. It provided security of tenure for tenants in unfurnished rented dwellings (furnished tenants were brought into the system in 1974), together with a system of registered fair rents. While starting, therefore, as the fulfillment of an election pledge to protect tenants against unscrupulous landlords, security of tenure soon became regarded as simply an ancillary prop to the fair rent system. It was argued that there was little point in providing machinery for the adjudication of fair rent if a tenant who had the temerity to invoke the procedure against his landlord could simply be evicted. Fair rent provisions without security could be too easily evaded.

Although such an observation may be so obvious as to be hardly worth the saying, it is equally the case that the obvious sometimes escapes attention. Security of tenure without fair rent provisions might equally provide the machinery for easy avoidance, yet that is exactly what pertains in the public sector. In the private sector security of tenure and regulation of rents are recognised as being closely connected, since the one could be made worthless without the other. Tenants using the fair rent machinery could be evicted, and security without fair rents could be evaded by arbitrary and uncontrolled increases in rents, forcing tenants to vacate. The scheme for public tenants in the Housing Act 1980 contains no such link and it may be asked whether it can work properly without one, especially in view of the current pressure on local authorities to reduce demands on the local population by increasing rates. So far as local authority rents are concerned, authorities have a wide discretion to fix rents in respect of particular tenancies as well as classes of tenancy (Housing Act 1957, s. 111(1)). If this discretion were to be used to fix an exorbitant rent for a dwelling or group of dwellings with the object of driving the tenants out, this would be subject to direct judicial control as an abuse of the statutory power, but such high court actions are expensive and, to date, not a single tenant has succeeded in one. Alternatively, the court, in an action for possession based on the ground of rent arrears, could refuse to grant an order on the basis that the rent, being unreasonable, was not lawfully due. It might be asked whether these safeguards are sufficient, given that they require the tenant to initiate or defend expensive, complex civil proceedings in the courts. In the private sector, it will be recalled, the rent adjudication procedure is conducted informally before a rent officer or a rent tribunal.

The notion that a landlord should be free to determine a periodic tenancy of residential accommodation, and should be free to refuse to renew a tenancy for a fixed term, has played some part in the attempts in the past, and under the 1980 Act, to justify the removal of security controls. It stems directly from the doctrine of freedom of contract and the concept of mutuality of termination rights between landlord and tenant. In the context of present-day landlord and tenant relations, however, to adhere to such concepts ignores the realities of the situation. It cannot now be possible to accept freedom of contract as a fact in the landlord-tenant relationship any more than it is in the mortgagor-mortgagee relationship in the owner-occupied market. One cannot base legal relationships in housing on theories of free economic competition when housing is in short supply. Equality of bargaining power between landlord and tenant becomes a fiction when one takes account of scarcity. Moreover, arguments of mutuality in landlord and tenant relations are weakened by the fact that the termination of a tenancy generally involves more serious economic and social consequences for the tenant than for the landlord. Not only is it very difficult to find alternative accommodation, but also the tenant must bear the cost of the move and the consequences of social upheaval. The landlord's task of filling vacant accommodation can scarcely be a difficult one in contemporary circumstances and so his costs are nearly always merely transactional. Thus it is obvious that reliance on the principles of a free market is not sufficient to preclude serious consideration of a concept of security of tenure.

There are also serious social implications in a system where tenants can be dislodged at will. While the landlord's interest in rented premises will generally be purely economic, a tenant will usually regard the premises as a home, and he may have a special attachment to the premises. Many commentators have noted that a secure home is a fundamental need for all families and all individuals[114]. Man's attitude to land, and to his home, is an irrational one and the law should not, therefore, be too anxious to reflect a purely economic model. It is a fallacy to start and finish with the assumption that one house is the same as another of similar size. Such a view ignores the sense of attachment which an occupier develops for his own particular piece of territory. Under primitive conditions the eviction of one man by another is a matter of physical strength. Social history and anthropology is full of

---

[114] Lyndal Evans, Minority Report *Report of the Committee on the Rent Acts* (Francis Report), 1971, Cmnd. 4609

cases in which man has sacrificed his life in defence of a piece of land. In a developed western society the trial of strength is conducted through the pricing mechanism and the richer bid away property from the poorer. There is no reason to think that the defeated and dispossessed feel this form of contest is any "fairer" than the fist fight[115]. Where termination of a tenancy can take place within a short period of time, and justification is not required, the tenant's social needs remain unfulfilled[116].

There is, in this respect, an analogy between security of tenure and security of employment and pension rights. An increasing range of employers now assume that people must be given security in their jobs, possibly until retirement and certainly for a considerable period ahead. At the least it is recognised that you cannot simply dismiss employees at will. For a family with children, whose education depends on continuing in the same school and whose welfare may depend upon preserving links between family and community, security in the home is just as important as job security[117]. Yet, in the most recent piece of U.K. legislation on the matter, security of tenure is sacrificed to the shibboleths of economic efficiency and freedom of property in the private sector, while in the public it is subject to such an obvious method of avoidance (the short fixed term letting) that any local authority who so wishes can, with comparative ease, defeat the purposes of the legislation.

There are other unfortunate practical manifestations which may arise from insecure tenancies. Tenants who have no certain right to remain in premises beyond a short-term period are less likely to be interested in maintaining the premises in good repair[118]. As long as all increases in value of the property inure to the benefit of landlords, tenants will be unwilling contributors to the cost of repairs or improvements. This attitude will be reinforced by the realisation that their interest in the premises may be terminated by the summary and arbitrary determination of the landlord. Further, tenants will be less likely to attempt to enforce their legal rights (for instance as to repairs, rent allowances, fair rents, health and safety standards, tenants' associations) as long as they are not granted a comprehensive right of security. Retaliatory eviction may be particularly difficult to prove where it is open to a landlord to terminate a tenancy for any reason whatsoever.

Landlords, and their spokesmen have advanced, over the years, a number of reasons why they feel tenant security is not desirable[119]. Some landlords

[115] A.A. Nevitt, *The Nature of Rent Controlling Legislation in the U.K.* Centre of Environment Studies, University Working Papers, Jan. 1970
[116] J. Rose, *Landlords and Tenants*, p.3
[117] See the anology drawn by Donnison between security of tenure and security of employment in: *Is there a Case for Rent Control?* Background Papers and Proceedings of a Canadian Council on Social Development Seminar on Rent Policy, 1973.
[118] Rose, *op. cit.*, p. 227.
[119] See *Letters from Landlords*, Small Landlords Association, 1980.

argue that, without security, unjustified terminations would not occur because it would not be in the landlord's best interest to terminate a tenancy without a very good reason for doing so. Rehabilitating the premises for a new tenant may cost money and may also involve a loss of rental income in the meantime. A particular variant of the "fair landlord" argument was used to justify the long-standing exemption for local authorities from the security of tenure provisions of the Rent Acts. Many doubted these protestations. Valiant attempts to utilise the common law of landlord and tenant, as well as public law procedures and remedies, were sometimes successful in establishing points of legal principle, but rarely of practical help and significance to the complainant tenants. These test cases did, however, serve one practical purpose. They dispelled the myth that public authorities were model landlords who ran their affairs in a benevolently paternalistic way. The "special relationship" between local authority and citizen, controllable through the ballot box was shown time and again to be a sham and a new climate was thus created in which arguments against the use of discretion, producing arbitrary decisions and the officious wielding of power, began to find favour until, finally, local authority tenants were granted security of tenure by the Housing Act 1980 although they do not, as has already been pointed out, have access to the fair rent machinery. The only attempt to subject council house tenants to fair rents was under the Housing Finance Act 1972. This measure met enormous opposition, largely because it was felt to be a piece of legislation aimed at increasing council house rents[120]. It was abandoned by the Labour government in 1975 before it had really got underway[121]. It may be that, if re-introduced today in the light of present local government and housing finance policies, fair rent legislation might have the effect of keeping rents down and operate as a useful corollary to public sector security. One then wonders whether its political fate would be the same.

The result of the reaction to local authority autocracy in the housing management field was a range of new laws dealing first with rent rebates, then homelessness, and now selection and security. Admittedly, this has been achieved at some cost. The growth of the public sector has been brought to a sharp halt – indeed many would say has been put into reverse. The state of repair of the public sector housing stock has given cause for adverse comment for some time; shortage of money has brought to a virtual standstill slum clearance and redevelopment programmes and the recent total ban on new building programmes, together with the right conferred by the Housing Act 1980 on council tenants to buy their rented houses, will have a rapid impact on the size of the public sector. Faced with this prospect many people are worried about what will take its place. The government

120   See Yates, [1972] Conv. (N.S.) 402.
121   See Yates, [1975] Conv. (N.S.) 387.

nopes that, by changing the Rent Act 1977, the supply of dwellings for rent in the private sector can be increased. That this view can still be held in a time when more property is falling into decay for want of repair and fewer new houses are being built than at any time since the war seems remarkable, but it explains the thinking behind the new forms of shorthold and assured tenancies created by the Housing Act 1980.

The shorthold provisions have been welcomed by landlords' associations, who see them as a method of combatting the effect of inflation upon income, providing the means of charging near market rents for a short period with the option of repossession and an opportunity of switching investments at the end. However, such "incentives" have been tried before, and failed. The lessons of the late 1950's and early 1960's have not, it seems, been learned.

The real difficulty facing policy makers when discussing security of tenure is that, on the one side, landlords are stereotyped as wealthy, frequently corporate oppressors of the working class and minority groups, and on the other as small time operators, widows, pensioners and the like who are only too ready to let their properties if only they could be guaranteed repossession if they need the property back again or cannot get on with their tenants. Such evidence as there is (the Studies of Cullingworth and Grieve, for example) demonstrates that these stereotypes bear little relation to the truth. Nevertheless, in particular areas of housing stress, abuses of power by a minority of landlords have been sufficently numerous to force successive Labour governments to increase and tighten controls over private landlordism. Necessary though these measures were to deal with a totally intolerable situation, they have further tarnished the image of the private landlord and have undoubtedly accelerated his decline.

The fallacy, however, is to believe that by lifting the controls the decline can be put into reverse. The real issue is whether private ownership of housing can be tolerated in areas of extreme housing stress and with what is the declining private sector to be replaced. The Francis Committee on the Rent Acts expressed their belief that it was essential to preserve the stock of privately rented accomodation – a view reiterated in the Green Paper of Housing Policy (Cmnd 6851, 1977) – "since there is a limit to what local authorities can do in the stress areas". The position was graphically put by one local authority witness to the Milner Holland Committee who, in discussing controls over multi-occupation, said that they were "creating a battlefield where the local authority cannot provide the ambulance service to take off the wounded".

In the light of this, present government policy, referred to earlier in this paper, which will inevitably result in a stabilisation, if not a contraction of the public sector, seems the more remarkable. The reason for this is not a conscious desire to increase housing stress but simply a disregard of the central issue of housing policy. Present thinking in government circles does not seem to be grappling with the problem of how the nation is to be housed, but rather how can local government autonomy be erroded and central control be imposed over hitherto locally-made decisions. Housing is simply one of several implements in this battle between central and local government, and the more cynical would argue that the conferring of security of tenure on public authority tenants is nothing to do with principles of justice and fair dealing but simply a means of checking the growth of public housing and thus government expenditure, and of providing a palliative for the savage cuts in building and improvement programmes. The last few years have seen many attacks on local government powers and autonomy in housing as in other local government activities. Central control now seems to be the order of the day. This process has been carried on by the Housing Act 1980, the forced sale of public housing to sitting tenants being, perhaps, the greatest imposition of central policy on local discretion.

However, the large issue of security, across the tenure boundaries, is one that must be treated on its own merits. Insecurity can be an even worse problem than high rents, particularly for elderly people and families with young children, especially where, as in Britain, the State may provide some financial assistance with rent payments. The problem is often dealt with through rent control, rather than being treated as a separate issue[122]. The two are obviously related but, with few exceptions, every residential tenant, whether protected by rent regulation or not, should be assured that if he pays his rent and observes the other terms, covenants and conditions of his tenancy agreement, he cannot be evicted from his home unless the landlord provides a fair and adequate alternative.

[122]   See L. Neville Brown, (1970) 19 I.C.L.Q. 205.

TENANTS PROTECTION IN SWEDEN
– THE SAME GRAPES BUT A DIFFERENT WINE

by

Anders Victorin

Introduction

What is striking from a Swedish point of view about Professor Yates' very well-written and interesting paper about security of tenure for tenants on the British scene is that most of what is in it is so familiar. Except for technicalities such as the methods of circumventing the law, which are always different in different countries, Swedish law deals with most of the issues raised by English law. There is a great similarity in values, although the legal solutions may differ in certain respects. I am sure that the similarity is greater than may be obvious from the paper – some of the differences may be attributed to a different focus of the debate emanating from a difference in the structure of housing between the two countries. Of course one may say that such similarity is only natural. The matter of security of tenure for rented housing automatically raises a number of points, but I think that the similarities go further than that. It is for the purpose of this conference obvious that security of tenure is so basic in the protection of the weaker party that it simply cannot be overlooked. Security of tenure is necessary in order for the weaker party to exercise all of his rights, which also Professor Yates' paper demonstrates with great clarity.

Some Basic Dissimilarities

There are some basic dissimilarities in the structure of the law which I would like to mention. One which always attracts attention is the fact that British legislation is usually much more detailed than legislation in Sweden. I shall not go into this in any depth, but I would only like to mention that this is not to say that the Swedish rule system by necessity has to be less detailed. Swedish legislation, at least legislation in the 20th century, has increasingly relied on *travaux préparatoires*. The statutory text itself only spells out the main rules, whereas the details and the rules on interpretation are to be found in Parliamentary Bills and in similar official documents.

There is another dissimilarity which may not be entirely clear to Englishmen or to Swedes and that is the fact that the rules on tenancy in Swedish law do not apply to housing cooperatives and similar arrangements, where the house is owned by an association in which the "tenants" are members. These cooperatives, which are juridical persons rather similar to shareholding companies, are treated separately, although the relationship between the cooperative as "landlord" and the member as "tenant" is similar to ordinary tenancy relations.

One further small point in this connection: Swedish law does not allow leases for more than 25 years in towns and 50 years in the countryside. Therefore the legal device of very long leases is not available in Sweden and to the extent it is, it is very seldom used, particularly since leases for dwellings must not be transferred for consideration.

With regard to the rules on security of tenure there are also certain basic dissimilarities in the structure. First, in Sweden there is no difference between the private and the public sector, at least not after the abolishment of the rent control system. Although I can well imagine that there may be a case for such differences, particularly when it comes to solving the housing problems for particular groups (see e.g. D 2 in Professor Yates' paper), there are no applicable statutory rules.

Secondly, the categories of tenancies in Sweden are not the same as in British legislation. A discussion on protected tenancies, statutory tenancies, assured tenancies, secure tenancies and restricted contracts under Swedish law would be pointless. I shall return to this presently.

Thirdly, the distinction between leases and licences is not known to Swedish law (and from what I have seen it seems doubtful whether it is clearly understood by English lawyers either). According to English law, however, the lease is a contract granting an interest in land, whereas a licence seems to be a type of contract, which has developed from a mere permission ("licence") not making staying on land unlawful trespassing, to a contract, not creating an interest in land, although in other respects rather similar to a lease. There seems also to be a requirement of exclusive occupation, but this seems to be a point of debate.

Therefore the basic structure of Swedish law is simpler in theory, although not necessarily in practice.

In general, the present Rent Act (Ch. 12 of the Land Code) only deals with the contractual relationship between the landlord and the tenant. There are complex rules dealing with the Case that there is a new landlord e.g. because the property is assigned to a new owner. I shall not go into these rules here, but I shall only mention that the rules on the right to a new contract which I shall touch upon presently also apply in such cases. According to Swedish law, tenancy according to contract is a property right which is protected by registration or by a duty of the owner to reserve the right when assigning the property. Should, however, the property right cease to exist the right to a new contract still remains. The main effect of this with regard to flats intended for housing purposes is that the terms of the contract may be changed to the detriment of the tenant, an effect which is however less important since most flats are subject to collective bargaining. (Cf. Victorin in *Law and the Weaker Party*, I, pp. 3 ff.)

There are other differences as well. In general the property or land right aspect of tenancy is less pronounced according to Swedish law. One example is the protection of tenancy when the apartment is damaged. According to English law the lease attaches to the land, which the licence does not do. However, according to Swedish law the contract expires in such a case (see ss. 10 and 16 of the Rent Act). There may arise a claim for damages. Another example is that usually there is no right to assign the tenancy. Therefore the contractual tenancy appears to be more personal according to Swedish law, although I understand that in England most leases contain a covenant for non-assignability. However, social considerations go in the other direction. According to Swedish law the tenant has a right to use the tenancy in a barter for a new dwelling, a right which I do not think exists in England. This is however regarded as an important part of tenants' protection in Sweden.

As I hinted earlier, the Swedish Rent Act does not make a distinction between contractual tenancies and statutory tenancies, i.e. there is no formal distinction between tenancy agreements which are made voluntarily and such agreements where the tenant has made the statutory protection apply. According to s. 51 of the Act a decision by the rent tribunal or the housing court granting the tenant the right to remain in the dwelling is to be regarded as an agreement concerning the conditions for a prolongation of the tenancy. What happens is therefore that the rent tribunal in a dispute between landlord and tenant is authorised to make a contract for the parties. This may happen again and again. Normally the contract is for a definite period of time (usually one year) and the rules on prolongation become operative at the expiry of the contract. What we have here is a kind of duty to make contracts by statutory intervention.

Basic Preconditions for Security of Tenure

According to the Swedish Rent Act, tenancies are protected if they meet certain basic preconditions spelled out in s. 1 of the Act. The exceptions are spelled out in s. 45. I shall return to them presently. According to s. 1 the Rent Act applies to agreements on the letting of a house or part of a house for consideration. Here we have the same points as those of English law. It concerns a house or a part of a house, it must be let by an agreement (contract) and there must be "rent" payable.

Breach of contract

Security of tenure according to the Swedish ways of looking at things comprises security of tenure according to the contracts as well as the right to a prolonged (new) contract. The English term "statutory tenancy" then corresponds to the rules on the right to a new contract. However, the Swedish Rent Act in s. 42 contains rules on the right of the landlord to terminate the contract before it expires, rules which are mandatory in favour of the tenant. The tenant has no right to a new contract when the contract has been terminated in accordance with s. 42.

According to s. 42 the tenancy is forfeited and the tenant has to move in 7 cases. These all constitute breach of contract, such as failure to pay the rent, assigning the contract or subletting without permission, using the flat for another purpose than the one stipulated in the agreement, etc. In all these cases there is a certain amount of discretion emanating from the fact that the tenancy is not forfeited if the breach of contract is minor. In most cases the tenancy is not forfeited if the breach of contract ceases before the landlord takes action. (Cf. s. 46 p. 2) There are special rules concerning failure to pay rent. The rules of s. 42 are exclusive – the tenancy cannot be forfeited in other cases. There is, however, a general provision in s. 42(7) stating that the tenancy is forfeited if there is a breach of a contractual obligation apart from those stated in the Rent Act and it must be considered exceptionally important for the landlord that the contractual obligations are fulfilled.

Right to a New Contract

The right to a new contract is – as I just mentioned – the corresponding feature to the statutory tenancy. The provisions in the Rent Act on the right to prolongation, however, do not apply (s. 45) for
(1) furnished flats or vacation lettings unless the contractual relationship ceases within 9 months,
(2) flats shared with the landlord,
(3) a tenancy that is forfeited and the landlord has brought an action.

The tenant may waive his right to a prolongation in a special contract. The particular rules on this waiver are rather curious. If the contract is made before the tenancy relationship has lasted more than 9 months the contract must be approved by the rent tribunal. The rationale behind these rules is that it is valuable if short-hold lettings are brought on the market. Otherwise landlords might prefer not to let flats that are vacant for a short period of time, e.g. when the landlord is away or when the flat is vacant because the house will be demolished.

The 9-month rule is curious, since there is absolutely no reason for a tenant to agree to a waiver once a tenancy relationship has been established. The rule seems to be the effect of a mistake in the drafting when the former rules restricting the right to prolongation to tenancies that had lasted for 9 months were abolished or – rather – limited to apply only to furnished apartments and to vacation lettings. It should be mentioned that the Act attaches effect to the length of the tenancy and not only to the length of the agreement or contract.

S. 46 of the Rent Act deals with reasons for not granting a right of prolongation. The starting point is that such a right exists except in certain cases. Here the similarities to the English legislation are quite remarkable.

S. 46 of the Rent Act deals with non-discretionary as well as discretionary grounds for possession. However, the distinction between non-discretionary and discretionary grounds is not really the same as in English law. Needless to say, there are differences as to what grounds are discretionary.

There are two grounds for possession that clearly are non-discretionary. Point 1 deals with the case when there is a breach of contract which is sufficient to constitute forfeiture of the lease and the tenant is still in breach of contract. In this case the landlord could have brought an action, but for some reason has waited until the contract has expired after the ordinary notice. Point 7 deals with certain employment contracts in connection with tenancies. There is no right for prolongation when the employment has ended in the following cases of employment:

(a) public (government or municipal) that is coupled with a duty to occupy a certain dwelling – ministers of religion is one group covered and possibly some officers of the armed forces,
(b) agricultural, or
(c) other employment where it is necessary for the employer to utilise the dwelling for the needs of employees who hold the same position as the one whose employment has ended. Here the functional relationship between the employment and the dwelling is very tangible. The cases covered are probably rather few.

There is a second group of cases occupying a position in between those which are non-discretional and those which are truly discretional. These grounds are the ones dealt with under p. 2 when there has been a breach of contract giving cause for forfeiture other than under p. 1 and the contract therefore should not reasonably be prolonged, and under p. 6 and 6a in which the same test applies concerning houses meant for one or two families or a rented condominium flat and the owner wants it back.

In simplified terms the point of departure here is that the tenancy normally should be terminated. The formula used, that the contract should not reasonably be prolonged, allows the rent tribunal to take the needs of the tenant into consideration and to weigh them against the interests of the landlord. Here, as in other cases involving a weighing of interests, the predominant factor concerns the lack of housing in the region. In the case of an acute housing shortage the tenancy may be prolonged, although perhaps on a short-term contract with a short period of notice, which gives the landlord a chance of terminating the tenancy as soon as the tenant has been able to solve his housing problems.

Finally, there are several cases where the point of departure is rather the opposite. The tenancy should be prolonged if the landlord does not have good reasons and it is not unreasonable to the tenant that the tenancy is terminated.

This also involves a weighing of interests which may be rather complex. The weighing may vary according to the reason for possession. The main consideration is also here that the tenant is not made homeless.

These cases include demolition of the house (p. 3), rebuilding (p. 4), changing use of the flat (p. 5). There are also rules along these lines for superintendents which give them increased protection after 3 years (p. 8), which is the same as the protection for ordinary employees (p. 9).

The rest of the cases are dealt with in a general clause (p. 10).

It is obvious from this review that most of the cases dealt with in English law are the same that are covered by the Swedish rules.

Policy Issues

The matter of security of tenure is not a hot issue in the Swedish debate anymore. The problem is rather one of increasing it still further for some categories, such as tenants caught in the sale of a block of flats in order to transfer it to condiminiums. The rationale of a piece of new legislation that has been recently passed is thus to prevent a flat rented to a tenant from being owned by an individual owner of the flat, something which would move the position of the tenant to p. 6a in s. 46 of the Rent Act recently discussed. Another category that deserves increased protection is those with secondary holdings.

Nor does it seem much of a debate going on right now on the position of private landlords. The position of Swedish private landlords is perhaps not as desperate as the one of British, but still there is very little incentive to build new private rented housing. (See my contribution to the 1979 seminar).

The focal point of interest in these days is rather the transfer of rented dwellings into condominiums and similar arrangements. It seems to be an almost worldwide movement in this direction propelled by conservative governments and the prospect of profits being made by owners as well as dwellers. There are several governmental commissions working with a view to putting forth new proposals on these matters, dealing with direct as well as indirect ownership. However, I shall not go into this here.

Perhaps one way of bringing out the basic differences with regard to Swedish and British policy is to ask the rather extreme question: Why should there be any restrictions at all on security of tenure except for those cases where an ultimate sanction against severe breaches of contract is needed?

In my view it is fairly obvious that the most important rationale for strong limitations on security of tenure has become irrelevant, since there is no market any more in the sense that the landlord is allowed to ask the highest price the market can fetch. Rent control in one way or another prevents that. This argument is equally valid in England and Sweden.

Now, of course, if one were to imagine a legal system with absolute security of tenure with one exception – that the tenant must move if he cannot meet the price offered by someone else, which presupposes of course that there is no rent control – one would probably find that one would have to look hard to find good reasons to defend other limitations. In the normal context of a landlord letting flats for profit there does not seem to be much more that can be asked for from the side of the landlord. Or does he really have a genuine interest in the property other than that of making a profit? This is the difficult part and if one should take the standpoint that some kind of rent control is needed, the argument will not change, although I suspect that the limitations on security of tenure may to some extent be explained by the fact that it has been felt necessary to provide the landlords with some kind of compensation.

Looking at the purportedly genuine property interests I think one can separate between three different groups:

(1) The sentimental interests. This argument goes like this. It is my house and I am entitled to benefit from my property e.g. by using my right to live there or let my family or relatives live there. I do not think such arguments carry much weight unless in cases such as the owner of a small house who has let the house with a view to returning there later and living there, or if you have cases of sharing with the landlord.

Here there is a difference with regard to the structure of housing in Sweden and Great Britain. In Sweden flats let for rent are predominantly found in rather large blocks of flats, whereas in England also rented housing is found to a great extent in rather small houses. Even an occasional visitor cannot fail to notice this difference. This also means that the landlord in Sweden in most cases has a very limited personal interest in his property apart from that of a mere business undertaking. The British landlord, on the other hand, seems typically to be a private person or a small-time business-man.

(2) The interest of efficient use of property. It is of overriding importance that the capital invested in land is put to efficient use. Houses must be renovated or sometimes demolished and rebuilt. Economically they should perhaps not be used for housing purposes any longer, etc. As long as it is a matter of preserving the housing stock I do not think there is much to be said against this line of argument. As a matter of fact this line of argument is the

most important argument against housing cooperatives or owned flats. It is difficult to manage the house in a reasonable way if renovation and rebuilding is prevented by ownership or non-terminable leases. When it comes to changing the use of the land there is another story. Here genuine public interests are involved expressed e.g. in zoning laws. But there is also a matter of weighing of interests not unlike the decisions made when introducing rent control. Changing use of land is sometimes a very efficient way of evading rent control.

(3) Special duties or interests vested in the landlord. Evidently, considerations of this kind play an important role in the English rules on security of tenure for public owners, such as the rules on homeless persons or persons seeking employment. Another example is the exemption for universities letting flats to students. In Sweden, on the other hand, they play only a minor role. This has of course to be accepted to a certain extent, although I have the feeling that public bodies are much too quick in seeking the necessity of providing special rules for their needs.

There is, however, a fourth line of argument which is partly connected with the argument of the efficient use of capital invested in land, although it is perhaps even more based on society's interest at large. Absolute security of tenure would in effect mean that the tenure comes very close to a property right which would in its turn mean that tenancy would come close to home ownership. Under a housing shortage in particular this would mean that the decisions concerning the distribution of housing would be taken by the tenants just as is the case with regard to home ownership. It seems, however, that there should be a sector of housing where decisions with regard to distribution of housing, at least to some extent, should be based on the needs of the tenant. It is for instance not acceptable that a large proportion of small flats are kept by businessmen using the flats as a substitute for hotel rooms during their stay in a particular city. Nor would it seem acceptable that flats are kept by tenants who do not actually need them but who sublet them to homeless persons. Under such circumstances it is felt that the decisions regarding the distribution of housing should be made by the landlords rather than by the tenants or even, in extreme cases, by local government housing exchange agencies (*bostadsförmedlingar*) as will probably be the case, e.g., with regard to the centre of Stockholm. Here, the argument touches upon the considerations of special duties vested in the landlord. On the other hand, such an argument will also lead to a situation where the would-be property right is transformed into a right not to be made home-less or even to be guaranteed housing of a similar standard. The considerations with regard to the right of the landlord to give notice to tenants, e.g. when the house is to be renovated under s. 46 of the Swedish Rent Act, has in effect led to such a situation. The contract must be prolonged unless the landlord offers another suitable flat for the tenant, i.e. a flat which is approximately equal with regard to size and standard (although not necessarily with equally low rent).

Home Ownership

Law and the Weaker Party

The phrase 'law and the weaker party' suggests a view of law being employed in order to regulate unequal social relationships. Law, in some sense is used to redress inherent inequality. Such inequality is particularly perceptible in private law transactions, especially between private individuals and large, usually corporate, institutions (or, to a lesser extent other private individuals who are richer, more powerful etc.). Thus, in the sphere of contractual relations, the law has taken cognisance of and sought to mitigate "the inequality of bargaining power". Similarly, a body of law has been developed aimed at expanding the basis upon which transactions may be set aside because of "undue influence". Another example is the enactment of unfair dismissal legislation, which provides a remedy to a dismissed employee even if the termination of his employment by the employer is permissible as a matter of contract.

In Britain, these developments originated both in case law and legislation. The balance is redressed either by overlaying a public law regime upon a private law system (as, in a sense, is the case in landlord-tenant and employer-employee relations) or by transforming the structure of private law (as was, in large measure, initially the case in what became consumer law). This perception of inherent inequality – the constitution of stronger and weaker parties in modern legal discourse – has commonly been expressed in terms of status: landlords and tenants, manufacturers-retailers and consumers, employers and workers. This mode of classification involves, of course, its own difficulties (some landlords are stronger than others etc.) but one of its advantages, from the point of view of policy formation, is that it enables consideration and open discussion of "tenants' rights", "consumers' rights" and so on – of what are acceptable social standards and what forms of regulation are required in order to achieve them. Secondly, such ways of formulating the issues are connected with the formation of common interest groups – tenants' associations – or of pressure groups which can defend the interests of or act as "watchdogs" for a particular social grouping – consumers associations. A third effect of such legal change is that it may encourage an existing collective body to take up a legally defined issue and incorporate it into its agenda or *raison d'être*, for example, trades unions and unfair dismissal.

HOME OWNERSHIP

by

W.T. Murphy

It may seem curious to depict the owner-occupied sector of housing as one which bears upon the theme of "law and the weaker party". In many countries access to owner-occupation of housing is associated with belonging to the more prosperous sections of society. It is true of Britain too that a significant percentage of the population have never or never will be able to embark upon owner-occupation, and are forced to spend their lives in the public or private rented parts of the housing sector. Some would suggest that this is a misfortune in itself – that those denied access to owner-occupation are deprived of enjoying the benefits of private property, and around such a view, a whole ideology of the value of "home ownership" has been assembled. Modern Britain it could be said, is a nation of home owners instead of shopkeepers. In each case, the generalisation never applied to everyone in the society, but captured a central feature of its operative ideology.

Yet this is not simply a matter of the British *mentalité*, a transposition of a peculiarly British (or English) affinity for *petit bourgeois* values. Home ownership is of great importance so far as access to housing in Britain is concerned, statistically as significant as the public and private rented sectors combined. Indeed, with the public sector relatively stagnant, it has become for many the only practicable means of entry into the housing sector[1].

Access to the owner-occupied sector is dominated by a specialised group of financial institutions, and, in particular, the building societes[2]. The practices of these institutions have tended to determine the costs of home purchase and the terms upon which it can be enjoyed. Yet these practices are only minimally regulated. State involvement in the provision of housing has, since the 1920's, led to increased governmental involvement in the macro-level decision making and planning of the building societies. But regulatory

---

[1] Martin Boddy's synthesis of the available statistics suggests the following changes in tenure: 1914: Owner-occupied 10%; Public rented 1%; Private rented 80%; 1951: Owner-occupied 29%; Public rented 18%; Private rented 45%; 1978: Owner-occupied 53.9%; Public rented 32.3%; Private rented 13.8%. (Other, relatively insignificant, forms of tenure have been excluded from the summary). The owner-occupier form of tenure, on Boddy's figures, reached the 50% mark in 1970. See Martin Boddy, *The Building Societies* (London, 1980).

[2] See Boddy, *op. cit.* and, for the definitive historical account, Eric Cleary, *The Building Society Movement* (London, 1965).

legislation concerned with the activities of building societies has concentrated upon the protection of investors, by requiring, for example, a relatively high degree of liquidity to be maintained by the societies, and by specifying what kinds of securities the societies may lend upon[3]. Regulation of the relationship between the societies and borrowers (i.e. home owners) has been minimal. Most building society mortgages fall outside the reach of recent consumer credit legislation; traditional equitable doctrines which modified oppressive mortgages have only a limited scope[4].

There is a second sense in which the theme of "law and the weaker party" can be illustrated by a consideration of the owner-occupied sector. This originates in the endeavours of the courts to formulate ways of resolving domestic disputes concerning the ownership or occupation of the home. In such disputes, women, or women and children, or the aged, have come (albeit unevenly) to be treated as "weaker parties", and to be protected at the expense of a relatively stronger party, usually male and possessing a greater income-earning capacity.

The way in which the law has constituted and protected the weaker party in owner-occupied housing is unsystematic and diffuse, although certain patterns can be discerned, which are discussed below. The reason for this is partly historical, though the lack of system is perhaps inherent in the distinctive Anglo-American tradition of legal development. In the absence of a comprehensive code, the applicable law is to be found in different areas of the law, in particular, the law of real property and family law. The law of the "family home" can be seen as a point of intersection between these two areas.

These two bodies of law are grounded in different concerns and their goals conflict as they converge in the owner-occupied sector. This conflict has transformed real property law so as to "accommodate" the goals of family law and policy. These are considered in the sections which follow.

Property Law: The 1925 Code
The present system of rules governing land ownership and transfer derives from the 1925 Property Code, the most monumental legislation ever enacted in Britain[5]. This code marked the culmination of a century of

---

[3]   Such intervention tended to take place following sometimes spectacular collapses of individual societies and the discovery of fraudulent management practice: see Cleary, *op. cit.* Chaps. 8 and 9. The primary codifying statute is the Building Societies Act 1962.
[4]   See, for example, the fairly narrow reach of *Cityland and Property (Holdings) Ltd* v *Dabrah* [1968] Ch. 166.
[5]   Although originally conceived as a single (and therefore, perhaps integrated) code, the final framework emerged in the form of a collection of separate statutes, comprising the Law of

debates on the reform of the land laws which can be traced back to the establishment of the Royal Commission on the Law of Real Property established in 1828. The 1925 code was intended to improve the machinery of land transfer in two ways. First, it sought to simplify and rationalise the concepts of land law; secondly, it aimed at simplifying and rationalising the investigations which exchange professionals, in particular solicitors, had to make on a transfer and thereby shorten the time, and the expense, involved. The role of solicitors in the formulation of these reform proposals was ambiguous; on the one hand "drudgery relief" was both desirable and in their professional interest; on the other hand, an excessive simplification might endanger their effective monopoly of the technical aspects of land transfer and in particular the preparation of conveyances. Because of this they opposed a full-scale modernisation of the system of land transfer in the form of compulsory nationwide registration of title[6].

In this sense the code embodied a compromise, but for all that, its focus was upon facilitating land transfer, which necessitated removing anachronisms and archaisms in the traditional law. The important point is that the changes it introduced were largely procedural or technical: it was only the mechanisms of land transfer which were altered. The reforms of 1925 did not involve a significant reorganisation or redefinition of the peculiar forms of ownership which characterised and continue to characterise English property law, especially the prevalence of split ownership and the use of various forms of *settlement*.

Settlement

Settlement involved the splitting of ownership into present and future interests, limiting the rights of those presently entitled to the settled property to income or revenue rights (usufructs) and postponing till the future

---

Property Act, the Land Registration Act, The Land Charges Act, and the Administration of Estates Act. Subsequent amending legislation has left the framework largely untouched. For British lawyers, the fragmentation of the legislation into separate statutes can lead to interpretive difficulties, particularly as regards the question of what guidance one statute can provide for the interpretation of another. For a vivid example, see *Midland Bank Trust Co. Ltd.* v *Green* [1981] A.C. 513. A continental lawyer would no doubt observe that this difficulty is connected with the hesitation of British lawyers to adopt a "teleological" mode of statutory interpretation. For an Anglicised version of such criticism, see Freeman (1980) 43 M.L.R. 692. A different assessment of how the English judiciary approach the task of statutory interpretation is offered in Murphy and Rawlings "After the *Ancien Regime*: The Writing of Judgments in the House of Lords 1979/80" (1981) 44 *M.L.R.* 617. Consequently, "the 1925 code" must be viewed as something of a metaphor, or, at least, a simplification.

[6] See especially Avner Offer "The origins of the Law of Property Acts 1910–25" (1977) 40 *M.L.R.* 505. For an overview of the historical dimensions of lawyer's position in the property market, see Avner Offer, *Property and Politics 1870-1914* (London, 1981).

tne right to absolute ownership. Although perpetual settlements of successive usufructs were not permitted by law, and settlements of particular property were customarily of limited duration, convention and circumstance often ensured that property remained settled through the generations. As one settlement ended or was terminated, the property contained in it was often resettled.

The function served by these settlements was to combine the provision of a secure income with the intergenerational preservation and transmission of capital (especially in the form of land or funds). The precise forms which settlements assumed varied, but for present purposes, two main forms can be distinguished: those associated with or facilitating partible inheritance, and those intended to achieve or maintain impartible, dynastic succession. The former type of settlement was commonly a settlement of funds, often made on a marriage, with the income from the fund settled upon the husband for his life, then to his wife for her life if she survived him, and then the trustees of the fund were directed to pay the capital to the children of the marriage equally or in such proportions as the husband or wife might direct. The latter kind of settlement, which enshrined the principle of primogeniture, were called strict settlements, and these were normally settlements of land. Such settlements were designed not only to regulate the mode of inheritance, but also to ensure that the particular property in question remained in the hands of the family. Strict settlements were thus designed to make land inalienable for the duration of the settlement. Formally, this was achieved by ensuring that no one had the power to sell the land in the settlement; practically, this result could ensue because such settlements were often extremely complex and the conveyancing problems involved in transfer could be immense. These settlements were thus of particular concern to those nineteenth century land reformers who sought to promote the free alienability of land, since it was commonly supposed in the nineteenth century that half the land in England was held under strict settlements[7]. The

---

[7] The facts of the matter remain far from clear; the ubiquitous nature of settlement has been doubted: see especially Eileen Spring "Landowners, Lawyers and Land Law Reform in Nineteenth Century England" [1977] *American Journal of Legal History* 40. However, the evils of strict settlement and the rules of primogeniture were a commonplace of nineteenth century political and economic debate, as F.M.L. Thompson has illuminatingly shown ("Land and Politics in England in the Nineteenth Century" (1965)*Transactions of the Royal Historical Society* 23; see also Harold Perkin "Land Reform and Class Conflict in Victorian Britain" in Butt and Clark (ed.) *The Victorians and Social Protest* (1973).) A very influential contemporary work exemplifying this view was George Brodrick, *English Land and English Landlords* (London, 1881). Changes in the law, especially concerning primogeniture, would, it was argued, transform the "reality" – typical is Frederick Pollock on the subject: ". . . the point actually at issue is on both sides well understood to be the symbol of much more . . . If the legal rule of primogeniture in the strict sense were abolished, the artificial primogeniture of our family settlements would not long survive it" *The Land Laws* (2nd ed., London 1887)

reformers legislated to override any obstacle to sale by ensuring first, that whatever the settlement provided, someone would have a statutory power to sell the land. Secondly, they modified both the conveyancing rules and the structure of some basic land law concepts in order to eliminate the technical difficulties which had in the past obstructed free transfer.

The architects of the 1925 conveyancing code were thus preoccupied with ironing out the creases in the law of property which were in large measure consequent upon the dynastic or at least inter-generational objectives of the nineteenth century propertied classes, which had required many lawyers to direct their expertise towards perfecting modes of settlement for personal and real property which reflected and embodied the "frame of mind" of the Victorian propertied classes.

The bare essentials of the 1925 scheme were first, to employ various forms of trust in order to preserve income security and intergenerational transmission but secondly, to keep such trusts "off the title" so that transfer of title was not affected by the multiplicity of interests comprised in settlements[8]. This largely eliminated the conveyancing difficulties associated with settlements of land. But the reforms were premissed upon these practices of settlement, and did not envisage the consequences of the growth of mass owner-occupation, on account of which many family disputes came to be filtered through a grid of ownership rights in the family home.

The Family Law Code: Its Origins

The area of family law which has most significantly impinged upon home ownership is the question of financial provision and property adjustment on divorce. The statutory law in this field can be traced back to the full secularisation of divorce in 1857[9]. It is important to see that the original framework for financial provision – which remained unaltered in its essentials for over a century – was rooted in the same practices of settlement discussed above.

Just as marriage settlements were concerned to provide a secure income during marriage, so the courts were empowered by the 1857 Act to order the provision of a secure income to divorcees on dissolution of the marriage. This included a power (after 1859)[10] to vary family settlements (permitting

p. 175. However, the prevalence of settlement was a centrepiece of debate and a central target for the movement for "free trade in land", and underscored the pressure for legislative reform which, when it came, continued through from the Settled Land Act 1882 to the 1925 code. Such a consensus about the shape of legal and social change permitted a distinguished conveyancer to observe that: ". . . but for [the Settled Land Act 1882] the greater part of the landed gentry of England would have been ruined". Underhill, (1935) 51 L.Q.R. 222, 224.

[8] The legal changes are summarised in Megarry and Wade, *The Law of Real Property* (4th ed., London 1975) Ch. 6.
[9] In the Matrimonial Causes Act 1857.
[10] Introduced by section 5 Matrimonial Causes Act 1859.

the court to require the family trustees to make separate payments from the settlement income to each former spouse). The divorce code further mirrored the structure and purposes of settlement by empowering the courts to settle property on the children of the divorced couple, thus giving expression to the intergenerational rationale of settlement[11].

The point is not simply to place the old law in its proper context, but rather to draw attention to the way in which the old statutory framework was assembled as a mirror of nineteenth century family settlements. The problems consequent upon divorce (as opposed to the ethico-religious problem posed by divorce) were essentially property problems, and property problems meant income security and intergenerational transmission. Thus, divorce was not simply *confined* to the upper classes (because of the expense of litigation etc.); it was designed for the upper classes and gave expression to their aspirations and concerns[12]. In this sense, its emphasis upon maintenance – income security – for the divorced wife, while signalling the dependency of upper class women, was rooted in the particular social reality of settlement.

By the 1950's, the focus upon maintenance came to seem anachronistic. It is doubtful if this was seriously connected with a growth in the idea of sexual equality and the unacceptability of perpetuating the element of dependency enshrined in maintenance. Rather, the development of mass divorce after the war, spurred on in part by the availability of legal aid from 1949, meant that a regime aimed at the needs and practices of the wealthy of an earlier time had to be used to make adjustments consequent upon the break-up of a working class or lower class marriage. Here, the only family income would be earned income (and generalising, the husband's income would be the more significant) and the only capital asset would be the family home acquired on an instalment mortgage, that is, by means of earned income. Moreover (and this is perhaps at the heart of the change) the capital asset – the home – did not yield or produce the family income. The position was reversed; the family income – wages and salaries – produced, went to purchse the family asset. At the time of divorce, that process of acquisition would often still be in motion.

The very different focus of modern family law was also inaugurated in embryonic form in the nineteenth century. For present purposes, the most significant steps were the enactment of the Married Women's Property Act 1870 – which gave a married woman a legal right in respect of her husband to

---

[11] Section 45 Matrimonial Causes Act 185 /. ⅰne power applied only over the property of a wife who was sued for divorce by her husband.

[12] Which is not to ignore the "double standard" enshrined in the original divorce law – for its broader ramifications, see Keith Thomas "The Double Standard" (1959) 20 *Journal of the History of Ideas* 199.

retain her earnings – and the Matrimonial Causes Act 1878, which empowered magistrates' courts to make orders that a wife was not obliged to cohabit with a husband convicted of criminal assault upon her. The scheme of this Act – separation order, maintenance order and custody of the children vested in wife – became the model for a frequently expanded jurisdiction contained in the Summary Jurisdiction (Separation and Maintenance) Acts 1895 to 1949[13].

These reforms aimed at ameliorating the conditions of working class families, with particular emphasis upon the conditions of life of wives and children. They also marked the beginnings of a complex network of surveillance of the family by different "expert" institutions. The orientation of these interventions could variously be expressed as enhancing social control or preserving children (sometimes with explicitly eugenicist overtones)[14]. Modern family law developed within this orientation, infused with a combination of moralism and demographic engineering. Thus the expense of the divorce regime (and the resulting lack of access for the lower classes) was condemned for encouraging lax moral standards[15]. Since the growth of mass divorce, and the consequent recognition of marital breakdown as a "social problem", confidence in the "fault" basis – the notion of matrimonial offence – of the grounds for divorce has been eroded. The basis of divorce was reformulated in 1969, "fault" being replaced with the more "liberal" irretrievable marital breakdown!·

For present purposes, however, it is the growth of state agencies focussed around the rearing and welfare of children which was significant. In this respect, reform spans juvenile justice, social security law and family allowances, which form part of a complex system designed to be instrumental in what Jacques Donzelot has aptly described as the "policing" of families[16]. The field of adjustment on divorce came increasingly to be subsumed within a prioritised concern with the destinies of children. In other words, as the *grounds* for divorce were "liberalised", the fate of children became progressively the guiding principle as to the *consequences* of divorce[17].

The development of these interventionist and regulatory strategies, centred perhaps around "the preservation of children", were in no sense directly aimed at the family home, although, since the 1930's, the promotion

[13] An excellent summary of the activities of what became known as the "police courts" can be found in the Royal Commission on One-Parent Families. For a discussion of their earlier operation, see Iris Minor, "Working-Class Women and Matrimonial Law Reform 1890-1914" in D. Martin and D. Rubinstein (ed.) *Ideology and the Labour Movement* (London, 1979).

[14] See Jane Lewis, *The Politics of Motherhood* (London, 1980).

[15] See, for example, E.S.P. Haynes *Divorce Problems of Today* (London, 1910) p.16.

[16] Donzelot, *The Policing of Families* (London, 1979).

[17] See, for example, Mervyn Murch, *Justice and Welfare in Divorce* (London, 1980) pp. 185-208.

of home ownership was explicity linked with the valorisation of family life[18]. At this point, the link must again be made with the changing structure of the housing sector. In the decades after the war, the steady growth of owner-occupation, displacing in particular the private rented sector, meant that increasingly, on a divorce, housing issues were entwined with property issues in the disposal of matrimonial disputes. Thus the question was not merely one of the appropriateness or viability of income awards out of earned rather than unearned income, but of the disposition of the family home against the background of a thoroughly transformed pattern of housing availability.

The proprietary form of owner-occupation and the practical difficulties of access to housing led the courts to develop in the interstices of property law a reallocative jurisdiction permitting them to vary the property entitlements of the spouses on divorce. In this way, family law and property law converged in the owner-occupied sector.

What lay behind the attempt to give the wife a share in the property? Under the pre-1969/1970 law, the court had no power to order that the wife and children remain in the family home after divorce. If the house was in the joint names of the spouses, it would be necessary, in the event of disagreement over whether the house should be sold, to apply to court for an order. By refusing such orders, the courts could thus ensure that the wife and children remained in the home. But without an express property entitlement, the court could only achieve this result if, by implication, the wife was found to have a share. In other words, the attempt to develop a set of concepts awarding her an implied interest, while couched in terms of marriage partnership and the wife's *quid pro quo*, made it possible to preserve the occupation of the wife and children in the family home[19].

Property Adjustment on Divorce and Home Ownership

It is diffcult to summarise in a satisfactory way how the courts in modern Britain deal with the question of property adjustment on divorce. Legislation introduced in 1970 establishes a set of criteria to be used by the courts, to be applied with the paramount objective of "[placing] the parties . . . in the financial position in which they would have been if the marriage had not broken down . . ."[20] The appellate courts have insisted that their decisions are to be treated by Registrars and Divorce judges as guidelines only, and the relatively small number of cases which reach that level can provide only a glimpse (and possibly a distorted one) of the process throughout the country as a whole. There is, to add to these difficulties, some evidence which

[18] Boddy *op. cit.* pp. 12-26; see also Alan A. Jackson, *Semi-Detached London* (London, 1973).
[19] An alternative, less severe method was to award a reduced maintenance for the wife conditional upon her being allowed to remain in the house.
[20] Section 25 Matrimonial Causes Act 1973.

suggests that there are considerable regional variations in the way in which property adjustment is processed. Thus the "account" which follows is a summary of the visible appellate guidelines rather than a description of the less visible day-to-day administration of divorce.

In *Wachtel* v *Wachtel*[21], the Court of Appeal developed the guideline of the one-third rule: a housewife was to take one-third of the husband's income by way of support and one-third of the capital assets. Since that time, there has been mounting criticism of perpetual maintenance, particularly because of the burden which it imposes upon the husband and any future woman he may subsequently marry[22]. The continued significance of maintenance has also been criticised as embodying a notion of female dependency which is incompatible with contemporary ideas about equal opportunity and sexual equality[23]. Echoing some of these sentiments, the Law Commission recommended in 1981 that the emphasis upon maintenance for wives be reduced[24]. To a limited extent, the Court of Appeal had earlier moved in a similar direction, by stressing the value of trying to effect, in appropriate cases, a "clean break" on marital dissolution, whereby the capital could be split (either 50/50 or otherwise) and no maintenance awarded[25].

The priority accorded to the welfare of children, discussed above, cuts across this apparent concern with female independence. Since, in the majority of cases, the wife will be awarded custody of any children, the question arises of where they are to live. At this point, again, the link can be made with owner-occupation. The courts developed what came to be called a *Mesher* order,[26] whereby, whatever property adjustment and support for a wife was ordered, the wife and children would be entitled to remain in the family home until the children were grown. It remains to be seen whether the courts will carry through the logic which underpins *Mesher* orders, and order a sale of the home when the children have left[27]. In its recent report, the Law Commission has also reaffirmed the primacy of the children's welfare, and indeed recommends that the legislation be amended so that this objective replaces the paramount goal of the 1970 statute[28].

[21] [1973] Fam 72.

[22] See Part III of the Law Commission's "Discussion Paper" on the Financial Consequences of Divorce (Law Com. No. 103, Cmnd 8041, 1980).

[23] The view has been expounded by Ruth Deech "The Principles of Maintenance" (1977) 8 *Family Law* 229; cf. the reply by Katherine O'Donovan (1978) 8 *Family Law* 180.

[24] Law Com. No. 112 (1981)

[25] See Lord Scarman's opinion in *Minton* v *Minton* [1979] A.C. 593. But cf. *Dipper* v *Dipper* [1980] 2 All E.R. 722. For a useful summary, see Gillian Douglas "The Clean Break on Divorce" (1981) 11 *Family Law* 42.

[26] [1980] 1 All E.R. 126. The case was decided in February 1973.

[27] See the change of focus in *Dunford* v *Dunford* [1980] 1 All E.R. 122 and, more recently, the comments of Ormrod, L.J. in *Carson* v *Carson* (1981) *The Times* July 7.

[28] Law Com. No. 112, para. 24.

Finally, mention should be made of consent orders. One feature of the present system is that if the parties do not agree a settlement, it will remain possible for either side to seek periodical review of maintenance awards. Conversely, if agreement is reached between the parties, it will only be binding if the agreement is approved by the judge or registrar. In such circumstances, a subsequent review is precluded. Again, consent orders may not be obtainable if there are young children; in other words, until they are grown, the position often remains open to review[29].

The transformation of property law and owner-occupation

Here I wish to emphasise the way in which some of the basic tools foɪ expressing property rights or resolving disputes arising out of the ownership of property have been transformed in the attempt to "do justice" in the context of the family home. The following discussion is based on the assumption that a house is vested or registered in the name or one person, and a spouse, lover or relative claims some ownership or occupation rights.

1. Trust

The claimant may assert that an implied trust of the property arises in his or her favour. If this is successful, it will lead to the claimant being awarded a share of the equity value of the house (that is, to simplify, a proportionate share of the value of the house minus the value of the building society's security).

The origin of this kind of implied trust was the resulting trust developed in the eighteenth century. The classic formulation of its juridical basis is that where a conveyance is taken in the name of another, a trust of the property will result to the person who provided the purchse money. The person whose name appears on the conveyance will thus be a mere nominee and the true "beneficial" owner, recognised by the courts of equity, will be entitled to call for a transfer of the estate to him if he so desires. Equity would not impose a trust in every case; if evidence suggested that a gift was intended, no trust would arise. In other words, the trust was imposed on the basis of what the court supposed was intended; hence it came to be described as the *presumption* of a resulting trust.

A counter-presumption arose where the nominee was a member of the family in a close dependent relationship with the person who put up the money. This was called the presumption of advancement. As the term denotes, this was based upon the idea that the dependent, in particular, wives or children, had "something coming to them". In other words, it was rooted in the norms of the propertied classes concerning pre-mortem inheritance, and part of the same matrix of expectations which we have already considered in relation to the practice of settlement.

[29] See Stephen Cretney, *Principles of Family Law* (3rd ed., London 1979) p. 374.

These presumptions are rather ungainly in the modern instalment mortgage context. The presumption of advancement is now viewed as anachronistic and old-fashioned; husbands are not presumed to be making advances to their wives, if, for example, the house is in her name but he pays off the mortgage. The real problem, though, concerns the resulting trust. Over a thirty year period, many views were canvassed in reported judgments as to how it could be "adapted" to meet modern conditions. One "progressive" view was that of the "joint venture" or viewing the home as a family asset[30]. The conservative objection to this, which technically prevailed, was that community property and anything resembling it was not known to English law. Eventually, the courts settled upon a test of common intention or consensus. The house would be owned in the shares in which the parties actually intended and called the proprietary modification involved the imposition of a resulting trust.

Though the question of the scope of the resulting trust came twice to the House of Lords[31], the question still gives rise to confusion and uncertainty[32]. The problem is simply this: once the resulting trust is something more than a device which simply credits the "real" purchaser as against the "nominal" purchaser, it is difficult to know what kind of contribution is required in order to bring it alive. In the context of the acquisition of the family home, it is particularly difficult to know what account is to be taken of domestic labour, contributions to family expenses and so on. Are they to be treated as "indirect" modes of paying towards the purchase price (which is what, in essence, the loan repayments are)? There is simply no agreement among the judiciary on these points. While, in the matrimonial context, they do not matter on divorce, since the enactment of the reallocation jurisdiction, the problems here are still germane in a non-marital dispute, and also arise for married couples if one of the spouses becomes bankrupt or defaults on a mortgage, or if, after a divorce, one spouse remarries without a property adjustment having taken place.

2. Licence

Originally, a licence was the term used to describe a permission to enter upon another's land, thereby negativing trespass. But it has been transformed so as to become a substantive right to possession of the property of another, exactly analogous with a lease with many of the same incidents, including, in some cases, payment of rent and exclusive possession of the

[30] See, for example, Lord Denning's judgment in *Rimmer* v *Rimmer* [1953] 1 Q.B. 63 and, more emphatically, in *Gissing* v *Gissing* [1969] 2 W.L.R. 525.
[31] *Pettitt* v *Pettitt* [1970] A.C. 777; *Gissing* v *Gissing* [1971] A.C. 886 – on each occasion, overruling the wider formulations in the Court of Appeal.
[32] See, in particular, the divergence of interpretation disclosed by *Cowcher* v *Cowcher* [1972] 1 W.L.R. 425, and *Re Densham (A Bankrupt)* [1975] 1 W.L.R. 1519.

property in question. The conceptual nature of such licences has been variously described as contractual (promise based) or equitable (reliance based). Applying these clear analytical distinctions is not easy: in *Tanner* v *Tanner*[33], for example, a woman gave up a rent controlled flat to live in a house bought by the father of her children. The Court of Appeal held that the purpose of this arrangement was to provide a home for her and the children until they were of school leaving age. But whether this is promise or reliance based is difficult to say[34].

3. *Estoppel*

"Proprietary estoppel" was a residual equitable device employed in fairly rare circumstances. For example, in *Dillwyn* v *Llewellyn*[35], a father either promised or represented to his son that if the son built a house on land belonging to the father he should have a conveyance of title to that land. The problem was that, if this was a contract, it was oral and so unenforceable; equally, it was not clear on the facts that there was a contract. Because of the expenditure of money in reliance, an "equity" arose in favour of the son. The equity could be satisfied by ordering the conveyance to be made, which the court duly did.

Estoppel has become increasingly fashionable in many areas of modern law and, it might be suggested, a substitute for a more rigorous (or "traditional") legal analysis. One speaks loosely of "equities" arising on the basis of conduct, and invokes Equity in a remedial way to do what is "just". In the home ownership context, this way of thinking has become quite common. The main examples will be given. In *Inwards* v *Baker*[36], a man built a bungalow on land belonging to his father on the understanding that he, the son, could live in it for his life. On the death of the father, his widow sought possession of the bungalow; an estoppel sufficed to deny her claim. In *Greaseley* v *Cooke*[37], a woman who had lived with a family for years had her occupation of the home protected for life. The basis here was her expectation of life-long occupancy, the work she had done for the family, and the opportunities she had foregone. Any need for expenditure of money (which had been present in the earlier decisions) was expressly denied. In *Pascoe* v *Turner*[38], a man bought a house for the woman to live in with whom he had a long relationship. He led her to believe that the house was hers. She spent her savings repairing it. The relationship broke up and he sought possession.

---

[33] [1975] 1 W.L.R. 1346.
[34] Some English scholars suggest, in effect, that this is a distinction without a difference – see especially P.S. Atiyah *The Rise and Fall of Freedom of Contract* (Oxford, 1979).
[35] (1862) 4 De GF & J 517.
[36] [1965] 2 Q.B. 29.
[37] [1980] 1 W.L.R. 1306.
[38] [1979] 1 W.L.R. 431.

The Court of Appeal ordered him to transfer the title of the house to her, so extensive was the "equity" which had arisen in her favour. Some of the reasoning of the Court in *Pascoe* is unusual, even for this area of judicial activism. The man was rich and the woman poor: ". . . the court has to look at all the circumstances. When the plaintiff left she was . . . a widow in her middle fifties. During the period that she lived with the plaintiff her capital was reduced from £4500 to £1000 . . . by the date of the trial she had only £300 left. Compared to her, on the evidence the plaintiff is a rich man[39]."

The Commercial Face of Property Law

The transformation of property law in the owner-occupied sector discussed above has mainly been effected by means of judicial decision, and come about outside of and independently of the framework established in the 1925 Property Code. But, as suggested above, the code was intended to provide a framework both for interests in family property and a new regime of land transfer. The latter was to be kept free of legal complexities which might arise by virtue of the former. In the modern context, however, what is to happen if the title to the house is in one person, and he mortgages the house and defaults on the debt, or becomes bankrupt, such that the home is one of the only potential realisable assets to meet outstanding debts? Here, the protection of family life collides with the legal certainty and simplicity required by the market. The question of how to decide between these competing claims of those wanting to remain in occupation and strangers, especially financial insititutions or creditors seeking a sale to realise their security, has proved to be difficult and contentious. The Court of Appeal and the House of Lords have recently leaned in favour of according priority to those in occupation; the English Law Commission is thought to be reviewing the position[40].

Summary

If a husband and wife or any two intending cohabitees buy a house together and have the house conveyed to them in their joint names, then they will in most circumstances be taken to be joint owners of the property. If the house is transferred to the husband alone, the wife may acquire some share in the equity value, especially if she goes out to work and her income goes toward paying the household expenses, or if she has contributed directly towards

[39] *Ibid.* at p. 438.
[40] See *Williams and Glyn's Bank* v *Boland* [1979] Ch. 312 (C.A.); [1980] 3 W.L.R. 138 (H.L.). For the position on bankruptcy, see n. *infra*. The debate about *priorities* should be distinguished from the question of whether claims for residential security should be protected by occupation as such or by means of public registration of rights. For a discussion of some of the issues here, see Murphy and Rawlings, "The Matrimonial Homes (Co-ownership) Bill: The Right Way Forward?" (1980) 10 Family Law 136.

financing the purchase, for example, by paying some or all of the deposit. Considerable uncertainty is involved in determining how large a share she should get if she is able to establish that she should get something; if a dispute arises on divorce, she may, as we have seen, get between one-third and one-half under the statutory jurisdiction, and have occupation protected until the children are of school leaving age. If a question as to her entitlement reaches the court because creditors of the husband have initiated litigation, she may find that the basis of her share is scrutinised more carefully by the courts, and she may further find that, even if she has a share of the property[41], the courts will order the property to be sold in order to meet the husband's debts[42]. Again, there is no consistent thread in the case-law on this point. If the husband abandons the wife and leaves her in the home, she can register a special charge which will, unless the husband becomes bankrupt, have the practical effect of freezing all dispositions by the husband of the property and thereby protect her occupation[43].

If, by contrast, the co-habitee is "a mistress" she may have much more difficulty in establishing that she has a share of the equity. Again, if she has paid towards the deposit or paid out directly towards the mortgage repayments, the same general principles should apply, although experience suggests that she will have more difficulty in staking out as large a share as a wife could. If her contributions are less "tangible" – for example her input takes the form of labour (assisting in the construction or repair of the property) – then it may be necessary for her, if precedent is to be followed, to show that initially when the property was bought the couple intended to marry as soon as they were able[44]. Unless the evidence suggests such an intention as regards their relationship, her labour or contribution towards household expenses may not result, as it could more easily in the case of a wife, in her acquiring a share of the equity. Rather, it is more likely that the courts would call her a licensee, which would generally leave only the question of the length of time that her occupation would be protected in the event of a subsequent dispute. If there are children of the relationship, then by unspoken analogy with the position on divorce, a deferred order might be made, by holding that the terms of a contractual relationship were that she should occupy until the children were of school leaving age[45]. Even if there are children, the position may be different if the man is also maintaining a

[41] *Re Densham, supra.*
[42] *Ibid.* But cf. the recent cases of *Re Holliday* [1981] Ch. 405 (where the Court of Appeal refused a sale) and *Re Lowrie* [1981] 3 All E.R. 353, where the Divisional Court of the Chancery Division distinguished *Holliday* and for most purposes restored the old practice.
[43] Matrimonial Homes Act 1967 as amended.
[44] See *Cooke* v *Head* [1972] 2 All E.R. 38 (C.A.) Lord Denning repeated the significance of the intention to marry in *Eves* v *Eves* [1975] 1 W.L.R. 1338.
[45] See *Tanner* v *Tanner, supra.* Cf. *Chandler* v *Kerley* [1978] 1 W.L.R. 693.

marriage, and dies insolvent: if he owns two houses but one must be sold in order to meet his debts, it may be more likely that the mistress must give way before the wife[46].

If the house is sold over the head of such a licensee, it remains to be seen whether the courts would seek to protect occupation or uphold the rights of property. But it does seem that if the occupant is not a mistress but an aged person, a purchaser who buys at a lower price subject to that person's occupation will be bound by the promise given to the vendor and not able to get possession from the licensee[47]. Equally an aged relative who had lent her nephew a substantial sum in order to acquire the property, on the under-standing that she could live there until the loan was repaid, would be able to defend an action for possession from the trustee in bankruptcy into whose hands title had passed on the failure of the nephew's business[48].

Conclusion

The changes discussed in this paper can in part be attributed to the extraor-dinary influence over the development of modern law of Lord Denning. They reflect his distinctive concern with promoting the values of family life and protecting the "weak". Yet, however great Lord Denning's influence, the transformations I have discussed do not simply illustrate "what one man can do". They should rather be understood by viewing the family home as the "point of intersection" between two movements: first, the attempt to reformulate property law, as owner-occupation has displaced family settle-ment from the centre of the stage, and secondly, the increased concern with the regulation of families. In this context the similarities between the approach to the statutory jurisdiction ("family law") and quasi-matrimonial disputes ("property law") are striking, especially so far as the impact of children is concerned. It should further be said that in the field of home ownership, the displacement of orthodox property law which has occurred has the consequence (and perhaps the objective) of insulating the "casual-ties" of domestic disputes from the need to rely upon public housing or, to some extent, social security. In this sense, "weaker parties" (women and children) are protected at the expense of an only relatively economically stronger (male) party, who himself is largely at the mercy of the financial institutions which in fact dominate the terms and conditions for many of access to housing.

[46] *Horrocks* v *Forray* [1976] 1 W.L.R. 230.
[47] *Binions* v *Evans* [1972] Ch. 359.
[48] *Re Sharpe* [1980] 1 W.L.R. 219.

HOME OWNERSHIP: A COMMENT

by

Carl Hemström

The theme of this book is "Law and the Weaker Party". This suggests, as Tim Murphy says, an idea of the law being used in order to regulate unequal bilateral relationships. Home ownership introduces a number of different parties, and it is not always a simple matter to determine which of these parties are strong and which weak. Furthermore, a party which is strong in one respect may be weak in another. As regards the relationship between home-owners and the institutions from which they borrow the money to acquire their homes, there is, however, no doubt that *it* to a high degree is a true "law and the weaker party" relationship. In considering the relationship between home owners and financial institutions as chiefly a consumer contract, Murphy has chosen the relationship within the family as the focus for his report. I, too, will begin in the same area. However, I will then continue with a few remarks on "law and the weaker party" problems as regards Swedish tenant-owners' societies (*bostadsrättsföreningar*). I do so in order that an English audience may learn about these societies, particularly since there are a great number of Swedes living in houses owned by such societies. Finally, I shall also discuss the possible introduction into Sweden of a notion corresponding to the phenomenon of freehold flats (*ägarlägenheter*), in American terminology *condominiums*.

Home Ownership and Matrimonial Property in Sweden

In his paper, Murphy points to the tension between the use of formal instruments to record property transactions and the legal effect of informal "family" arrangements. He gives in this connection a description of developments in English law over a rather long period. Let me confine my remarks here to saying that, in Sweden, husband and wife became legally equal parties in 1920. At the same time, each spouse was given a right to half of the matrimonial property on the termination of the marriage.

The legal rules regulating marriage are still contained in the Marriage Code of 1920. However the Code has undergone great changes since then; especially concerning the commencement and dissolution of marriage. The rules on the economic relations between spouses are still awaiting revision. A governmental committee is expected soon to publish its proposals on some of the issues which will be discussed here[1].

One of the reasons for the alterations that the Marriage Code and other legislation have undergone during the last few decades, and which might lead to further alterations in the future, is a new way of looking at marriage as such. It is nowadays very common that men and women live together as couples without having been formally married; *i.e.* as cohabitees[2]. To a great extent the legislature has tried to make rules that apply neutrally to married couples and cohabitees. As regards the economic relations between the parties, there is, however, still a clear difference between married and non-married couples. Thus, in a marriage the spouses usually have matrimonial property, which is, it is to be observed, not co-owned during the marriage (although a spouse is not free to do exactly what he/she wants with his/her property) but is to be divided (in principle) equally when the marriage is ended through death or dissolution. However one, or both, of the spouses might also have private property, which the other party will not usually get any part of when the marriage is over. Private property may, for example, be established through a marriage contract between the parties. For cohabitees there are no corresponding rules[3].

Against this background I shall now turn to the division of the common home (dwelling) upon the divorce/separation or the death of one of the parties. My description of the Swedish system will start with the situation obtaining for married couples, and then go on with the situation for cohabitees.

A man and his wife, or either of the spouses, are free to decide when they wish to end the marriage – even if they sometimes have to wait for the expiration of a reconsideration period of six months before they can get a divorce. However, even if marriage is looked upon as a contract, such contracts have to be ended through a court decision. When such a case comes up, the court may have to rule on the common dwelling – the family home – until the property is divided. In this situation it does not matter if the dwelling is a house or a dwelling held with a tenant-ownership right (*infra* "tenant-owner dwelling") or a rented apartment. Nor does it probably matter if the house in fact belongs to the other spouse as his or her private

[1] The proposal was published in December 1981, see *Äktenskapsbalk* (Marriage Code), *Förslag av familjelagssakkunniga* (The Family Law Reform Commission), (SOU 1981: 85) Stockholm 1981.

[2] It is estimated that in 1980 roughly 20 per cent of all couples living together were not married. See SOU 1981: 85, at p. 618.

[3] In view of the fact that the institution of marriage still has a dominating position the Family Law Reform Commission has come to the conclusion "that there is no need for legislation which treats cohabitation as an alternative to marriage", SOU 1981: 85 at p. 622. This does not, however, mean that there is no need for protection of the weaker party on the dissolution of cohabitation. Cf. *infra* p. 71 footnote 10.

property[4]. The spouse who gets the right to use the dwelling until the property is finally divided is usually under no obligation to pay any rent to the other spouse even if the dwelling belongs to that spouse. If this continues for a substantial period of time the opposite might, however, be true[5]. As to the final division of the property, the rules concerning the dwelling of the family are to be found in an Act of 1959 with Special Regulations Concerning the Common Dwelling of Married Couples. This Act lays down that the spouse who needs the dwelling most has (with some exceptions) the right to it if this seems fair considering the circumstances of the case, unless the dwelling is a house which is real property and unless that house belongs to the other spouse as his or her private property. This means that the right encompasses not only houses which are not private property, but all tenant-owner dwellings and also all rented apartments.

I have said that the spouse who needs the dwelling most usually has the right to it if this seems fair considering the circumstances of the case. *Fairness* in this connection was illustrated in a case decided by the Supreme Court fifteen years ago[6]. The question arose in this case whether it was fair to decide that a wife should get a tenant-owner dwelling when the tenant-ownership right had been made the husband's private property through a marriage contract on the re-marriage (to each other) of the spouses, and the wife had, through unfaithfulness, grossly injured her husband. The Supreme Court decided that the wife should; nevertheless, have the tenant-ownership right, since she needed the dwelling for her and her two children (one of which was not the child of the man in question). The courts would no doubt – or rather *a fortiori* – come to the same conclusion to-day, as the legislature has since repealed the rules of the Marriage Code which earlier gave weight to whom was responsible for a divorce.

If the value of the home exceeds the amount that the spouse who needs the dwelling most is entitled to – in principle half of the matrimonial property (cf.*supra*) – he/she may get the dwelling in any event, if he/she pays the difference in cash. If, however, the party who gets this privilege does not fulfil this obligation, and the non-execution of the obligation is not of merely minor importance, then the division of the property, including the home, will be cancelled[7].

What I have said here with reference to the situation when spouses are divorced is *mutatis mutandis*, equally true when one of them is deceased.

[4] *Cf.* SvJT (Svensk Juristtidning) 1965 rf. ("Judgments of Courts of Appeal") p. 1. See also Beckman-Höglund, *Svensk familjerättspraxis*, (ed. 6, 1977) p. 53.
[5] *Cf.* NJA (Nytt Juridiskt Arkiv, "Judgments of the Supreme Court") 1968 p. 197.
[6] NJA 1966 p. 1.
[7] NJA 1975 p. 699.

Cohabitation and Home Ownership

As I have already pointed out, the Swedish legislature has, to a certain extent, tried to be neutral as regards marriage and cohabitation. This can be illustrated by legislation enacted in 1973 with rules similar to the ones applicable to married couples. Also, as regards common dwellings of cohabitees, the party who needs it most will get the dwelling if this seems fair considering the circumstances of the case: usually, however, only if they have, or have had, a child together. This rule reflects the fact that, in these cases, the legislature has tried to see to the interests of the children. The party who gets a dwelling that is held by the other party with some right has, however, to pay that party the value of the right. The difference between the 1959 and 1973 Acts is mainly (apart the fact that the 1973 Act is usually applicable only when the man and the woman have, or have had, a child together) that the 1973 Act does not give a cohabitee the right to obtain real property which belongs to the other cohabitee. In that sense, the 1973 Act can be said to treat all real property belonging to the cohabitees as private property of the spouses in a marriage.

So much for these rules for the moment. However, exactly as in English law, the question might arise whether these rules must not be supplemented by some informal rules. It might be difficult to establish justice with formal rules alone, and Murphy's paper points to a trust, a licence, and an estoppel as means to "do justice" in the context of the family home. As regards home ownership, the problems in Swedish law are mainly to be found in the area of real property, but as regards ownership, as such, of any kind of property, the same problem might have to be solved. Indeed, these are problems that we also meet within English law, where, for example, a claimant may assert that an implied trust of property arises in his or her favour. If this is successful it will lead, Murphy says, to the claimant being awarded a share of the equity value of the house. The judicial basis here is that, where a conveyance is taken in the name of another, a trust of the property will result to the person who provided the purchase money. If, on the other hand, a gift was intended, no trust would arise. But, Murphy asks, what kind of contribution is required to establish such a trust? How about domestic labour; how about contributions to family expenses; and so on? Exactly the same questions might be asked in Swedish law when a party has contributed domestic labour, or has paid parts of the expenses of the family, or, maybe, even part of the interest on the mortgage for the family home, while the other person in the family or the cohabitation relationship had the same dwelling registered in his or her name. The first party might, in these cases, claim that a house or a tenant-ownership right was, in reality, bought and owned by both of them with joint ownership *(samäganderätt)*, which is the main tool that the Swedish courts use to get a fair result. Indeed, there are some decisions by Swedish courts where a plaintiff has won such cases. The latest are from 1980 and 1981[8].

In the first of these cases, the Supreme Court declared that a woman who for more than 25 years had been living together with a man with whom she had a child, was the joint owner of a house which was registered in the man's name. But these were not the only circumstances of interest in the case. The Court of Appeal whose decision was, with one minor addition, accepted by the Supreme Court, drew attention to the fact that (1) the man and the woman had been living together like man and wife for more than 25 years; (2) they had, to start with, lived in an apartment rented by the woman; (3) the property was bought mainly to be used as the common dwelling of the parties; (4) the woman had paid only a fraction of the cost of the property but that, on the other hand, the brother of the woman had lent her and the man part of the necessary money when the property was bought, and the employer of the woman had guaranteed another loan; (5) the loan from the brother would not have been given unless the woman was one of the borrowers; (6) both the woman and the man had, at the time of the purchase of the land, paid instalments, the man slightly more than the woman; and (7) the woman had contributed during the cohabitation by buying almost all the furniture, as well as paying for other common expenses.

The 1981 case, on the other hand, concerns a married couple, who had made a marriage contract to the effect that all property which the spouses acquired should be the private property of the spouse who had acquired *that* property. Some time later, the man bought a piece of land from his father-in-law and built himself a pre-fabricated house on the land, assisted *inter alia* by his wife. The man was registered as owner of the land. Some years later, in connection with their divorce, the wife found out that the land and the house were the private property of her husband. She claimed that the land and the house were jointly owned by her and her former husband. The Supreme Court agreed. The court pointed to the fact that the piece of land had been bought, and the house built, to be used as the common dwelling of the spouses and their children. The land was sold by the father of the woman and at a much lower price than the market value. The father did not know of, or, anyhow, did not recall, the marriage contract, and he had intended that each of the spouses should get the same right to the land. The spouses discussed at the time of the acquisition neither the marriage contract nor which of them should be the registered owner of the land. The main work on the house was done by an uncle of the woman (who was however, paid for the work), but the man, the woman and her father all assisted in its construction. The man did much more of the construction work than the woman, but she also took care of the paperwork in connection with the construction and she took care of their home and children as well. The initial instalment was mainly made through a loan. Both the man and the woman had been working outside the home: the man all the time, the woman during certain periods. The man had paid amortisation payments and interest on the loan, but, beyond that, the incomes of both of the parties had been used mainly for their common living and for their home. Finally, the court pointed to the fact (1) that there was reason to believe the wife when she said that she had

[8] NJA 1980 p. 705; NJA 1981 p. 693.

believed that she had acquired part of the property at the time the house was built; and (2) that the man had agreed that his being registered owner was merely accidental and that there was reason to believe that he, too, thought that the land and the house were acquired by both of them and to the same degree.

The question now arises how many of the factors that we meet in these two cases are necessary before there is a joint ownership. That is difficult to answer. It seems however as if the Supreme Court has not accepted a rule for joint ownership such as has been found in two earlier Court of Appeal decisions[9]: namely (i) that the property was bought for the common use of the parties; (ii) that the party not registered as owner shall have made the acquisition possible through direct or indirect (*i.e.* working in the home) contributions to the common economy; and (iii) that there is no agreement between the parties to the effect that the party registered as owner is also the sole owner?

After the discussion – based, as far as Swedish law is concerned, on joint ownership – I should, however, add that, if a person pays all the costs of a house but lets his/her spouse be registered as owner, it is possible that the property might, nevertheless, belong to the person who paid the money.

Among questions that have to be asked in this connection are: When will direct or indirect contributions to the common economy be deemed extensive enough to justify ownership of the common dwelling? There might also be other items which have, instead, been bought with or because of these contributions, and which were intended for common use (*e.g.* food or other things which have been consumed). However, it could also happen that other items have been bought by the party not registered as owner; items intended for his or her private use. Furthermore, what rule should be applied when a party registered as owner had money enough to buy the property without any economic assistance from the other spouse or cohabitee? In addition what weight should be given to the time factor: *i.e.* how long the man and the woman have been living together? Finally should any weight be given to the fact if they have, or do not have, a child together[10]?

---

[9] See Agell, samboende utan äktenskap, (1982) p. 41–42 and compare his critical analysis of these decisions.

[10] It may in this connection be mentioned that the Family Law Reform Commission in its proposal for a new Marriage Code (SOU 1981: 85) proposes that "at the division of property, /the matrimonial home and the household goods which have been acquired for common use/ . . . are treated as the joint property of the spouses, each of whom owns a half share. It is /according to the proposal/ not possible to make such assets the private property of one of the spouses by means of a general marriage contract"(p. 618). At the division of the property "the matrimonial home . . . can be transferred to the spouse who has the greater need of a place to live" (same page). And as to cohabitation without marriage, the Commission declares that "as regards the home and the household goods that have been acquired for the common use of the cohabitants, the same considerations as in the case of the spouses can be applied. Consequently, the Commission considers that these assets should be regarded as owned jointly by the cohabitants, and should ordinarily be shared equally" (p. 622).

I mentioned earlier that the main tool in Swedish law to accomplish fair results in this area has been the use of joint ownership. I wish, however, finally to point to the possible use of the notion of *unjust enrichment* as another tool[11].

We have, so far, only discussed the relationship between spouses and cohabitees. However, the rules that regulate the relationship between them have to be supplemented – and indeed they are – by rules which solve the problem in relation to the landlord when there is a rented apartment, and in relation to the tenant-owners' society when there is a dwelling held with a tenant-ownership right. But the landlord might also be under an obligation to accept a tenant under other conditions. For example, if a person who is married or cohabiting and is the sole tenant either ends or forfeits the tenancy, then the other spouse or cohabitee has the right to become the tenant in his place, provided that the remaining spouse or cohabitee lives in the apartment and is acceptable. Furthermore, if two persons are both tenants, they are often both protected.

Finally, if a spouse has let a house to a third party and that house is matrimonial property and the spouses' common dwelling, or if a spouse has let or transferred a rented or tenant-owner dwelling to a third party, then the other spouse may, under certain conditions, have that lease or transfer cancelled. The same rule applies to cohabitees as regards rented and tenant-owner dwellings. To this should be added the fact that real property which is not private property is protected against being sold or mortgaged, since the sale or mortgage of such property needs the written consent of the other spouse.

To sum up, therefore, as in English law, legal developments in Sweden as regards dwellings have been towards the protection of the weaker party: usually women and children. Several problems remain, however, to be solved. One such is to determine when the party not registered as owner should get a right to that property and when he should not. Another problem is to what extent the rules should be applied in the same way as to married spouses and unmarried cohabitees. This also poses the question of how to define cohabitation.

Rights of Tenant-Ownership
I said when I started this comment that I would also say a few words about both dwellings held with tenant-ownership right and freehold flats.

There are at present governmental committees working in Sweden in both these fields. I will only briefly comment here on the 1971 Swedish Act on Tenant-Owners' Societies. Instead, I shall take up problems which are at

[11] *Cf. Agell, op. cit.*, p. 51.

present under discussion, and which will perhaps lead to legislation in the future.

As regards "law and the weaker party", the legislature of the 1971 Act on Tenant-Owners' Societies has been quite aware of the problems that tenant-owners might run into. Therefore, the rules of the Act are mandatory unless the Act itself indicates otherwise. The rules adopted for the protection of tenant-owners include a combination of rules from the Act on Societies and the Rent Restriction Act. Both of these areas include regulation to protect the weaker party, and they are therefore of relevance in this connection. Which, then, is the weaker party in this relation? To start with, it is, no doubt, the person who intends to pay an instalment to the society in connection with the forming of the society and the construction of the house. In this situation, the individual needs protection against economic ventures which are either dangerous or too expensive for him. Thus, the Act tries to see to it that everybody who is interested in acquiring a share in the society can rely on the calculations that are made. Nevertheless, calculations one year may cause problems in a later year in times of quickly rising building costs. Therefore, the Act contains rules concerning conditions under which members can be released from a society and the costs in connection with the apartment. The Act also contains rules regarding the transfer of a tenant-ownership right to a new member: what conditions may be applied by the society, etc. As regards the relationship between those living in the dwellings and the housing society, the rules are, to a great extent, similar to those of the landlord and tenant relationship. I shall, however, not go into further details of the Act here. Instead, I am going to point to some questions which we are discussing in Sweden at present.

Nowadays, a tenant-owners' society is normally created in connection with the construction of one building or several houses on an estate. The possibility of transforming, and the right for tenants to transform, an apartment house into such a society causes, however, problems of other kinds. Under what conditions, if any, should, for example, a landlord be compelled to accept the transfer of his property (the apartment house) to a tenant-owners' society? Should the same rules apply to all kinds of landlords, or should some be excluded? And what about the tenants? Is it enough if a minority of the tenants in a house want to form a society, or should a majority be required? And in that case, what majority? Under what conditions should a member be freed from his or her undertaking to become a member? The opposite problem might also appear: Should a tenant-owners' society be allowed to exclude any of the old tenants from membership? It should be mentioned in this connection that the protection for tenants in an apartment house that is transformed into a housing society was recently strengthened. In October 1981, an amendment of the Act on Tenant-Owners' Societies became effective. This amendment excludes (with one exception) the possibility of making a rented dwelling a cooperative dwelling as long as the tenancy goes on regarding that dwelling. To return to problems in the area: How can tenants get the economic assistance that is usually necessary if they are to be able to become members of a tenant-owners' society which is being transformed from an ordinary apartment house? And to what degree should the societies be allowed to make arrangements that force a member of the society who wants to sell his tenant-ownership right to sell it to, for example, the local community?

Let me just conclude my comments by saying that, to a very high degree, the problems that I have now mentioned with regard to tenant-owners' societies are also applicable as regards freehold flats: Who should have the right to start a conversion process, the old landlord or only the tenants? And what percentage of the tenants should be required? What protection do those who stay as tenants need, and what do the owners of the freehold flats need? The similarity of the problems to be solved makes it natural to ask the question: What is it that the form of freehold flats offers which the form of tenant-owners' societies cannot?

As for English law in this area, I can conclude by saying that it seems as if the legislature has been more interested in giving housing associations economic means to provide accomodation than in deciding what forms the dwellers should be organised into and what kind of influence they should get.

(Written for a symposium in Stockholm in the Autumn of 1981; footnotes added later.)

PART II

CONSUMER LAW

THE APPLICABILITY OF GENERAL RULES OF PRIVATE LAW TO CONSUMER DISPUTES

by

Francis Reynolds

In England, and no doubt in most if not all Western countries, the law of contract is assumed to be of general application: that is to say, all contract disputes of whatever nature should be soluble by the application of the same basic principles. It is true that contracts for the transfer and lease of land tend to be considered separately. This is partly because of different historical development, association with a separate jurisdiction (the Court of Chancery) and with the practice of conveyancers and (in the case of leases) the amount of statutory control to which they are subject. But the present trend is towards assimilating them into the general fabric[1]. The contract of employment, also, has taken its own route historically, and now has much statutory overlay: but again the present tendency is to seek to assimilate its governing principles, at any rate, into the general fabric[2].

The existence on the Continent of Europe and elsewhere of Commercial Codes suggests that need has at some time been perceived for the modification of the basic principles of contract to the special requirements of commercial disputes. Such codes can of course also be accounted for by the specialised nature of commercial litigation in particular countries. They are in any case on the decrease rather than the increase (if one excludes the Uniform Commercial Code, which, despite its title, is not confined to purely commercial transactions). The general principles of English contract law (which is almost entirely derived from case-law) are, however, already heavily commercially oriented. This has to some degree always been so: many of the early great cases stemmed from the efforts of Lord Mansfield to

---

[1] *E.g.* the strict effect of stipulations as to time in the renewal of a lease was relaxed, by reference to commercial principles, in *United Scientific Holdings Ltd v Burnley B.C.* [1978] A.C. 904; a view that in certain situations in connection with the sale of land it was not possible to rescind and claim damages was overruled in *Johnson v Agnew* [1980] A.C. 367; and it was held in *National Carriers Ltd v Panalpina (Northern) Ltd* [1981] A.C. 675 that the parties to a lease of land might be released from their obligations by a fundamental change of circumstances, under the doctrine of frustration.

[2] The main problems have concerned whether the principles of discharge (termination) are different in employment contracts: *Thomas Marshall (Exports) Ltd v Guinlé* [1979] Ch. 227; *Gunton v Richmond L.B.C.* [1981] Ch. 448; *London Transport Executive v Clarke* [1981] I.C.R. 355.

assimilate commercial disputes into the general common law in the eighteenth century, and from the commercial judges, such as Lord Blackburn, of the nineteenth century. But it seems to have become even more true of late and the understanding of this fact is very important for the proper appreciation of the contemporary English rules, at least as they are customarily expounded. Many of the leading cases which students learn and analyse for the purpose of extracting basic principles concern litigation on international trade and shipping in general: many of them involve no English litigants or facts at all. Thus one of the leading decisions of waiver of contractual rights concerns rejection of a bill of lading, relating to a shipment from Brazil to Antwerp, for wrong dating[3]; the leading decision on exclusion of liability clauses was for some fifteen years that in a case on a consecutive voyage charter for the carriage of coal in a Swiss-owned ship from the United States to the continent of Europe[4]; recent decisions relevant to economic duress concern Dr Armand Hammer's chartering operations[5] and a contract for the building of a ship for a Liberian company in South Korea[6]. A leading case on illegality in the performance of a contract concerns an overloaded grain ship[7]; four key decisions on the extension of the benefit of exclusion clauses to persons not party to the contract in which it is contained involve the Hague Rules[8]; a group of significant decisions of recent years concerning discharge of contract by breach ("termination", "rescission") relate to bulk commodity shipments[9], tramp ship chartering[10] and shipbuilding in Japan[11]; probably half the cases on frustration (release of the parties from a contract by supervening change of circumstances) deal with ships affected by warlike situations[12] (the other major cataclysm of the twentieth century leading to litigation on this topic being the cancellation of the coronation processions of King Edward VII in 1902); and the leading case on the principles of damages assessment concerns carriage of sugar in bulk from Constantza to

[3] *Panchaud Frères S.A.* v *Et. General Grain Co.* [1970] 1 Lloyd's Rep. 53.
[4] *Suisse Atlantique Société d'Armement Maritime* v *N.V. Rotterdamsche Kolen Centrale* [1967] 1 A.C. 361.
[5] *Occidental Worldwide Investment Cpn.* v *Skibs A/S Avanti (The Siboen and Sibotre)* [1976] 1 Lloyd's Rep. 293.
[6] *North Ocean Shipping Co. Ltd.* v *Hyundai Heavy Industries Co. Ltd. (The Atlantic Baron)* [1979] Q.B. 705.
[7] *St. John Shipping Cpn* v *Joseph Rank Ltd.* [1957] 1 Q.B. 267.
[8] *Pyrene Co. Ltd* v *Scindia Navigation Ltd.* [1954] 2 Q.B. 402; *Midland Silicones Ltd* v *Scruttons Ltd* [1962] A.C. 446; *A.M. Satterthwaite & Co. Ltd* v *New Zealand Shipping Co. Ltd. (The Eurymedon)* [1975] A.C. 154; *Salmond & Spraggon (Australia) Pty. Ltd* v *Port Jackson Stevedoring Co. Ltd (The New York Star)* [1981] 1 W.L.R. 138.
[9] *Cehave N.V.* v *Bremer Handelsgesellschaft m.b.H. (The Hansa Nord)* [1976] Q.B. 44 (citrus pulp pellets); *Bunge Cpn* v *Tradax Export S.A.* [1981] 1 W.L.R. 711 (soya bean meal).
' *Hong Kong Fir Shipping Co. Ltd* v *Kawasaki Kisen Kaisha Ltd.* [1962] 2 Q.B. 26. *Reardon Smith Line Ltd* v *Yngvar Hansen-Tangen (The Diana Prosperity)* [1976] 1 W.L.R. 989.
[12] There are too many to list.

Basra[13]. I once heard Professor Karl Llewellyn say that he did not under-stand English contract law until he discovered Lloyd's Reports.

On the whole, the tendency of these cases is towards strict interpretation of contractual duties, particularly where (as is of course normal in commer-cial cases) the contract is written. The desirability of such interpretation is indeed something of an article of faith among English commercial judges. Lord Wilberforce, in a domestic case relating to a lease, recently said "I think that the movement of the law of contract is away from a rigid theory of autonomy towards the discovery – or I do not hesitate to say imposition – by the courts of just solutions, which can be ascribed to reasonable men in the position of the parties"[14]. But two months later Lord Bridge, in a case relating to payment of hire under a time charter, thought it important that the courts should "strive to follow clear and consistent principles and stead-fastly refuse to be blown off course by the supposed merits of individual cases"[15].

What is the reason for the predominance of such case-law? Its existence can be accounted for by the fact that London has long been a centre of international trade, shipping and insurance, and therefore also of arbitration and litigation. This explains the presence of such cases, but not the relative absence of other types of litigation at appellate level. Litigation involving land, which is prominent in common law jurisdictions where there is less commercial business, has, as already mentioned, in England taken a differ-ent route, partly because it is to no small extent conducted by a specialised group of barristers and judges in what is now the Chancery Division of the High Court. Only at the appellate level do the streams mix more easily, and there have been, as already mentioned, some recent appellate decisions which may lead towards unifying the principles to some extent. Construction and engineering disputes, which seem conspicuous in the United States, do not seem to proceed easily to appeal: they tend to come before a special type of judge, an Official Referee, from whose decisions appeals for some reason do not seem common[16]. Commercial cases too, come before a specialised court, the Commercial Court (which is however part of the Queen's Bench Division of the High Court of Justice): but here appeals are frequent.

The results of this overall orientation towards the supposed needs of international commercial litigation is that it can strongly be argued that the law of contract as it is understood in England (and other common law jurisdictions which pay attention to English precedents) is totally unsuited to

[13] *C. Czarnikow Ltd* v *Koufos (The Heron II)* [1969] 1 A.C. 350.

[14] *National Carriers Ltd* v *Panalpina (Northern) Ltd., (supra,* note 1) at p. 60.

[15] *A/S Awilco of Oslo* v *Fulvia S.p.A. di Navigazione of Cagliari (The Chikuma)* [1981] 1 W.L.R. 314, 322.

[16] Though a leading recent decision is *Woodar Investment Development Ltd* v *Wimpey Con-struction U.K. Ltd* [1980] 1 W.L.R. 277.

consumer disputes, the special nature of which is a fairly recent discovery, but is now of course generally acknowledged. To resume for a moment the former catalogue in a more specialised context, a leading decision on the requisite degree of conformity of goods sold with their description concerns Russian timber[17]; and the most recent leading cases on the "merchantable quality" which the Sale of Goods Act requires of goods sold concern Brazilian groundnut extraction[18], citrus pulp pellets[19] and cloth bought in commercial quantities[20].

As Professor Hellner pointed out a few years ago[21], there are various courses which a legal system can follow when confronted with a problem of this sort. One is to seek to make the general law suitable for private transactions, and add special rules for commercial cases by way of a Commercial Code. This is the case in Germany, where the special rules appear, not surprisingly, to be stricter than the normal rules[22]. It would not be at all appropriate in England, where the general rules are themselves strict. The most extreme converse position would involve the drafting and implementation of some sort of Consumer Code, and it is perhaps worth considering the merits of this solution first.

An obvious point in favour of such a Code is political. It would represent a famous victory for consumer bodies and a clear recognition of the special needs of the consumer, and as such would tie in with the various manifestoes of consumer rights that have from time to time been promulgated. It would facilitate concentration on the appropriate rules for the regulation of consumer transactions, and would probably enable the assimilation and improvement of the law as to consumer credit and perhaps also other transactions (such as hire) which regularly involve consumers. Attention has recently been drawn in England to the defects for general analysis in the classical model of the not-yet-performed contract involving reciprocal promises directed towards the making of profit, and to the limits imposed by the notion of promise[23]. Many consumer disputes involve instant or "quick-hand" transactions which do not relate easily to the notion of promise – and furthermore should arguably involve the liability of a person (the manufacturer) with whom there is no direct contact, and who is not involved in the transaction[24]. Concentration on the special nature of consumer law would facilitate the proper analysis of these problems, including some of

[17] *Arcos Ltd.* v *E.A. Ronaasen & Son* [1933] A.C. 470.
[18] *Henry Kendall & Sons* v *William Lillico & Sons Ltd* [1969] 2 A.C. 31.
[19] *The Hansa Nord (supra*, note 9).
[20] *B.S. Brown & Son* v *Craiks Ltd* [1970] 1 W.L.R. 750.
[21] [1978] *Scandinavian Studies in Law*, 55, 59-60.
[22] HGB, arts. 373-382.
[23] Atiyah, 94 L.Q. Rev. 193 (1978); *The Rise and Fall of Freedom of Contract* (Clarendon Press, Oxford, 1979).
[24] See *Jolowicz*, 32 M.L.R. 1 (1969).

those of product liability, whereas the application of the general law of contract at present distorts them.

As against this it may be said that to erect special categories immediately presents (as in the case of commercial sales and tribunals, and special rules and tribunals for disputes involving public bodies) technical problems, unconnected with the merits of the dispute in question, of determining whether a particular matter comes within the special category or not. Preliminary to this are the problems of deciding whether these special rules should apply also to disputes between consumers, and to disputes where the consumer is the seller. Furthermore, examples can easily be produced of consumers who are more powerful commercially than the concerns with which they are dealing: and of commercial dealers who are in as weak a position as any consumer and just as much in need of protection – indeed more in need of protection than some consumers. They are not however an identifiable category: there is a sliding progression from the strong to the weak. It may reasonably be asked also whether the group of consumers really has sufficiently indentifiable characteristics to receive special treatment, to the possible distortion of other areas of private law. In size the group is even larger than those of employees and tenants (groups which do not aspire to a complete Code): in fact every individual has a private capacity in which he belongs to it. Again, the consumer has, at least in a Western economy[25], more choice available to him than the tenant or the employee: in most (but not all) situations he can acquire what he wants by other means, and can improve quality or terms of contract by allotting more economic resources to it. On general grounds there are, finally, arguments that simple basic principles, of self-evident moral, practical or economic value, should be seen to lie at the back of, and justify, all dispute settlement, even if their application is different in different spheres of human activity. A consumer code may be thought to carry implications of fundamental reorganisation of legal techniques for which the case is not at present made out.

The lesser alternatives would seem to be two[26]. The first is to supplement the general rules of law by special rules for consumers, as in the Swedish Consumer Sales Act of 1973 and in the proposed consumer services legislation. The second, if general legislation already exists, is to incorporate provisions protecting consumers into it. This can itself be done in two ways. First, special provisions applicable to consumers or consumer situations designated by that name can be incorporated into the legislation: some of them can be made mandatory (e.g. those relating to exclusions of liability). The second way requires simply that the general techniques and concepts

---

[25] Contrast the position in Socialist systems: Eörsi, *International Encyclopedia of Comparative Law*, vol. VII, Chap. 16, pp. 153 *et seq*.

[26] *Hellner, op. cit. (supra*, note 21).

used be reconsidered and if necessary reformulated with a view to making sure that they are adaptable to the special problems of consumer disputes, which may not have been present to the minds of the original draftsman. A technique sometimes used in England which could be employed here is the insertion of guidelines for the application of "open-textured" notions, for example that of "merchantable" or "reasonable quality", to which I shall return[27].

I propose to consider these possibilities in connection with some well-worn problems relating to the sale of movable goods to consumers. The sale of land, which in England almost always requires the intervention of lawyers, attracts too many special considerations to be of use here: and the problems of consumer services transactions are so new to systematic study that any work, such as that of the recent Swedish commission, must be pathfinding. Problems of housing and employment law are in any case the subject of separate considerations at the present meetings.

Although the general law of contract is in England based on case-law, sale of goods is regulated by a statute into which special terms for consumers could be inserted, so that either of the techniques referred to in the previous paragraph could be implemented. The Sale of Goods Act 1893, which was re-enacted in 1979 for the purpose of consolidating into it the various amendments made up to that date, is not far off in time from the Swedish Act of 1905, and the now obsolete American Uniform Sales Act of 1906 followed it closely while seeking to improve on it. It applies to all sales, whether between oil companies or private individuals, by a large business concern to a consumer, by a large business concern to a small business concern, or by a consumer to a business concern. There is no provision for any special type of transaction other than the confining of the implied promises as to quality to professional sellers[28] (there being no requirement as to who is the buyer). The Act has very much the same slant towards commodity sales between traders as Professor Hellner attributes to the Swedish Act[29]. It should be noted at once however that a considerable problem relevant to consumers, that of unfair contract terms, has in England been hived off by the Unfair Contract Terms Act 1977. As I have pointed out elsewhere[30], this applies only to clauses excluding or restricting liability: it does not cover all types of unfair contract term, nor all consumer transac-

---

[27] This practice, and certain connected questions of technique, are discussed by Treitel, *Doctrine and discretion in the law of contract* (Clarendon Press, Oxford, 1981). Its application in England has hitherto been insufficiently systematic.

[28] S. 14.

[29] *Op. cit. (supra,* note 21) at p. 58.

[30] *F. Reynolds,* "Unfair Contract Terms: A Comment", in Alan C. Neal (ed.) *Law and the Weaker Party, Volume I* (Abingdon 1981) pp. 95-103; see also *Benjamin's Sale of Goods,* (2nd ed., 1981), ss. 985, 1027.

tions, nor all situations where standard terms are used. These are however difficulties at the fringe: the Act certainly provides for a large central area where consumers (and others) may need protection. The result of the Swedish Act to Prohibit Improper Contract Terms is presumably similar.

If we take the basic duties of the seller, they are in the English Act to supply goods of the contract description, which he has the right to sell, and which are of merchantable quality and reasonably fit for their purpose[31]. I omit at this stage questions of time of performance as being less often relevant to consumer situations.

The first duty, to supply goods conforming with description, has largely been litigated in connection with technical specifications in commodity contracts, *e.g.* as to measurements of timber, or the meaning of "Hard Amber Durum Wheat[32]:" and its application has been strict[33]. Cases in which consumers have found it useful to rely on this provision are few[34], and most of them in fact settle for rather a loose interpretation of this requirement, in the context of determining (prior to the 1977 Act) that an exclusion clause cannot limit the seller's duty below a certain minimal compliance[35]. The requirement of conformity with description is not always separately formulated in sales legislation (except sometimes in connection with delivery of the wrong quantity) and seems to give rise to no special problems in the context of consumer sales.

The consumer is more likely to complain of the quality of goods: and here there are two provisions, restricted to professional sellers but not to consumer buyers, requiring the goods to be "merchantable" and "reasonably fit for their purpose".[36] The first term is on its face directed towards the requirements of merchants, who can dispose of goods for varying purposes, rather than those of the consumer, who is likely to want them for one self-evident purpose and to have very limited opportunities of resale or use for another purpose. Although its scope is made reasonably wide by a recent statutory definition[37], it is much criticised by consumer organisations on the basis that its interpretation is dominated by the assumption that goods not

---

[31] Sale of Goods Act 1979 ss. 12, 13, 14.
[32] *Toepfer* v *Continental Grain Co.* [1974] 1 Lloyd's Rep. 11.
[33] As in the Russian timber case *(supra,* note 17).
[34] An example is *Beale* v *Taylor* [1967] 1 W.L.R. 1193, where a car was advertised as "Herald Convertible, white, 1961." It was in fact an amalgam of two cars of different dates welded together. The seller argued that the buyer had bought the metal contrivance in which he attempted to drive away: but the court held that the advertisement contained the description of what was sold.
[35] See*Coote*, 50 Aus. L.J. 17 (1976) criticising *Ashington Piggeries Ltd* v *Christopher Hill Ltd* [1972] A.C. 441, where Norwegian herring meal contaminated in such a way as to be poisonous to mink was held still to be herring meal.
[36] Sale of Goods Act 1979, s. 14 (1) (2).
[37] S.14(6).

satisfactory for one purpose may be sold or used for another. The leading
cases, indeed, concern, as already mentioned, Brazilian groundnut extraction and citrus pulp pellets[38], goods not regularly used by consumers. The
definition, and also the requirement of reasonable fitness for purpose, are
said to concentrate too much on whether goods can be *used*, and to provide
insufficient indication that consumer acceptability should be pitched at a
higher level – that consumers reasonably expect goods in perfect condition,
without scratches, dents or defects (an example often used is that of the new
car in which the cigarette lighter does not work).

In my view these criticisms are rather laboured and could be met by a
reformulation avoiding reference to the word "merchantable", which seems
to have been used with the juries of merchants that heard commercial cases in
the nineteenth century in mind. The existing formulation is not in my view
antipathetic to these factors being taken into account and it does not seem
clear that the more general provisions on latent defects in Civil Codes[39] are
necessarily much of an improvement. But there is no doubt that it is quite
difficult, at any rate where the seller is uncooperative, for a consumer to
reject goods on the ground of defective quality; it seems rare for a new car to
be successfully rejected after litigation[40]. One reason is that the attitude of
the courts may be articulated in a commercial case where a buyer was
seeking to reject on unmeritorious grounds[41]: the requirement may then be
pitched rather high (bearing in mind that in English law damages would also
be available if an express term is broken). Such a case may well, by virtue of
the amount of intellectual input and output generated by the amount of
money at stake, become a leading case, and what is decided and what is said
in it may not be helpful to consumers.

The difficulty in English law is then that if the goods are not bad enough to
be rejected there is no remedy at all (unless special contract terms provide
it). This is because of the special technique of English law, criticised but
recently strongly reaffirmed[42], which designates certain principal terms in
contracts as "conditions". This use of the word is unusual and misleading,

---

[38] *Supra*, notes 18 and 19.
[39] CC, art. 1641; Quebec CC, art. 1522; BGB, art. 459.
[40] A recent failure to reject appears in *Leaves* v *Wadham Stringer (Cliftons) Ltd* [1980] R.T.R.
308 (defects in braking system). Rejection has been easier where the car was known to be
required for a special purpose: e.g. *Spencer* v *Claud Rye (Vehicles) Ltd,* quoted by *Whincup*,
38 M.L.R. 660 (1975), where a car bought for a honeymoon involving the crossing of the
Alps proved to be prone to boil. The purchaser, a barrister, appeared in person.
[41] Thus was probably the case in *The Hansa Nord* (*supra*, note 9) where the Dutch buyer
rejected the goods and then, when they had been sold by order of the court, apparently
bought them in through a nominee. On the other hand there are also non-consumer cases
where rejection may have been permitted too easily: see those cited *in infra*, note 54, where
the defects could easily have been cured.
[42] *Bunge Cpn* v *Tradax Export S.A.* (*supra*, note 9).

but the result of a term being so designated is that *any* breach of it entitles the party prejudiced to terminate the contract (and sue for damages). This gives powerful rights if the term is broken, and is a mainstay of the strict techniques applicable to commercial contracts already mentioned. But if the relevant term is "open-textured", as is the condition of merchantable quality, it may not be broken at all: hence there may be no remedy at all.

One way of meeting the difficulty would be to improve and (perhaps) tighten up on the definition of the general requirement of reasonable quality and then provide a general rule (as does the 1980 Vienna Convention on the Sale of Goods)[43] that only a major or "fundamental" breach entitles rejection of the goods by the buyer. This would be the general commercial rule: and it could then be modified by special rules, rather as in the Swedish Consumer Sales Act, making rejection rather easier for the consumer (perhaps subject to the seller's right, and/or the buyer's duty, to attempt to cure defects). This might be unacceptable in England as diminishing the strict rights of rejection in commercial cases, to which much importance has been attached: indeed the unfavourable attitude of the Convention towards rejection (also to be seen in the Uniform Commercial Code, at least in non-consumer transactions) may make English legal and commercial interests hostile to it. It can also be said that it is odd to remove a right to reject, only to replace it later, albeit in a limited form.

Another course, which might be more acceptable, is to sharpen up the general definition of the required quality in a more discriminating fashion (there is of course no reason why the uncommon word "merchantable" should be retained) by the addition of guidelines indicating the factors to be taken (non-exclusively) into account. Such guidelines already effectively appear in the Uniform Commercial Code[44] and in the Vienna Convention[45]: but the typical technique now used in England is to provide that in determining a specified question "regard shall be had in particular to . . .". Some of these could be drafted specifically to refer to the needs of consumers, and refer to matters such as suitability for immediate use, possession of the characteristics of appearance and finish appropriate to consumer goods sold as new, etc. This would in my view be a proper use of guidelines, pointing the court, within the framework of a general concept or notion, towards factors which might otherwise, because the existing case-law arises in a different context or against a different social or historical background, be overlooked. Any consequent claim by the retailer or wholesaler against the manufacturer could be made simpler by the inclusion of further criteria formulated with such claims in mind. It is obvious that it is not enough to draft provisions

[43] Art. 49.
[33] S. 2-314(2).
[45] Art. 35.

favourable to consumers if the duties of the person selling to the retailer are not framed with an eye to the consumer claims which the retailer may have to meet.

A point frequently raised in connection with consumer sales is that of durability. Consumers buy for use, not resale: and hence the life-span of a product is important to them. For commercial purposes, and in my view for all true analytical purposes, the durability is inherent in the quality on original sale: *i.e.*, the fact that the goods break down or deteriorate soon after purchase indicates that they were not of an appropriate quality or in an appropriate condition when sold. But the point is regularly put that this is in practice not enough for consumer disputes: what is needed is some overt recognition, to brandish before the seller or the court, that the law cares about durability. At the risk of some illogicality, therefore, it may be desirable to add this as a special term, rather than to write something to the effect into the guidelines to which I refer above. Since the breach of such a term may only be apparent by accumulation over a period, the special technique of designating the term as a condition is inappropriate: this term is not sufficiently sharp to be isolated as one any breach of which entitles rejection. It should therefore probably be subsumed into the category, sometimes called in England "innominate terms" – viz., ordinary terms breach of which may entitle rejection, but only if sufficiently substantial or fundamental: otherwise there will be an entitlement to damages only[46]. One must then ask, should such a term, inserted to meet the perceived needs of consumer complaints and litigation, therefore be confined to consumers? It seems in principle wrong for it to be so limited. There must be others, e.g. commercial buyers of fleet vehicles, farmers buying tractors, dentists buying drills and so forth, who expect durable products and would like help in the case of a dispute. If such a duty is to be formulated it is difficult to find conclusive reasons for confining it to consumer transactions.

Problems of non-delivery and late delivery are not differentiated in common law jurisdictions to the same extent as may occur in some civil law systems, though commercial contracts are of course more likely to contain specific provisions as to time of performance. The English approach is to say that time is likely to be "of the essence" in commercial contracts: otherwise something like a *mahnung* or *nachfrist* may be the only way of establishing a breach of contract[47]. It is difficult to see that there is or should be any

---

[46]   But the test is pitched so as to make rejection rather difficult: the deficiency must be "frustrating", not merely "unreasonable": See the *Hong Kong Fir* case (*supra*, note 10). As so often in this area, the factual background to the leading cases is far from the world of the consumer.

[47]   *E.g. Charles Rickards Ltd* v *Oppenhaim* [1950] 1 K.B. 616, where a custom-built Rolls-Royce was delivered late. But see also *McDougall* v *Aeromarine of Emsworth Ltd* [1958] 1 W.L.R. 1126 (time clause in contract for building of pleasure yacht).

difference of principle for consumer transactions, though there will of course be differences of application. The same seems to be true of the stipulation as to the seller's right to sell, though some protection may be needed as regards transfer of title to bona fide purchasers in consumer or private transactions[48]. The rules as to partial performance are strict in English law[49], but the difficulties may be solved by a right to cure to which I refer below.

If we proceed from duties to remedies, it next becomes appropriate to consider whether or not the normal remedies laid down for breach of contract are appropriate for consumers, or whether a special regime is needed, and if so, what form it should take. I propose in this connection to ignore the remedy of enforced or specific performance. In common law countries this is taken to mean an order of the court, enforceable by imprisonment, that a contract be performed, and is rare, though less rare than it used to be. It is on the whole confined to articles of unique value or which are in short supply, and would not be thought of as a suitable run-of-the-mill remedy for consumer cases. Its availability can also have repercussions in bankruptcy law, which noticeably complicates the issue. Consideration of the extent to which a more general approach favouring the enforcement of a duty to perform leads to different emphasis and results in matters such as entitlement to the price or the property, rights to cure and to have cured, rights to resell or to make cover purchases on the other party's account, etc., is a complex exercise in comparative law which would not be immediately relevant to the question here discussed[50]. It may be noted, however, that in Socialist legal systems, where cover purchases may not be so easy, the emphasis on enforced performance, at the expense of termination or rescission, seems to be considerable[51].

I start therefore with the right to reject, alternative terms for which include "termination", "rescission" and (though not in common law) "avoidance". Karl Llewellyn regarded this as the appropriate remedy for consumers but not for commercial men. "It fits the case of the wallpaper which is just enough off-colour, or the radio which is just enough off-true, to edge the nerves"[52]. Although this judgment as to interests in rescission is perhaps a little simplistic[53] (and I have never thought of the wallpaper example as

[48] There is special provision for hirers and conditional buyers of motor vehicles in Part III of the Hire Purchase Act 1964.
[49] Sale of Goods Act 1979, s. 30: an entire consignment may be rejected for short or excessive delivery.
[50] See Treitel, *International Encyclopedia of Comparative Law*, vol. VII, Chap. 16 at pp. 6 *et seq*.
[51] Eörsi, *op. cit.(supra*, note 50) at pp. 153 *et seq*., 162 *et seq*.
[52] 37 Col. L. Rev. 341, 388 (1937).
[53] *Priest*, 91 Harvard L. Rev. 960 (1978). For example a commercial seller may not be able easily to resell: a consumer buyer may not fail to notice a chance of escaping from a bad bargain, or may be able to cure the defect himself. "There will be a continuum of merchants' and consumers' resale costs, so that any broad distinction between merchants and consumers, while efficient in general, will fail in particular cases" (p. 974).

providing on its face a very strong ground for rejection) it seems reasonable to assume that to reject the goods and buy again is often the simplest course for a Western consumer. On the basis of supposed commercial needs, and in disagreement with Llewellyn's view, English law on its face tends to favour rejection in *all* cases. If a term is designated as a condition any breach of it, however slight, and whether or not it causes inconvenience or loss, entitles rejection. The only modification to this occurs, as has been seen, where the term is itself "open-textured" (or where it is not designated as a condition at all). Paradoxically, this is a considerable exception and makes rejection more difficult for the consumer (who has to rely on the "open-textured" provisions) than the commercial man.

If the terms as to the seller's duties were sharpened so as more readily to apply to consumer disputes, it might however be thought that it would then become too easy for the consumer to reject. Tiresome as car dealers may be, it is surely undesirable that a new car can be completely rejected for some small fault which can easily be rectified and which the seller is equipped and prepared to rectify. In the case of complex artefacts it can be argued that the price is so set as to allow for detailed inspection and testing by the consumer rather than the manufacturer, and rectification on demand within a set of guaranteed period. Excessive quality control would raise the cost to the ultimate purchaser. English books usually cite two (non-consumer) cases where goods were successfully rejected for miniscule defects which could have been rectified: one where a computing scale had a broken glass on the dial of the scale, and one where a thicknessing machine had a broken shield and set-screws[54]. Neither seems on its face very satisfactory, because in each, cure was easily possible.

It would hardly be practicable to provide that consumers must exercise their rights reasonably, whereas commercial men need not, even though the results of such a surprising principle might not be out of line with practice in certain spheres of activity such as commodity markets. Much more appropriate therefore, if one has complex artefacts in mind, is to give the seller some right to cure defects, which, because of the threat of rejection he will doubtless in most cases be zealous to exercise. Since the tender of non-conforming goods may sometimes be a breach, at common law such a general right would need to be created by statute. But this again it would be difficult to confine to consumer sales: for a start, it might well be politically unacceptable to consumer organisations that consumers alone had to submit to a right to cure, the exercise of which might often prove slow and tiresome.

[54] *I.B.M. Co. Ltd.*, v *Shcherban* [1925] 1 D.L.R. 864 (cost of glass 30c: the seller offered to pay the buyer to replace it); *Winsley Bros* v *Woodfield Importing Co.* [1929] N.Z.L.R. 480 (cost of cure £1: but the machine would not work without these items). The leading English case is *Jackson* v *Rotax Motor and Cycle Co. Ltd.* [1910] 2 K.B. 937 (dented and scratched motor horns rejectable though cost of cure "trifling").

But in many commercial situations, *e.g.* machinery specially manufactured, farm machinery, boxes of cheap plastic goods delivered to a small retailer, such a right would be equally appropriate: indeed, it is provided for in the Uniform Commercial Code[55], which of course covers both types of transaction, and in the Vienna Convention[56], which does not apply to consumer sales at all.

Therefore it would seem that such a right to cure (which might perhaps sometimes be discharged by an offer of a reduced price but should probably not prejudice the right to damages where loss can be proved) should not be confined to consumers, but must be limited by general criteria only, such as are found in the Uniform Commercial Code, the Vienna Convention and the Swedish Consumer Sales Act. Under the Uniform Commercial Code the right to cure varies in accordance with whether the time for performance has expired or not: if it has, the right is less likely to be exercisable. It seems to me however that the more general phraseology applicable to the right to cure after the time for performance has expired would serve both purposes: it requires the seller to have "reason to believe" that the tender would be acceptable with or without money allowance. Not dissimilarly the Swedish Act permits cure if it can be effected immediately and without the buyer being subjected to any costs or substantial inconvenience: and the legislation proposed by the Ontario Law Reform Commision permits it "if the nonconformity can be cured without reasonable prejudice, risk or inconvenience to the buyer; and if the type of cure offered by the seller is reasonable in the circumstances"[57]. All these formulations, whichever one may prefer as a matter of drafting, seem to me principles reasonably applicable to all types of transaction: and as an outsider I am not clear why the provision (and indeed other provisions) of the Swedish Act should be confined to consumers.

The right to cure is plainly introduced having in mind minor defects which do not seem without more to justify rejection: but it is arguable that not only should it not be restricted to consumers, it should not be restricted to minor matters either. A major defect may sometimes be curable (e.g. by complete replacement) more easily than a minor one. Nor does it seem that there is any reason of principle which would confine the right to defects in the goods as opposed to partial performance (where the English rules are strict against the seller) and late performance (where they may not be). There may be differences of application, but that does not mean that there should be differences in principle.

[55] S. 2–508(2). On its face this only allows the substitution of a "confirming tender": but see White and Summers, *Uniform Commercial Code* (2nd ed.) pp. 322–323.
[56] Art. 48.
[57] Report of the Ontario Law Reform Commission on Sale of Goods (1979), vol. III, Draft Statute, s. 7.7.

The Ontario Law Reform Commission conclude that if there is to be a seller's right to cure there should be a complementary right in the buyer to demand cure[58]: and in the context of consumers (who may have difficulty in proving damages) this appears at first sight reasonable. It would however be less appropriate for commercial dealings, where unscrupulous buyers might force upon distant sellers quite inappropriate demands for cure unless a further set of criteria as to reasonableness was devised. Perhaps simpler in this area is to treat the right to reject as primary, which can sometimes be averted by the exercise of the right to cure. The reciprocal view looks neat and logical, but economy of means may give better results. However, what all this may show is that the introduction of such a right requires complete legislative provisions (as in the Ontario Draft Bill) or vaguer provisions leaving a lot to subsequent case-law (as in the Uniform Commercial Code).

The right to reject the goods cannot continue indefinitely: it must be lost at some point. Some civil law systems are accustomed to an absolute bar on rejection for non-conformity calculated by time, i.e. a special limitation or prescription period, as was the case with the aedilician actions of Roman Law. Indeed the Vienna Convention contains a two-year bar in this respect[59]. Such limits are unknown to the English common law, and it is difficult to see one being introduced unless considerable effort is made to educate the public to knowledge of such a bar, which will affect more ordinary citizens than the normal rules on limitation of actions. Perhaps a three-year limit might be considered, on the analogy of the three-year limitation period which operates in England in actions for personal injuries[60], which affects many ordinary citizens and probably is not well known. But this is subject to exceptions when the injury is not reasonably discoverable within the period, and in certain other situations that cause great difficulty[61]. Consumer organisations might similarly wish to defer the running of the peroid to the time when the defect ought to have been known of, which would generate similar problems. Again, more general principles seem appropriate.

The applicable principles at common law proceed on the basis that the right to reject is lost on "acceptance" of the goods. As an organising notion this seems reasonably to accord with common thought, and it does not seem to me that the negative formulation of which the Uniform Commercial Code makes some use, "fails to make an effective rejection"[62], advances the matter to any considerable extent. The drafting of the provisions relating to acceptance in the Sale of Goods Act has caused difficulties for English

---

[58] *Op. cit.(supra*, note 57) vol. II, pp. 465-467.
[59] Art. 39(2). Cf. UCC s. 2-607(3) (reasonable time).
[60] Law Reform (Limitation of Actions) Act 1954.
[61] See Limitation Act 1975.
[62] S. 2-606(1).

lawyers which I shall not go into: but broadly the intention of the relevant provisions is that the right to reject is lost (i) by words, viz. by stating that the goods are not rejected and are acceptable: (ii) by conduct, viz. by acting in a way inconsistent with an intention to exercise the right to reject; and (iii) by inactivity, viz. by retaining the goods for "a reasonable time". The second of these is subject to an opportunity to examine the goods: the first and third are not[63].

Such general rules are difficult to fault, though their application may cause problems. But from the consumer point of view three special problems arise. First, the consumer does not normally have facilities or expertise for testing goods, and is to some extent entitled to assume that the goods are in perfect order. Second, there may be a danger that a consumer who does not reject but allows the seller to go on trying to remedy the defect may get himself into a position in which he may be held to have accepted by conduct[64]. And third, a consumer who expressly states that he accepts goods may be ill-advised in so doing – particularly where he signs in haste or imprudence some form of delivery note acknowledging the receipt in good order of goods which he had not examined.

The first two are matters that could arise in any transaction, even if it is in consumer transactions that they are more likely to cause difficulty. They can be taken into account by careful reconsideration of the wording of the provisions as to inconsistent conduct and reasonable time, so as to demand of the consumer less vigilance than is expected of the businessman. It may even be possible to insert guidelines, though the economy of means which I am in general urging throughout this paper suggests not doing this unless it seems absolutely necessary for the purpose of drawing attention to considerations which are in serious danger of being overlooked. The Uniform Commercial Code again takes account of these points by setting two stages, this time for returning the goods. The first, rejection of non-conforming goods, can be effected quite easily. The second, revocation of acceptance, is more difficult to justify: it requires more substantial defects and is conditioned on such factors as the expectation that the defect will be cured, difficulties of detecting the defect, and the seller's assurances concerning it[65]. It seems that consumers have more often succeeded in a revocation suit than have commercial concerns, which is not surprising[66]: but the right is not confined to consumers, nor does there seem any reason why it should be. The argument here is again one of simplicity and economy of means: whether it is necessary to reflect the obvious increasing difficulty of rejection as time passes by means of separate rules, or whether the whole problem can be subsumed (as I would prefer) under more general criteria. The provisions

[63] Sale of Goods Act 1979, ss 11, 34, 35.
[64] As perhaps in *Jackson* v *Chrysler Acceptances Ltd.* [1978] R.T.R. 474.
[65] S. 2-608.

as to remedies in the Uniform Commercial Code are far from easy for a lawyer, let alone for a consumer who would like to have a thumb-nail sketch of his rights and the ideas by which they are justified[67].

The third point is however rather different. Here it is sought (as in the case of unfair contract terms) to release a person from the consequences of clear actions, on the ground that he is in such a position that he should be protected against the results of his own imprudence. One way of accomodating it might lie in the inclusion of some general statement to the effect that an express indication of acceptance will not of itself be conclusive that the goods are accepted – this might or might not be made dependent on the fact that they could not reasonably have been inspected. But if it is desired to attack the special social problem (if there is one) of delivery notes (which in England may not be caught by the Unfair Contract Terms Act) then this must be done under the general heading of control of improper or unfair marketing practices, such as is found in most Western countries.

The final remedy in the consumer's armoury is his action for damages. The breadth of the general principles which regulate these in the common law (which regards damages as the primary remedy in all contractual actions) is very considerable[68]. There is virtually no difference of principle between damages for delay and for other breaches; the limited awards of the *actio quanti minoris*, of course, have no place; liability in damages does not usually (and hardly ever in sales) depend on fault; there is now in principle no objection to *dommage moral* if its occurrence was within the contemplation of the parties. Only punitive damages are excluded.

In most situations the consumer, like the businessman, can make a cover purchase. The main form of damage which the consumer will suffer which a commercial buyer might not will be the disappointment, inconvenience and frustration which come from having an unsatisfactory consumer product, the product being bought for use and not redisposal. Although the Sale of Goods Act 1979 does little more than refer in general terms to the loss directly and naturally resulting from the breach[69], which has long been taken to mean the foreseeable loss within the contemplation of the parties as likely to result from the breach, the courts seem to be edging forward in this area. Thus damages have been obtained in respect of a holiday spoiled by repeated trouble with a car[70], and the "expense and frustration" caused by car

---

[66] See *Priest, op. cit.* (*supra*, note 53) at pp. 979, 995.
[67] See *Peters*, 73 Yale L.J. 199 (1963).
[68] The general principles are usually taken as having been laid down in *The Heron II* (*supra*, note 13). For a view that the principles are unsatisfactory, and that the Court should formally be given a discretion, see *Sir Robin Cooke* (a judge of the Court of Appeal of New Zealand) [1978] C.L.J. 288. The New Zealand Contractual Remedies Act 1979 gives the court discretion as to *all* remedies and is a most interesting experiment.
[69] Ss 51(2), 53(2).
[70] *Jackson* v *Chrysler Acceptances Ltd* (*supra*, note 64).

breakdown in normal domestic use[71] and there are other examples in the context of the travel industry. This problem does not require any special rules as to damages for consumers: detailed rules as to damages are conspicuously absent in the common law. The difficulty here is more likely to be a procedural one: whether it is worth the consumer's trouble to make claims which may well be difficult to bring home if the suit is energetically defended. Only if it is desired to make consumer damages perform some sort of cautionary or "policing" function is it desirable to have special rules: but such a proposal is outside the scope of this discussion.

My conclusion, then, on the basis of this particular analysis, is that not only is a Consumer Code inappropriate, but that in general the special problems of consumers can be and should be accomodated within the general rules. Many of the problems identified by consumer organisations seem likely to be problems which hit commercial men too (a point made by the English Law Commission in connection with proposals for special rules as to disclosure in insurance contracts involving consumers)[72]. Many of them result only from the emphasis of legislation and case-law which dates from a time before the consumer revolution was envisaged, and the use as precedent of case-law from commercial contexts. Some of them (like the problem of damages) can be dealt with by the normal general forward movement of the law; some by emerging doctrines of economic duress and unconscionability; some by the reformulation or reslanting of key notions or concepts, perhaps assisted in some cases by the use of guidelines. Occasionally consumer problems may demonstrate (as in the case of the seller's right to cure) that adjustments to the general rules are needed: but it does not follow that such adjustments should be confined to consumer transactions. Abuses which require correction regardless of the general rules may have to be dealt with by legislation on market practices, fair trading or specific types of transaction. Only in the areas of unfair contract terms and acceptance (where it may be appropriate to release parties from the results of clear, but imprudent, actions), and perhaps of statements and representations by manufacturers and retailers making claims for their goods (if this is a proper sphere for private law) is there, I suggest, an obvious need for special rules of private law – and even these may raise problems common to several areas of activity (e.g. the general problems of standard contract terms and of unfair advertising) which may make and has made appropriate their separate treatment. I am even, respectfully, dubious about the usefulness, except as a temporary expedient, of statutes creating a small number of special rules for consumer transactions, and should be interested by discussion as to why most of the provisions of the Swedish Consumer Sales Act would not be fairly applied to

---

[71] *Gascoigne* v *British Credit Trust* [1978] C.L.Y. s. 711.
[72] See Law Com. No. 104, Cmnd 8064 (1980), pp. 42-46.

sales in general. It is worth noting that the sales section (Section 2) of the Uniform Commercial Code applies to consumers, and has no significant provisions specifically for them: and the recent exhaustive study by the Ontario Law Reform Commission suggests no special regime for consumers[73]. It may however be that this view is connected with a generality of approach which is bred by a law of contract dependent on case-law for its basic principles; and with a mistrust of detailed statutory regulation.

I should stress in any case that this analysis refers to the basic rules of private law only: it does not seek to touch on general powers of control over marketing practices, nor on statutory regulation of particular types of transaction; nor on problems of consumer remedies, which are the subject of another paper. As a nineteenth-century Secretary of State in the English Colonial Office said: "A man may starve, and yet have the best right of action that a special pleader could wish for.[74]"

---

[73] *Supra*, note 57.
[74] Sir J. Stephen, quoted by Atiyah, *Rise and Fall of Freedom of Contract* (1979) p. 554.

THE APPLICABILITY OF GENERAL RULES OF PRIVATE LAW TO CONSUMER DISPUTES: A COMMENT

by

Jan Hellner

112

The topic of Mr Reynolds' paper reminds us that in the United Kingdom most of the recent reform of contract law deals with contracts (or sales) in general, whereas in Sweden reform has largely been limited to the merchant-consumer relation. This fact might be thought to provide a Swede with the opportunity to challenge Mr Reynolds' contention that on the whole the same principles should apply to consumer disputes as to contractual disputes in general. However, the limitation of the Swedish legislation is largely due to circumstances that have no great bearing on questions of principle. The control of standard terms – which was established by one of the first pieces of legislation in this field – is largely associated with the activity of the Consumer Ombudsman, who deals only with consumer interests. Partly because it was easy to stick to the limitation that had thus been introduced, and partly because protection of consumer interests has a stronger political appeal than other professed aims of new legislation, the original limitation characterises most of the legislation that followed. However, it is assumed throughout that to a large, but uncertain, extent the principles that have been codified for the merchant-consumer relation are also suitable to contracts in general. We are thus free to discuss the principles without feeling bound by the legislation that exists.

Some main questions concern the quality of goods. Mr Reynolds argues that the concept of "merchantability", which embodies a fundamental requirement when goods are sold by a professional seller under English law, could be reformulated in order to cover also the needs of a consumer, while retaining its meaning for professional buyers. The same goes for the requirement of "reasonable fitness for purpose". Technically, this problem is even easier to solve under Swedish law than under English law, as Swedish law does not contain any general statutory rules regarding the quality of goods sold. To decide when the goods are "conforming" or, looking at the matter from another angle, what constitutes a "defect" in goods sold, is decided in Sweden by case law. The principles applied in Swedish case law coincide largely with what is stated explicitly in the English Sale of Goods Act, and they allow for all the flexibility that can be wished.

However, there is an underlying question of policy. Even if we disregard the commodity sales between traders – to which there is no counterpart in the sales to consumers – it remains to ask whether with respect to durable goods there should be a difference between the demands that can reasonably be made by enterprises and those that can be made by consumers. It can be argued – as Mr Reynolds mentions – that consumers have demands other than enterprises have, especially with regard to the "cosmetic" qualities of the goods. A new car should not have any scratches or dents that mar its looks, even if they do not change its driving qualities. But even in this respect I cannot see any reason for drawing a substantial distinction between consumers and other buyers. If an enterprise buys a car for its managing director, its demands will not be lower than those of a private person. On the other hand, the looks of a machine that is used in production may be insignificant to the enterprise that buys it, unless a scratch perhaps indicates that the machine that was sold as new had been subject to some misadventure before being delivered to this buyer. The conclusion that can be drawn is simple but important: the requirements of quality must depend on the functions, in a wide sense, of the goods that are bought. In so far as these functions coincide for consumers and for enterprises, the rules of law ought to be the same.

The questions regarding durability do not seem to be the same in Sweden as in the United Kingdom. Most of the problems that we meet concern the construction and the consequences of the "guarantees" that regularly form part of the sellers' promises when selling durable goods, whether to enterprises or to consumers. The guarantees issued to consumers are – or perhaps rather were, before consumer protection legislation was introduced – sometimes worthless, because they principally limit the sellers' responsibility for defects. In other cases the guarantee may confer certain advantages to the buyer but yet be limited to defects that existed at least *in nuce* when the goods were handed over to the buyer. The guarantee may then in fact be a limitation of the responsibility of the seller for the durability of the goods. On this point I am inclined to believe that there are good grounds for distinguishing between sales to consumers and those to enterprises. Consumers need protection against guarantees that are worthless, or appear on the surface to be more valuable than they are in fact. The need for protection and for hard-and-fast rules justifies the introduction of fairly simple, mandatory rules. With regard to enterprises, there may also be a need for protection. Against this need must be weighed the fact that the situations for which guarantees are given may differ considerably, even when the buyers are small and weak enterprises. I therefore find it hard to justify the imposition of strict mandatory rules. This view may be applicable to other situations as well.

With regard to the remedies that should be available to a buyer, there are certainly important differences of opinion. However, they seem to be less concerned with distinctions between consumer buyers and other buyers than with deep-going divergences between legal systems. Specific performance can be set aside: its practical importance does not justify an attempt at analysis.

There is a strong tendency in Swedish law to allow rejection of the goods because of the seller's breach of contract only when the breach is fundamental. This tendency has been reinforced by the attitude of the UN Convention (and the earlier ULIS). A right of rejection without regard to fundamental breach may be appropriate for sales of commodities but fundamental breach should be a condition for rejection both for commercial sales of machinery and similar products and for consumer sales.

The point on which a difference between commercial sales and consumer sales might be justified is the one concerning the right of a seller to deprive the buyer of the right of rejection by use of a contract clause. On this point the Swedish Consumer Sales Act is firm: the seller may not deprive the buyer of his right of rejection when the breach is fundamental (there is, however, a special provision requiring "strong fundamentality" for rejection when the goods have been fabricated especially for the buyer's needs). With regard to commercial sales, the use of mandatory rules upholding the buyer's right to reject the goods seems too risky. Whenever goods are manufactured specially for the buyer, or when they are transported long distances at great cost, a right of rejection may hit the seller unduly hard. A discussion of the appropriate remedies must take account of the extent to which the parties are allowed to deviate by agreement from the legal rules.

As Mr Reynolds points out, the right to reject goods cannot be separated from the seller's right to cure. The Swedish Consumer Sales Act gives the seller a substantial right to cure. An underlying idea is that the buyer should not have access to a remedy, which may be as severe to the seller as rejection can be, unless the seller has at first had the opportunity to cure a defect. There does not seem to be any good reason for making a difference between commercial sales and consumer sales. The fact that the Swedish Sale of Goods Act is less favourable to the seller on this point is to be ascribed simply to its age: for the products that were considered in 1905 – such as commodities, timber, agricultural products and horses – there is generally no other possibility of cure than the delivery of new goods instead of the defective ones.

Mr Reynolds mentions the duty of a buyer to examine the goods, with the risk that if he omits to do so he cannot reject goods because of a defect which would have been discovered upon examination. Swedish law, like several other legal systems, requires a commercial buyer to undertake such an examination. On this point I believe that a difference between consumer buyers and others is called for. Even if the law requires the consumer buyer to examine the goods, it is likely that the rule often will not be observed in practice. An inefficient rule is likely to cause more harm than good.

In my opinion, damages to the buyer is the most difficult and the most controversial point in the whole comparison. Once again, sales of commodities between traders need not be considered. Damages based on cover transactions can be awarded only if the goods are rejected, and the right to such damages is therefore limited by the same rules as limit the right of rejection. On the other hand, if goods are rightfully rejected, damages based on cover seem to be equally called for in commercial and in consumer transactions. What causes trouble is the indemnity for consequential loss. Such loss in the consumer field may consist in having to do more work in the household, prolonged travels to and from work, spoiled holidays, etc. These are entirely different from the sort of consequential loss that a commercial buyer may suffer, such as loss of profit (or reduced profit) from a later transaction, standstill of a factory, loss of customers, etc. There may be a similarity as regards products liability, but I leave that aside, as I assume that products liability is to be judged under tort rules.

Even if there are no definite obstacles under current principles to awarding damages to consumers for the kinds of consequential loss that were mentioned, I doubt whether it is desirable to allow such damages. The amount of the damages may differ considerably according to the personal circumstances of the buyer, it will often be difficult to compute the damages, and it is likely that there will be serious disagreements between sellers and buyers as to the correct amount of the damages. Not only a law suit for such damages but also the handling of a private claim will cause much trouble and unnecessary expense. At the same time, the losses are rarely of the kind that will seriously affect the buyers economically. It is possible that only a limited number of buyers, and not necessarily those who deserve them most, will be able to collect the damages which in theory are due to all of them. A right to damages may on the whole cost buyers more than the right is worth.

For reasons such as those that are mentioned, the Swedish Consumer Sales Act permits the sellers to exempt themselves from liability for consequential loss, and the sellers to a large extent make use of this permission. However, even if we accept the view just taken, it is not certain that it would lead to any difference in the treatment of consumer sales and commercial sales. Even for commercial sales, there are often good grounds for restricting the seller's liability for consequential loss, although these reasons are not the same as for consumer transactions. Exemption clauses relating to consequential loss should therefore on the whole be held valid. See my development of this theme in "Consequential Loss and Exemption Clauses", Vol. 1. Oxford Jnl. of Legal Studies, 13 (1981).

In conclusion I agree on the whole with Mr Reynolds on the point that the same principles should apply to consumer sales and to commercial sales, assuming that the principles of contract law arc flexible enough to allow for differences between goods of various kinds, between the requirements of various buyers, etc. The main problem concerns the extent to which freedom of contract should be restricted, by mandatory rules, by the power of the courts to set aside contract clauses that are considered inequitable, etc. I hold no firm opinion as to the solution to this problem. It can well be argued that consumers are not the only ones who are in need of protection against the superior power of influential contract partners. But the precise way in which a weaker party should be protected is a major problem of modern contract law, and one that goes beyond the scope of the present discussion.

118

SOME PROBLEMS OF INDIVIDUAL AND COLLECTIVE CONSUMER REDRESS IN ENGLISH LAW

by

C.J. Miller

It is only relatively recently that English lawyers have come to regard Consumer Law as a distinct subject worthy of study in its own right along with such subjects as Commercial Law, Labour Law and Family Law. However it is now attracting a great deal of attention, especially from academics for whom it has the dubious attraction of demanding a general acquaintance with a wide range of materials, both legal and extra-legal[1]. The legislature has been similarly active and both Conservative and Labour governments have promoted or supported an impressive number of Acts and regulations. These include the Trade Descriptions Act 1968, Fair Trading Act 1973, Consumer Credit Act 1974, Unfair Contract Terms Act 1977 and the Consumer Safety Act 1978, together with regulations controlling *inter alia* "bargain offer" claims[2] and truth in lending[3]. Legislative reform is under discussion in other areas, notably product liability[4] and contracts for the supply of goods[5] and services[6]. However there is no immediate likelihood of our enacting either a separate Consumer Sales and Services Act or a

[1] Some of the main texts include Cranston, *Consumers and the Law*, Weidenfeld, 1978; Borrie and Diamond, *The Consumer, Society and the Law*, Penguin Books, 4th ed., 1981; Harvey, *The Law of Consumer Protection and Fair Trading*, Butterworths, 1978; Mickleburgh, *Consumer Protection*, Professional Books, 1979; Lowe and Woodroffe, *Consumer Law and Practice*, Sweet and Maxwell, 1980. See also Cranston, *Regulating Business*, Macmillan, 1979.

[2] See the Price Marking (Bargain Offers) Order 1979, SI 1979 No. 364 as amended by SI 1979 Nos 633 and 1124.

[3] See the Consumer Credit (Advertisements) Regulations 1980, SI 1980 No. 54 and the Consumer Credit (Quotations) Regulations 1980, SI 1980 No. 55.

[4] Here the main subject of debate is the proposal for an EEC directive relating to the approximation of the laws, regulations and administrative provisions of the Member States concerning liability for defective products (Com. (79) 415 final).

[5] See the Law Commission report "Implied Terms in Contracts for the Supply of Goods", Law Com. No 95, July 1979. The Law Commission is also considering possible amendments to the implied terms as to quality and fitness and the remedies which follow on their breach. These issues are discussed by Francis Reynolds in his paper "The Applicability of General Rules of Private Law to Consumer Disputes": see p. 77, above.

[6] See the National Consumer Council report "Service Please – Services and the Law" [October 1981]. A Private Members' Bill (Supply of Goods and Services Bill) has been introduced in the present Parliamentary session to cover contracts for the supply of both goods and services.

general broadly-expressed provision controlling unfair or unconscionable trading practices.

As a separate development we have seen a rapid growth in the number of Codes of Practice agreed between trade associations and the Office of Fair Trading and intended "to refresh those parts of business life that laws cannot reach"[7]. Although no-one claims that these codes have been an unqualified success[8] there is general agreement that they have played an important part in improving standards, especially in the travel industry. Indeed some would go so far as to say that in this area at least the United Kingdom is well in advance of the rest of Europe.

Compared with this proliferation of laws and codes intended to benefit consumers there has been far less of an improvement in what is now popularly termed "access to justice". Of course this balance is not confined to the United Kingdom. Other jurisdictions have shown a similar preference for reforming substantive law rather than procedure. Nonetheless the result has been unfortunate. As the New Law Journal commented in September 1979:

> "If legislation specifically enacted for the protection of ordinary consumers is not to be seen as a mere 'paper tiger', changes in procedural law are likely to be required in aid of its enforcement. Without such changes, substantive law reform may well prove a pointless exercise. It is a measure of the failure of existing procedures that recourse to the courts is not universally available to wronged individuals. In that situation, it is manifestly a fraudulent claim that equality of access to justice is one of the hallmarks of our legal system."

The importance of recourse to the courts for individual claimants is only part of the picture. It is similarly important that legal systems have mechanisms or agencies possessed of the necessary funds and commitment to ensure that changes in substantive laws are reflected in changes in practice. Legislation is not self-implementing as to its effect and compliance with the law is not automatic even where criminal penalties are involved. The divergence between the law on the statute book and the law in practice is likely to be even more marked where the obligation is civil in nature. To take but one example, businesses will not invariably modify their standard-form contracts to give effect to a new Unfair Contract Terms Act and there is indeed no lack

---

[7] See *Gordon Borrie*, "Laws and Codes for Consumers" (1977) JBL 315, 322. At the time of writing some twenty codes of practice have been concluded under the auspices of the Office of Fair Trading. These cover such areas as electrical goods and services, the motor industry, footwear, launderers and dry cleaners, furniture, photography, mail order, package holidays, tele-communications and postal services and even funerals.

[8] For a general discussion see J.F. Pickering and D.C. Cousins, "The Benefits and Costs of Voluntary Codes of Practice", 1980. See also Mitchell, "Government Approved Codes of Practice" (1978) 2 Journal of Consumer Policy, p. 144. The results of monitoring exercises are published by the Office of Fair Trading as "Beeline" Special Edition Research Papers.

of evidence suggesting that many reputable firms have not in fact done so[9]. It is no more than a truism to suggest that an effective law for consumers must both facilitate access to justice for individuals and ensure that there is no marked divergence between the law and commercial practice. Only the complacent would contend that English law is beyond reproach in this respect.

It is substantially certain that the problems of individual and collective consumer redress will be at the forefront of discussion in the nineteen eighties. Indeed the National Consumer Council is currently engaged on a major research project with a view to formulating policy recommendations[10]. Attention will probably be focussed on such matters as the most appropriate forum for the adjudication of "small claims", the use and abuse of class actions, the role of the consumer organisations and official agencies, and the issue of *locus standi* in seeking injunctive and declaratory relief. The purpose of this paper is to describe some relatively recent developments in English law and outline some of the future possibilities[11].

The Forum for Adjudication

In post-war years the English legal system has seen a marked growth in the number of specialist courts and tribunals created to adjudicate on disputes in particular areas. These have included the Restrictive Practices Court, industrial tribunals and rent assessment committees. There has been pressure for a Family court. A common feature of such adjudicative bodies is that they normally consist of lay members sitting alongside legally qualified chairmen. Although there are good arguments for creating equivalent tribunals to hear consumer complaints, as in the case of some Australian states and the Swedish Market Court, there does not seem to have been significant pressure to this end in the United Kingdom. Rather two main developments have occurred, one within the traditional court system and the other outside it[12].

---

[9] Significantly the first unreported cases decided under the 1977 Act seem to hold consistently in the consumer's favour: see e.g. *Woodman* v *Photo Trade Processing Ltd* (May 1981, Exeter County Court); *Waldron-Kelly* v *British Railways Board* (March 1981, Stockport County Court).

[10] See the report of the sixth National Consumer Congress held in Cardiff in 1981.

[11] In undertaking this task I have benefitted considerably from reading some of the (as yet) unpublished papers prepared for the National Consumer Council, notably that of Richard Tur of Oriel College Oxford on "Public Interest, Litigation and the Consumer". There is also a wealth of comparative material in Cappelletti, *Access to Justice* (1979) and Cappelletti, *Access to Justice and the Welfare State* (1981).

[12] A further development has been at local level where one has seen the establishment and demise of *inter alia* the Manchester Arbitration Scheme for Small Claims and the London (Westminster) Small Claims Court. See generally, Foster, "Problems with Small Claims", (1974) 2 British Jo. of Law and Society, p. 75; *Egerton*, "The Birth and Death of the London Small Claims Court", (1980) 130 NLJ, p. 488; "Simple Justice. A consumer view of small claims procedures in England and Wales", National Consumer Council, 1979, ch. 11 especially; George Appleby, "Small Claims in England and Wales" in *Access to Justice* (editors Cappelletti and Weisner) Vol. II, Book II, (1979), 685, at pp. 743-751, 757-763.

The first, which is now well documented[13], has seen the adaptation of county court procedures in an attempt to make them more responsive to the adjudication of small claims. The Consumer Council and latterly the National Consumer Council deserve substantial credit for these changes[14]. Since 1972 there has been provision for a pre-trial review by county court registrars which may either assist the parties to reach a settlement or, failing that, prepare the case for a hearing. Provision has been made also for referral to arbitration within certain financial limits (now £500)[15] initially on request by a party to the dispute but since 21 April 1981 automatically, unless the registrar rescinds the referral. This he may do if he is satisfied that (a) a difficult question of law or a question of fact of exceptional complexity is involved; or (b) a charge of fraud is in issue; or (c) the parties are agreed that the dispute should be tried in court; or (d) it would be unreasonable for the claim to proceed to arbitration having regard to its subject matter, the circumstances of the parties or the interests of any other person likely to be affected by the award[16]. Richard Thomas, the Legal Officer of the National Consumer Council, summarises the position by saying:

> "In broad terms, the new rules will create and emphasise a sharper distinction between cases which will go to arbitration (the majority of claims below £500) and those which will go to trial (the majority of claims above £500 and a few below that). It is intended that arbitrated small claims should follow a simple, informal and flexible procedure. An almost absolute no-costs rule will discourage legal representation[17]. On the other hand, where a case proceeds to formal trial legal costs *will* be allowed, even where the claim falls below £500."[18]

The simplified no-costs rule should discourage businesses from availing themselves of legal representation and this in turn should help arbitrators to achieve the desired informality and flexibility of procedure. Whether the rules go far enough (or for that matter too far) is open to debate. One strand of criticism suggests that at least the more articulate and knowledgeable consumer is badly served by a system of automatic reference which typically

[13] See, e.g., "Simple Justice" (1979) and Appleby "Small Claims in England and Wales (1979), above, note 12).

[14] The Consumer Council Study "Justice out of Reach: A case for Small Claims Courts", HMSO 1970, was influential in prompting developments in the early nineteen-seventies. The National Consumer Council study "Simple Justice" (1979) took matters further, forming the basis for a consultative paper issued by the Lord Chancellor's Department for the guidance of the County Court Rule Committee. This led in turn to the recent changes in the law which are noted below.

[15] See the County Court (Amendment No. 3) Rules 1980, SI 1980 No, 1807, Order 19, rule 1(4).

[16] Order 19, rule 1(5).

[17] By Order 19, rule 1(11) "No solicitor's charges shall be allowed as between party and party in respect of any proceedings referred to arbitration under Order 19, r.1(4), except for (a) the costs stated on the summons; (b) the costs of enforcing the award; and (c) such costs as are certified by the arbitrator to have been incurred through the unreasonable conduct of the opposite party in relation to the proceedings or the claim therein."

[18] See "Small Claims – The New Arrangements" (1981) 131 NLJ, p. 429.

denies access to a county court judge. Another view accepts the general principle of arbitration but would like to see the rules removed from the Green Book and expressed in a separate document to be administered by a distinct small claims division operating within the county court system. This is essentially the view of the National Consumer Council which has published a "Model Code of Procedure for Small Claims Divisions of County Courts" (May 1980). However its proposal did not find favour with the County Court Rule Committee which regarded it as "unnecessary and undesirable"[19]. Others would go further and press (at least as a long-term objective) for specialised courts or tribunals which deal only with consumer claims[20].

The second main development has been sectoral rather than general and has accompanied the growing number of codes of practice to which reference was made above. All such codes contain procedures intended to facilitate the resolution of disputes through conciliation, and the majority has a further provision for arbitration as an alternative to using the normal court procedure. According to a recent consultative document issued by the Office of Fair Trading, arbitrations under codes of practice have been concerned almost exclusively with motor cars and package holidays[21].

The Office of Fair Trading supports the continued availability of such alternative methods of pursuing redress, pointing, for example, to the convenience of a typically documents-only procedure and noting that many claims could be for sums in excess of the present county court limit for arbitration (now £500)". However the National Consumer Council has been less than fully convinced of the benefits of arbitration under codes, suggesting that the Office of Fair Trading should consider whether codes should stop at the point of conciliation[23]. Certainly most interested parties agree that it is important to avoid a repetition of (admittedly isolated) incidents in which unsuccessful consumer claimants have been saddled with

---

[19] See para. 2 of the consultative paper referred to in note 14, above.

[20] A quite distinct problem for individual consumers is that of enforcing county court judgments. One might be forgiven for assuming that the enforcement of judgments was the responsibility of the court system rather than that of successful claimants. This is true of fines imposed by magistrates' courts but it is not the case with ordinary judgment debts where responsibility for enforcement rests with the individual judgment creditors. See, in general, "Simple Justice" (1979), ch. 6, and Michael Birks, "Enforcing Money Judgments in the County Court: How to obtain payment without a solicitor", April 1980.

[21] See "Redress Procedures under Codes of Practice: A Consultative Document (1980) para. 1.5, where it is noted that it was "recently estimated that some 1000 code arbitrations have been conducted during the last 5 years, with the Motor and ABTA Codes accounting roughly equally for all but 15 or so of these. The present high cost of purchasing and repairing motor vehicles or booking a family holiday no doubt stimulates consumers to pursue some disputes to the arbitration stage".

[22] *Ibid.*, para. 1.3.

[23] See "Simple Justice" (1979), ch. 10, at p. 81.

a heavy liability in costs[24]. For this reason there should be a cautious welcome for the Office of Fair Trading's recommendation that "all arbitrations under codes of practice should be on a documents-only basis, except in the very limited circumstances when the arbitrator is able to arrange a local hearing at no additional cost to the parties involved in the dispute[25]."

Class Actions and Collective Redress

The developments noted above should facilitate access to the courts by individual litigants pursuing small claims. However there are cases where either a representative or a collective approach may seem more apposite, as when an otherwise unconnected group of consumers has relied on the same advertisement, contracted for the same holiday, or been damaged (whether physically or financially) by a product, for example a drug, contraceptive device or motor car, which, it is alleged, is defective or unmerchantable in design. In such cases the various claimants are likely to have sufficient points in common to make it sensible to think in terms of a unified approach rather than an approach which envisages distinct actions by individuals.

Class Actions

As is well known, American courts have sanctioned the development of the class action to deal with such cases. This has recently been described by the Australian Law Reform Commission as,

"a legal procedure which enables the claims of a number of persons against the same defendant to be determined in the one action. In a class action one or more persons ('the plaintiff') may sue on his own behalf and on behalf of a large number of other persons (the class) who have the same interest in the subject matter of the action as the plaintiff. The class members are not usually named as individual parties but are merely described. Although they do not usually take any active part in the litigation, they may nevertheless be bound by the result. It is, thus, a device for multi-party litigation where the interests of a number of parties can be combined in one suit[26]"

The Commission recognises that the procedure is open to abuse, but

---

[24] In "Simple Justice" reference is made to a "well publicised case where lawyers acting for a holidaymaker and his colleagues took a case involving a disputed holiday in Crete to an attended arbitration hearing which lasted five days. The entire arbitration costs were awarded against the holidaymakers, amounting to £1,700. In addition they were required to pay two-fifths of the legal costs amounting to a further £1,800": *ibid.*, at p. 74.

[25] See "Redress Procedures under Codes of Practice: Conclusions following a review by the Office of Fair Trading (December, 1981), para. 2.4.

[26] See "Access to the Courts – II, Class Actions", Discussion Paper No. 11, June 1979, p. 4. The whole paper is highly informative and persuasive as is Discussion Paper No. 4, "Access to the Courts – I, Standing Public Interest Suits". See also A. Miller, "Of Frankenstein Monsters and Shining Knights", 92 Harvard L.R. 664 (1979); Bates, "A Case for the Introduction of Class Actions into English Law", (1980) New Law Journal, p. 560; Cranston, "Access to Justice for Consumers" (1979) *Journal of Consumer Policy*, p. 291 *et seq*.

nonetheless believes that "so long as the courts are vigilant in ensuring that the class action remains manageable a proper balance could be preserved between the competing interests of plaintiffs and defendants"[27]. Elsewhere in common law jurisdictions the Ontario Court of Appeal has sanctioned a similar approach in a case where the plaintiffs were alleging that Firenza motor vehicles manufactured in 1971 and 1972 and sold in Ontario did not match up to the standards expressly warranted in General Motors advertising campaign[28].

English law has a number of procedural devices which might be called in aid or adapted to deal with similar situations. However we have tended to emphasise individual rather than collective or indeed generalised rights. At times this has been carried to extremes, so much so that the established rule (and it must indeed appear strange to the layman) is that a third party cannot adduce evidence of even a central finding of fact in a judgment in an action between two other parties with whom he is not privy[29]. Placed in the present context this means that if an individual consumer (A) succeeds in establishing that B is in breach of contract or that his product is defective in design the judgment will not in principle be admissable in evidence (let alone conclusive) where a third party (C) has an identical complaint. C must in theory begin again, calling his own expert witnesses as necessary.

Lord Denning, M.R., has recently challenged the correctness of this view asserting in a somewhat different context that if the defendant has had "a full and fair opportunity of contesting the issue . . . in the first action he should be stopped from disputing it in the second action"[30]. Although there are good arguments in favour of such an approach it cannot be said with confidence that it is in accordance with the present state of English Law. Of course in any such situation the defendant may agree to treat the first action as a "test case"[31], but this is far removed from the type of class action procedure familiar in the American courts. Apart from any other considerations it depends on the consent and often on the goodwill of the defendant and it may impose an unfair burden as to costs on the plaintiff.

---

[27] *Ibid.*, at p. 38.
[28] See *Naken* v *General Motors of Canada Ltd.* (1979) 21 O.R. (2d) 780.
[29] See *Hollington* v *Hewthorn & Co. Ltd.* [1943] KB 587, [1943] 2 All ER 35. The rule has been reversed by statute where it is sought to adduce evidence of a conviction in subsequent civil proceedings: see the Civil Evidence Act 1968, s. 11. The same Act also alters the position with respect to findings of adultery and paternity and in the case of defamation proceedings.
[30] See *McIlkenny* v *Chief Constable of West Midlands Police Force* [1980] 2 All E.R. 227, 238, CA (claim for damages for assualt following the conviction of the plaintiffs in respect of the murder of some 21 persons through causing a bomb explosion). An appeal has subsequently been dismissed: *Hunter* v *Chief Constable of West Midlands* [1981] 3 All E.R. 727, H.L.
[31] Modern examples may be said to include *Dougan* v *Rangers F.C.* [1974] SLT (Sh. Ct.) 34 (personal injury at the Ibrox football disaster) and *Congreve* v *Home Office* [1976] 1 All E.R. 697, at p. 706, CA (the television licence case.)

Another recognised procedural device is the representative action. This is provided for by Order 15, Rule 12(1) of the Rules of the Supreme Court which states in part that,

> "where numerous persons have the same interest in any proceedings ... the proceedings may be begun and unless the Court otherwise orders, continued, by or against any one or more of them as representing all except one or more of them."

This procedure has been used in a number of well-known cases involving such persons as producers of Champagne and stallholders in Covent Garden market[32]. In the latter case Lord Macnaghten stated that the basic requirements of the action were that "Given a common interest and a common grievance, a representative suit was in order if the relief sought was in its nature beneficial to all whom the plaintiff proposed to represent.[33]" However this fairly general requirement has sometimes been construed narrowly so that the full potential of the action has not been developed. In particular it came to be accepted that the requirement of a "common interest" would not be satisfied where the complainants had separate contracts with the defendant and it was also thought that the procedure was appropriate only where the relief sought was declaratory or injunctive in nature[34].

In recent cases a more liberal approach has been adopted by two first instance judges. The first case, *Prudential Assurance Co. Ltd* v *Newman Industries Ltd*,[35] involved protracted and costly litigation which was greatly complicated by the fact that the relevant class comprised the shareholders of a company. The plaintiff, a minority shareholder in the company, was at one stage seeking to bring a direct representative action on behalf of itself and the other shareholders, claiming, *inter alia*, damages for conspiracy. The intention, it seems, was to avoid the rule in *Foss* v *Harbottle*[36] whereby the proper plaintiff in respect of a wrong allegedly done to a company is the company itself. Allowing amendments to the writ and statement of claim so as to permit the action to proceed, Vinelott, J. summarised the position after a thorough review of the authorities by saying:-[37]

> "It is clear on authority and principle that a representative action can be brought by a plaintiff, suing on behalf of himself and all other members of a class, each

---

[32]   See, respectively, *Bollinger* v *Costa Brava Wine Co. Ltd* [1960] Ch. 262; [1961] 1 W.L.R. 277 and *Duke of Bedford* v *Ellis* [1901] AC 1.

[33]   *Ibid.*, at p. 9.

[34]   See *Markt & Co. Ltd.* v *Knight Steamship Co. Ltd* [1910] 2 KB 1021. It has frequently been pointed out that the latter point does not form part of the *ratio* of the case.

[35]   [1979] 3 All ER 507.

[36]   (1843) 2 Hare 461, 67 ER 189. See in this respect *Prudential Assurance Co. Ltd* v *Newman Industries Ltd* (No 2) [1980] 2 All ER 841 (Vinelott, J.) and [1982] 1 All ER 354 (CA).

[37]   [1979] 3 All ER 507, 520.

member of which, including the plaintiff, is alleged to have a separate cause of action in tort, provided that three conditions are satisfied. The first I have already stated. No order can properly be made in such a representative action if the effect might in any circumstances be to confer a right of action on a member of the class represented who would not otherwise have been able to assert such a right in separate proceedings, or to bar a defence which might otherwise have been available to the defendant in such a separate action. Normally, therefore, if not invariably, the only relief that will be capable of being obtained by the plaintiff in his representative capacity will be declaratory relief, though, of course, he may join with it a personal claim for damages . . .

The second condition is that there must be an 'interest' shared by all members of the class. In relation to a representative action in which it is claimed that every member of the class has a separate cause of action in tort, this condition requires, as I see it, that there must be a common ingredient in the cause of action of each member of the class. In the present case that requirement is clearly satisfied . . . The third and related condition is that the court must be satisfied that it is for the benefit of the class that the plaintiff be permitted to sue in a representative capacity. The court must, therefore, be satisfied that the issues common to every member of the class will be decided after full discovery and in the light of all the evidence capable of being adduced in favour of the claim. For unless this condition is satisfied it would be wrong (as Fletcher Moulton L.J., remarked in *Markt*) to permit the representative plaintiff 'to conduct litigation on behalf of another without his leave and yet so as to bind him'."

At the trial of the action Vinelott, J., held that there was a good cause of action in conspiracy in the personal and representative claims, although the action proceeded thereafter on a "derivative" basis[38].

The judgment in the *Prudential Assurance* case envisages a split procedure in which the representative action concludes with a declaration as to an entitlement to damages. Matters were taken somewhat further in *E.M.I. Records Ltd* v *Riley*[39] where the defendant market trader had distributed "pirate" cassettes in breach of copyright and the action was brought by the plaintiff company acting on behalf of itself and other members of the British Phonographic Industry (B.P.I.). Dillon, J., noted the dominant position of the B.P.I. in the trade and emphasised that "This is not a case of a small number of manufacturers getting together as a self-constituted association where there would be a serious likelihood that other pirated cassettes which the defendants may have sold would have nothing to do with the members of the association". Accordingly he was willing to grant both an injunction and an inquiry as to damages for infringement of copyright etc., the damages to be paid to E.M.I. to be held on trust for all members of the B.P.I. On the facts of the case this was clearly the most convenient outcome. Nothing was

[38] For discussion of this aspect of the case see *Wedderburn*, (1981) 44 MLR 202.
[39] [1981] 1 WLR 923.

to be gained from requiring all the individual complainants to institute separate proceedings for the purposes of assessing damages.

Although the *Prudential Assurance* and *E.M.I.* cases both show that the representative action has the capacity for development in English law (at least where the action is framed in tort rather than contract)[40] it is possible that its full potential can be developed only through a somewhat more systematic approach. If this occurs a number of familiar questions will have to be answered. For example, it will be necessary to make provision for publicising actions and notifying potential class members where appropriate. Attention will also have to be paid to the issue of whether individual members are to be required to "opt in" or "opt out" of the proceedings. The decision on this point will be likely to affect their entitlement to sue in their own right and their liability to contribute to the costs of an unsuccessful action no less than their entitlement to benefit from the rewards of a successful one. The difficulties of quantifying and awarding damages will also have to be faced as will the basic issue of how class actions are to be funded. It will not have escaped notice that recent developments in the United Kingdom have been associated with corporate plaintiffs and indeed there is a strong case for arguing that the use of the procedure in the U.S.A. is associated closely with the contingent fee system. Certainly this system provides a financial incentive for taking on and managing what is often costly and difficult litigation[41]. It is not immediately obvious that class actions can operate on a regular basis if the matter is left to individual (and often unorganised) plaintiffs and their legal advisers. This point will be considered further when discussing the potential role of consumer organisations.

Although this is not an appropriate place for a detailed discussion of the development of class actions in the U.S.A., it may be said that American courts have sometimes appeared particularly flexible in their approach to awarding damages. The conventional insistence on an itemised assessment of an individual plaintiff's loss has been supplemented by class-wide assessments using broad statistical and computer techniques, and by "fluid recovery" and cy-près schemes to absorb unallocated damages[42]. It is unlikely that English law will adopt similar approaches; yet it is equally difficult to see how without them the law can deal effectively with those potential defendants whose civil wrongs are committed at the expense of numerous small claimants.

A similar willingness on the part of American courts to re-examine

[40] Here developments are hampered by the decision in the *Markt* case, above note 34.
[41] The point is discussed by the Australian Law Reform Commission at p. 28 *et seq*. of its discussion paper on class actions, above, note 26.
[42] Examples cited by the Australian Law Reform Commission include *In re Co-ordinated Pretrial Proceedings in Antibiotics Antitrust Actions*, 333 F. Supp. 278 (1971) and *Daar* v *Yellow Cab Co.*, 63 Cal. Rep. 274 (1967).

conventional approaches has begun to appear also in cases where the plaintiff is unable to identify which of several potential defendants was responsible for causing damage in his or her case. This seems to have caused particular problems in the case of such a drug as diethylstilbestrol (DES) which may cause cancerous growths in the adolescent daughters of mothers who have taken it in pregnancy to prevent a miscarriage. *Sindell* v *Abbott Laboratories*[43] was such a case. Here the plaintiff's class action was on behalf of herself and "Girls and women who are residents of California and who have been exposed to DES before birth and who may or may not know the fact or the danger". At least two hundred companies produced DES to an identical formula and the defendants were ultimately some five or so companies which, it was alleged, had ninety per cent of the market. The plaintiff was unable to identify which, if any, of these companies supplied the drug taken by her mother. Nonetheless the Supreme Court of California was prepared to permit the continuation of the action, the majority stating, *inter alia* that[44]:

> "We hold it to be reasonable in the present context to measure the likelihood that any of the defendants supplied the product which allegedly injured plaintiff by the percentage which the DES sold by each of them for the purpose of preventing miscarriage bears to the entire production of the drug sold by all for that purpose . . .
>
> "If plaintiff joins in the action the manufacturers of a substantial share of the DES which her mother might have taken, the injustice of shifting the burden of proof to defendants to demonstrate that they could not have made the substance which injured plaintiff is significantly diminished . . .
>
> "The presence in the action of a substantial share of the appropriate market also provides a ready means to apportion damages among the defendants. Each defendant will be held liable for the proportion of the judgment represented by its share of that market unless it demonstrates that it could not have made the product which caused plaintiff's injuries . . .[45]"

This may seem a very rough and ready form of justice, but again it is thought that the disinterested lay observer would regard it as preferable to a solution which denied any recourse to the injured plaintiff. The court was careful not to place too precise a limit on the requirement that the several defendants should share a "substantial percentage" of the market.

Consumer Organisations and Public Agencies
The above discussion has concentrated on collective remedies through class

---

[43]   163 Cal. Rep. 132, 607 P(2d) 924 (1980).
[44]   607 P(2d) 924, 937.
[45]   Alternative theories of liability were rejected and other State Courts may insist on all potential defendants being before the court. See, e.g. the New Jersey case of *Namm* v *Charles E. Frost* (March 1981) noted in (1981) New Law Journal, at p. 598.

actions in circumstances in which an individual plaintiff has a clear legal and financial interest in pursuing a claim. However there are cases in which these features will not necessarily be present and where an alternative approach may be needed. For example, it was noted earlier that exemption clauses may be unenforceable under the Unfair Contract Terms Act 1977 and yet remarkably effective in practice in the absence of a mechanism for ensuring that changes in the law are reflected in changes in commercial practice. The validity of such clauses in standard-form contracts is, it may be thought, too important a matter to be left to the happenchance of litigation by a individual consumer. Again, it has been noted that there are other cases where a rational consumer will allow a valid legal claim to go by default, notably with goods or services of low value where the "opportunity cost" of litigation may outweigh any financial or other rewards.

If this occurs in numerous individual cases the wrongdoer will break the law with impunity and profit thereby, subject only to the operation of market forces and conceivably the criminal law. Some writers argue that it is quite acceptable to invoke the criminal law as a means of ensuring that shoddy goods (and presumably services) are not marketed[46], but this is not my view. Nor do I believe it should be invoked too readily as a means of underpinning other obligations under the civil law. In any event alternative approaches are needed.

In the situations outlined above there are strong and indeed obvious arguments for allowing either consumer organisations or a public official to institute proceedings in the interests of consumers generally. Many continental (and other) jurisdictions make specific provisions for this. For example, in France the Loi Royer of 1973 entitles authorised consumer groups to bring actions, typically for injunctive of declaratory relief. According to *Le Monde*[47] there were some fifteen national organisations in being in November 1980 of which the most influential is the Union Federale des Consommateurs (UFC). This group also publishes *Que Choisir?* providing information along the lines of our own *Which?* The collective power of French consumers was in evidence in such campaigns as that involving the veal boycott. In West Germany also provision is made for authorised consumer associations to bring proceedings in defence of the consumer interest. Thus the Law Against Unfair Competition of 1965 enabled associations to seek injunctions restraining alleged breaches of the Act. More recently the Law on Standard Contract Terms of 1976 contains similar powers in the case of traders using invalid contract terms. A similar approach is adopted in other jurisdictions, some of which confer powers on public officials. As

---

[46] This seems to be the view of Ross Cranston as expressed in his book *Consumers and the Law* (1978), at p. 240.
[47] See *Le Monde*, 16 November 1980, XI X.

Professor Hellner noted in his paper on "Unfair Contract Terms" this is true of Sweden, where the Consumer Ombudsman is empowered to appear before the Market Court to restrain individual traders from using improper contract terms[48].

In the United Kingdom the Consumers' Association has a notable record in promoting legislation and it occasionally sponsors test-cases. Indeed its Legal Officer, David Tench, recently appeared before the Exeter County Court qua solicitor to argue one of the first cases decided under the Unfair Contract Terms Act 1977[49]. However, neither it nor any other consumer organisation, has, so far as I am aware, sought injunctive or declaratory relief in its own name and in the interests of its members or indeed of consumers generally. Were it to do so in circumstances in which the defendant's conduct was "unlawful" it would have to establish that it had a sufficient interest in the matter to be allowed to proceed.

The general principle is that private individuals and (where appropriate) interest groups may prosecute in respect of criminal offences[50], yet cannot (simply as members of the public) seek injunctions to restrain breaches of the criminal law. The Attorney-General's consent to relator proceedings is required [51]. In the field of administrative law, where the action is against a public authority, the rules in relation to *locus standi* have been relaxed in recent years. For example, a local residents' association has been held to have a sufficient interest to challenge the granting of planning permission in its locality[52], although the National Federation of Self-employed and Small Businesses did not, on inquiry into the facts of the case, have a sufficient interest to challenge the decision of the Inland Revenue Commissioners to grant an amnesty to casual workers in Fleet Street[53]. This latter decision of the House of Lords is especially important as indicating that the rules in relation to standing to sue are not to be determined in isolation from the matter to which the application relates. However, although it is unfashionable as an idea, there still remains a divide between the assertion of "public law" rights and assertions of "private law" concerns which happen to affect the public generally. Were it to seek an injunction or a declaration that a term in a standard-form contract was void, or that a consumer product was

---

[48] See *Hellner*, "Unfair Contract Terms" in A.C. Neal (ed.) *Law and the Weaker Party*, Vol. 1, 1981, pp. 89-92.

[49] *Woodman* v *Photo Trade Processing Ltd* (May, 1981).

[50] For a general discussion of this point see Research Study No. 10 on Prosecutions by Private Individuals and Non-Police Agencies, prepared for the Royal Commission on Criminal Procedure.

[51] *Gouriet* v *Union of Post Office Workers* [1977] 3 All ER 70.

[52] See, e.g. *Turner* v *Secretary of State for Environment* (1974) 28 P. & C.R. 123 and, more recently, *Covent Garden Community Association Ltd* v *G.L.C.* (Woolf, J., April 1980).

[53] *Commissioners of Inland Revenue* v *National Federation of Self-Employed and Small Businesses Ltd* [1981] 2 All ER 93, H.L. (the famous Mickey-Mouse or Fleet Street casuals' case).

unmerchantable or defective in design, a body like the Consumers' Association or the National Consumer Council could hardly be categorised as a mere "busybody". Yet it is unlikely that it would be regarded as having a sufficient interest to entitle it to a remedy. In any event the point is sufficiently unclear for it to be desirable to have it clarified.

If consumer organisations are to be involved more systematically in collective redress this will do little more than parallel development in other areas. Thus it has been noted that such bodies as local authorities, trade associations and tenants' associations have already been recognised,[54] as of course have the trade unions. However a number of questions remain open. For example, it will be necessary to decide whether the organisation can claim only injunctive or declaratory relief or whether in addition it can sue for damages to be held on trust for its members or a wider class of consumers. In the latter event a system of licensing might seem to be required in order to ensure that the organisation is both representative and financially secure. It will be necessary also to decide whether organisations may be brought into existence solely to deal with the aftermath of a particular event (for example, an airline disaster or injury associated with a particular drug) or whether they must have a somewhat more permanent existence. However these are essentially points of detail, albeit important ones. The important point is that statutory recognition be accorded.

Turning briefly to the position of public officials, the Director-General of Fair Trading has been accorded wide ranging powers and duties under the Fair Trading Act 1973. These include the negotiating and drawing up of codes of practice[55], the setting in train of a procedure under Part II of the Act to penalise consumer trade practices which have been shown to be detrimental to the economic interests of consumers[56], and the powers conferred by Part III of the Act. These latter powers enable the Director-General to seek assurances from (and, where necessary, to obtain injunctions against) individual traders who have persisted in a course of conduct which is detrimental to the interests of consumers and to be regarded as unfair to them. The notion of "unfairness" is defined by s. 34(2) and (3) of the Act in terms of breaches of both criminal and civil obligations, although it does not go further than this. Hence the continued use of void contract terms would not

---

[54]   See e.g. the Local Government Act 1972, s. 222 (Local Authority entitlement to sue); Retail Prices Act 1976, s. 15(c) (trade association); Housing Act 1972 (tenants' association); and the cases cited above note 52 for residents' associations. The point is made in the admirable paper on "Public Interest, Litigation and the Consumer" prepared by Richard Tur for the National Consumer Council: see above note 11. Indeed it has even been held that a local authority is entitled to sue in its own name in defamation: see *Bognor Regis U.D.C.* v *Campion* [1972] 2 Q.B. 169.
[55]   See above, p. 101.
[56]   See sections 13-33 of the Act.

generally and *per se* constitute unfairness for the purposes of Part III[57]. There seems to be general agreement that these provisions are useful as a means of according direct and personal control over the activities of some of the worst of the "rogue traders", but they have obvious limitations. In particular it is unlikely that the Office of Fair Trading will always have sufficient resources effectively to monitor all assurances recorded over the years.

Control at a more general level is possible under Part II of the Act but the provisions have been used only rarely. So whereas it is a criminal offence to display notices etc. which purport to take away a consumers' statutory rights to receive goods of merchantable quality it is not an offence to contract on similarly void terms which purport to exclude liability for death or personal injury caused by negligence[59]. In any event there are limits to the extent to which the criminal law can be properly invoked in this area. In particular there can hardly be any question of invoking it where the relevant contract term is invalid only if it is unreasonable in relation to the particular contract in which it is used. Similarly it must be conceded that there are difficulties in a system of prior validation or subsequent vetting of such terms since the test of "reasonableness" does not lend itself readily to being applied in the abstract[60]. Nevertheless the difficulties can be overstated and more mischief is likely to be caused by the continued use of such terms than by controlling their use in consumer transactions over stringently.

If there be general agreement over the need to make more effective provision for collective consumer redress through organisations (and this is doubtful) there is likely to be much less agreement as to the form this provision should take. Many would argue that the task should be given to a public agency like the Office of Fair Trading, but it is not clear that it would welcome this additional role and there are good reasons for preferring the involvement of bodies which are avowedly in business as consumer advocates. Official agencies are likely to be staffed in practice by civil servants on short term secondment and whilst this may help to prevent their being claimed by "the system", they may be less than fully committed to the task. In any event there is nothing to preclude the dual involvement of both public agencies and consumer organisations.

As in many other areas the main practical difficulty is likely to be one of

[57] In certain circumstances it may however be an offence under the Consumer Transactions (Restriction on Statements) Order 1976, S.I. 1976 No. 1813 made under Part II of the Act. For that reason it might then be "unfair" for the purpose of s. 34.
[58] See the Consumer Transactions (Restrictions on Statements) Order 1976, S.I. 1976 No 1813 as amended by S.I. 1978 No. 127.
[59] Such terms are void by virtue of s. 2(1) of the Unfair Contract Terms Act 1977.
[60] See the second report of the Law Commission, "Exemption Clauses", Law Com. No. 69 (1975), para. 290 *et seq*.

funding. In so far as public agencies like the Office of Fair Trading are concerned the issue is not one of principle, but rather one of priorities. The same is true of the National Consumer Council which is also publically funded. Here again there seems no good reason why such funds should not be used for advancing the consumer interest through litigation as much as through promoting legislation. Thereafter a somewhat more innovative approach may be needed and Michael Zander has suggested that there are two possible ways ahead[61]. One is to extend legal aid to proceedings brought by groups which are competent to represent the interests of their members. The other is to use public funds to support private practice. As Zander notes,

> "It has now been accepted in many countries that public moneys can legitimately be provided to support 'ordinary' law centres. The next step will be to use public finds to support lawyers working in a more focused way on the legal problems of particular groups whose problems are felt to deserve special attention[62]"

Although the current economic climate hardly seems conducive to an increased funding of the consumer cause it should not preclude an adjustment in the ways in which existing funds are spent.

[61] See Zander, *Legal Services for the Community* (1978), p. 230
[62] *Ibid.*, at p. 232.

CONSUMER REDRESS: A COMMENT

by

Lars Heuman

In this paper, I shall mainly discuss problems concerning "access to justice" and the most appropriate forum for the adjudication of small claims. Collective redress is not very common in Sweden, and I would also like to make some remarks on the subject. My comments are based mainly upon an investigation of the Public Complaints Board and Private Insurance Boards, published at the end of 1980[1].

Individual Consumer Redress
According to modern consumer policy, it is of great importance to see that consumer *disputes do not arise in the first place*. For example, deceptive or unclear standard contracts ought to be changed or forbidden. Consumer disputes can be reduced if retailers are not allowed to sell dangerous or defective products. I shall not deal here with the question of what possibilities the various courts have in this respect. When a consumer dispute does arise, the parties should first try to conciliate. Consumers can consult civil servants at the district courts, the Public Complaints Board, or the Municipal Consumer Counsellor before they accept a settlement. This is an inexpensive way of resolving disputes, both for the parties and for the government. However the consumer often runs the risk of losing out when he approves an agreement. During the negotiations the consumer is at a disadvantage in relation to the retailer, who often has experience of litigation[2].

For a long time legislators have tried to make the procedures *simple, inexpensive* and *rapid*. During the 1970's they also attempted to make the new procedures *flexible*. This means that the court or the board adapts the proceedings to the special circumstances of each case; e.g. the redress demanded or the need for evidence. If you want to make the procedure flexible, you cannot provide detailed rules. You must allow the legally-qualified Chairman to solve the problems. There is always the risk that he might not see the problem, or that he might not realise its importance and complications. A flexible procedure presupposes that the Chairman knows a

[1] L. Heuman, *Reklamationsnämnder och försäkringsnämnder* (Stockholm 1980). See also SOU 1978: 40 with a Summary in English, pp. 15-19.
[2] Heuman, *Ibid.*, p. 556 and p. 802 f., and L. Heuman., *Rättsforum*, 23/24 p. 22.

great deal of procedural law. You must not forget the need for legal predic-
tability, when you try to improve the judicial process[3].

I think that there will be a new trend not only in consumer policy but also
in legislation and adjudication in general. Most of the countries of Western
Europe have financial problems. Governments must *cut down on the costs of
public activities*. Even the courts must work more effectively. Fees for
various applications increase. However, grants for public legal aid cannot
increase as fast as inflation. This cost-conscious way of thinking can also
affect the interpretation and application of certain rules; e.g. rules in the Act
on Public Legal Aid. During the last decade the Swedish government has
given ample grants to improve consumer protection. Now when cuts have to
be made, it is important that this should not hit the weakest groups among
consumers. Simplifications and rationalisations of proceedings could be
dangerous, because it is very difficult to foresee the effects on consumers in
the long run.

Adjudication of Consumer Disputes in Sweden

According to the *Code of Judicial Procedure*, proceedings are oral; both in
the pre-trial and the main hearings. The procedure is so complicated that the
parties are usually represented by lawyers. The high legal fees make the
procedure rather expensive. If the party is not entitled to public legal aid, he
himself will be responsible for his lawyer's fee. If the party loses his case, he
will be obliged to pay the other side's costs. In the past, it was often too
hazardous to litigate in small claims disputes.

In order to improve access to justice, the *Small Claims Act* was enacted in
1974. As in England, a no-costs rule makes the procedure less expensive and
discourages legal representation. In small claims cases the court cannot
prohibit a party from using a lawyer. However, if a party prefers legal
representation, he must pay his lawyer's fee. Public legal aid does not cover
this cost.

The parties can obtain information and certain guidance from the court,
enabling them to litigate without help from lawyers. Nevertheless retailers
often employ lawyers in small claims cases, in order to put the consumer in a
relatively weak position.

The small claims procedure is mainly oral – although the court can
demand documents from the parties – and is more informal and flexible than
in normal cases. The court has to apply the Small Claims Act in cases where
the plaintiff is claiming less than £700. This financial limit is index-linked.
The parties are obliged to observe the Act in small claims cases, and may not
agree to adopt the usual form of proceedings. The reason for this is that the

[3] Heuman, *Reklamationsnämnder och försäkringsnämnder*, p. 5 ff. and p. 810 ff.

small claims procedure is less expensive for the government, since the parties cannot obtain public legal aid.

Arbitration clauses in consumer contracts will not be valid, since arbitration is too expensive for the parties. This is due to the fact that they will have to pay fees to the arbitrators a case for which they cannot get compensation from legal aid[4].

However retailers often undertake in advance to observe the decisions of the Board. Such undertakings can be included in standard contracts, or may be given effect through provisions in the regulations of trade organisations.

The *Public Complaints Board* adjudicates in disputes between consumers and retailers but only at the request of the consumer. The consumer can also bring a legal action. The form of adjudication can be chosen by the consumer but not by the retailer.

The Complaints Board has different departments for special kinds of disputes. It can deal with complaints concerning *inter alia* cars, boats, private insurance, holiday travels, T.V. sets, furniture, clothes and shoes. The Board has no competence to adjudicate in certain kinds of complicated disputes: e.g. concerning the purchase of real property, doctors' services, and lawyers' work. Such disputes cannot be tried in a simple way. However this represents a gap in consumer protection[5].

When determining disputes, the Complaints Board is made up of a legally qualified Chairman together with an equal number of representatives for consumers and for retailers. These representatives are often experts in technical problems which are dealt with by the Ministry in question: e.g. in disputes concerning defective cars. From this point of view, the Board is a kind of specialist court[6].

The proceedings are based solely on documents. The parties and witnesses cannot be examined[7]. Decisions of the Board are only recommendations and cannot be executed. If a retailer refuses to make the suggested rectification, his name will be published in the newspapers[8]. A party who is dissatisfied with a recommendation may commence an action. Retailers do so very rarely because they are afraid of adverse publicity. This is so even in cases where they are convinced that the court will overturn the decision of the Board[9].

Improving the Effectiveness of Adjudication

In order to achieve effectiveness in adjudication, it is of great importance

4 L. Heuman, *Specialprocess Utsökning och Konkurs*, (Lund 1981) p. 23 ff.
5 L. Heuman, *Reklamantionsnämnder och försäkringsnämnder*, pp. 39 ff and 798 ff.
6 *Ibid.*, p. 107 ff
7 *Ibid.*, p. 391 ff
8 *Ibid.*, p. 11 ff, 636 ff and 827 ff.
9 *Ibid.*, p. 552 ff.

that disputes are well-distributed between courts, arbitrators and Boards. Legislation in Sweden has tried to improve access to justice without paying sufficient attention to the need for rationalisation. The present economic situation makes this problem more important. I think that one cannot pay attention only to the fact that consumers normally prefer to go to the Board rather than to the district court. From a *functional point of view*, one must consider what kind of evidence the parties will present[10].

From the outset, the Complaints Board determined disputes concerning defective *products which the consumer could send to the Board*; e.g. shoes, furs and clothes. The experts on the Board examined the products and were able to decide the cases rather rapidly. All these special cases were concentrated to the Board. Disputes could be resolved in one to three months. This kind of adjudication was a successful rationalisation.

Subsequently the jurisdiction of the Board was widened to include disputes concerning *products which could not be sent in to the Board*: e.g. cars and boats. The consumer had to obtain an *expert opinion* before the Board could give a recommendation. The Board cannot adjudicate these disputes more rapidly and simply than a court. One advantage with the Board procedure, however, is that the Board has expert members.

The Board also tries a third kind of dispute which a court could adjudicate much better. This is any *dispute where oral evidence* is of importance; e.g. concerning oral agreements. The Board should refer this kind of litigation to the courts, but does so too late – often after several months. The oral procedure has two advantages in these cases. First, the oral pre-trial hearing can shorten the time needed for the exchange of documents, especially in complicated disputes. Secondly, the courts can obtain much better evidence, since they are able to examine the parties and the witnesses. In this kind of case, the court procedure is more rapid than the Board procedure. However, even in consumer disputes, the Board in general needs more time than do the courts to decide disputes: about six months, as opposed to the courts – four[11].

Financial limits are often an ungainly and a clumsy basis upon which to distribute disputes between different forums. Several circumstances must be met in order to make a suitable distribution. This means that a lawyer must decide to which forum the case shall be referred: it is difficult for the consumer to choose the best form of adjudication.

In Sweden there is, on the one hand, a system used by the courts when dealing with normal civil litigation and consumer disputes, and, on the other hand, the complaints procedure, which can be employed only in consumer

[10] *Ibid.*, p. 836 ff.
[11] *Ibid.*, p. 221 ff and *Bernitz*, "Consumer Protection" (1976) Scandinavian Studies in Law p. 21 ff.

disputes. The *concept "consumer"* is here of decisive importance in differentiating between court procedure and complaints procedure. In Sweden, the authority of the Public Complaints Board is decided in accordance with the civil consumer concept. One may ask if this is expedient from a procedural point of view.

The consumer concept can be determined either in an *objective or a subjective way*. If one is of the opinion that consumer buying exists only when a private person has bought a typical consumer article, then one can speak of an objective consumer concept. To give an example: a purchaser is considered a consumer when he buys a vacuum cleaner, but not when he buys a steam shovel which he plans to use in his spare time.

In the Swedish civil consumer statutes, the consumer concept has been defined in accordance with the *subjective method*. A person is considered a consumer when he acquires a product *intended primarily for his own private use* from a retailer acting within his professional capacity. Thus, the decisive element here is the intention of the purchaser regarding the acquisition. It is of no importance in theory if the purchaser has actually used the product in a manner other than he had intended when he bought it; e.g. if he has used a car professionally, even though he had intended to use the product privately, does it matter if the seller believes otherwise: e.g. when he sells a small tractor to someone who gardens as a hobby?

It is often *difficult to prove the purpose* behind a purchase, as the parties to an agreement usually do not discuss how the product is to be used. The *burden of proof* that he planned to use the product privately is *considered to lie with the purchaser*. He does not have to prove that he made his purpose clear to the seller in a way that the seller could understand; e.g. through various external circumstances at the time of the purchase. The purchaser can advert to the purpose of the purchase through the testimony of people who heard him say that he intended to use the product privately. In this way, the application of the Consumer Purchases Act can come as a *surprise for the seller*, as well as the fact that certain terms of the agreement therefore do not apply to the purchaser. In practice however, the nature of the article and its actual usage ought to be of great importance in deciding whether or not the buyer proved the intention behind the purchase.

From the point of view of procedure, the civil law consumer concept is not expedient in two ways. Assume that a purchaser can prove that he had intended to use an article privately, even though it is commonly used in industrial activities; e.g. a steam shovel or some other *complicated article*. If a dispute arises between the buyer and the seller, it is a consumer dispute which, according to principle, falls under the authority of the Complaints Board. These disputes have had to be *removed in different ways from the authority of the Complaints Board* as it is far too difficult for the Board to adjudicate them within the framework of a simplified procedure.

Another weakness in allowing the Complaints Board's authority to be determined by the civil law consumer concept is that the Board cannot adjudicate disputes between private persons concerning typical consumer articles; e.g. disputes revolving around the purchase of used cars. One of the strong points in the Board's activities is that there are experts there who are experienced in judging certain technical issues, as, for example, those concerning cars. Thus when a dispute about an engine fault arises, the Board can often assess the technical issues better than a court, regardless of whether the seller is a car dealer or a private person. As the Board, at least for the present, cannot settle disputes between private persons, its potential for quickly reviewing technical questions is not fully utilised. One more general problem concerns the possibilities of *simplifying adjudication*. This can be done in many ways. The interpretation and application of civil law rules take a long time when several issues of law have to be resolved. The presentation and evaluation of evidence can also be simplified. I shall develop this further.

The civil law rules often start from the incorrect assumption that the circumstances are non-contentious. The court cannot base the judgment on contentious facts, but must resolve this problem according to rules on the burden of proof. This often means that one party gets everything and the other nothing. I think that the parties usually do not like this kind of adjudication. *The parties prefer compromises*. They want a reasonable division to be made, which is why they prefer settlements and arbitration. This kind of adjudication can be more simple and rapid than the usual one. We must look into this issue if we are to increase the possibilities of this kind of adjudication. A tendency in that direction can be observed in the Board, especially in small claims cases concerning several issues. The Board can form a general opinion and balance out issues against each other, eliminating the need to solve all the small problems concerning a few pounds[12]. However, there is an imperfection in the Swedish system. The recommendations of the Board can be changed by a court, which must follow the traditional methods of adjudication. In my opinion, different forums should not use different methods of application in the same case. Before the procedure begins, it must be decided which kind of adjudication is to be used.

It is difficult for the consumer to know what kind of evidence he must present, especially in technical issues. Perhaps it would be better if retailers were forced to *contribute to the submission of evidence, even in cases where the consumer has the burden of proof*[13]. Often disputes raise very compli-

[12]   *Ibid.*, p. 614
[13]   *Ibid.*, p. 472 ff.

cated technical problems, which can make it difficult to investigate all the details. In small claims cases, the Board can make a general common-sense consideration, without resolving all of the minor issues. If, for example, the engine of a second-hand car breaks down soon after purchase, the buyer often claims that the engine was defective before purchase. The seller usually denies this. Instead of a careful technical argumentation, the Board, on the basis of a presumption, states that the engine must have been defective before the purchase. With such presumptions, adjudication can be facilitated[14].

In Sweden, disputes below £10 or £20 cannot be tried by the Board. The normal legal system is not to be used in cases of minor importance[15]. However, a claim of £20 can mean much for a poor consumer, but almost nothing for a rich one. The weakest consumers will be those most affected by the financial limit. The Board cannot carry out its preventive function in the field of small purchases.

When a consumer receives advice from a court or the Board, he can no longer have a lawyer's fee paid by Public Legal Aid. Grants to legal aid must be kept down. All the new flexible procedures have *restricted the possibilities of legal aid*. This restriction hits the weakest consumers hardest, especially in complicated disputes[16].

Class Actions and Collective Redress
In Sweden we do not have anything like the American system of class action, but we have problems with collective redress. These problems are reduced by the possibility of prohibiting a retailer from using onerous contract terms in the future. First the Consumer Ombudsman negotiates with the retailer and tries to come to an agreement. If the Consumer Ombudsman does not succeed in getting acceptable results, he can commence an action before the Market Court. This court can prohibit the retailer, under threat of a contingent fine, from using contract terms. The Consumer Ombudsman and the Market Court can also prohibit improper marketing and dangerous products, but have no jurisdiction to handle disputes when a consumer seeks redress[17].

The Consumer Ombudsman cannot represent an individual consumer before the district courts and the Complaints Board. However, a committee has proposed that the Consumer Ombudsman should be able to represent a consumer in the courts, if the judgment will be important from a general consumer point of view. The committee has discussed mainly two kinds of

[14] *Ibid.*, p. 549 f.
[15] Compare Prop. 1979/80: 114, p. 28 and SOU 1978: 40, p. 147 and *Lagutskottets Betänkande* 1980/81: 23 p. 27 (tax enforcement).
[16] Heuman, *Ibid.*, p. 694 ff.
[17] *Bernitz* in *An Introduction to Swedish Law* (ed. Strömholm, Stockholm 1981) p. 242 ff.

methods. One possibility, which was rejected, was that the action should contain abstract issues of law, without connection to any particular case. The other method proposed that the consumer should authorise the Consumer Ombudsman to represent him and to commence an action. These problems will be considered further[18].

The system with power of attorney has been used in package holidays disputes. The Complaints Board tried only claims from complaining travellers, who had authorised one of their group to act as their representative. Travellers who did not claim redress were not asked to do so, even in cases where the Board had received a list of the travellers' names[19].

Finally, I would like to deal with a group of current cases.

After some dentists had filled some cavities, a few patients contracted a curious disease. Many of these patients have now engaged lawyers, who claim that the National Social Welfare Board is responsible for the disease. The lawyers have commenced actions against the government at many different courts. The government, of course, would prefer that one test case be determined first. It is difficult and expensive for the government to litigate before several courts.

The cases cannot be attached to one district court. Furthermore, it is not certain that the courts can always suspend disputes until one test case is determined.

The National Board of Court Administration has tried to hold back legal aid until there is a leading judgment. As the circumstances are not exactly the same in the various cases, however, a lot of plaintiffs will obtain legal aid.

The government has presented a Bill aimed at limiting the possibilities for legal aid when there are many cases of a homogeneous nature and there is no guiding decision concerning the assessment of a matter of fact or law which is the same for the different cases[20]. Legal aid will not be granted in the similar cases until one (or a few) test case(s) have been adjudicated. However, under the Bill, legal aid can be granted immediately for perpetuating evidence concerning the individual's claim; e.g. personal injury which he has suffered.

The government's proposal has been severely criticised and will probably not be approved by Parliament. Critics have felt that it goes counter to the principle of equality in the Consitution[21]: that in the same type of case it will allow some persons to receive legal aid, while others must wait, in some cases up to several years, for decisions in the test cases. The vaguely formulated principle of equality in the Constitution does, however, allow for citizens to

[18] SOU 1978: 40, p. 181 ff.
[19] Heuman, *Ibid.*, p. 246 ff.
[20] Prop. 1981/82: 28. p. 22 ff.
[21] *Regeringsformen* 1:2

be treated in different ways in accordance with *inter alia* their different economic needs. According to the Bill, however, citizens are treated differently depending on the interest of the government in limiting legal aid, not on the individual situation of each claimant. In cases which are of interest from the point of view of precedents, though, the claimant is given certain benefits in accordance with the current legislation. This inequality in the way citizens are treated has most probably been accepted, as it was believed that certain persons were given certain benefits, not that certain persons were deprived of benefits which others were guaranteed.

Many different problems must be examined more closely before a reform of the type presented by the government can be made. For example, can the government limit legal aid costs in ways other than through reduced legal aid? Or, can costs be limited by passing new rules about staying proceedings, transferring cases to one court, having common attorneys with requirements for special jurisdiction, making a more stringent examination of fees, and so on? If changes of the type in the Bill are nevertheless effected, problems will arise if the party who has legal aid wants to make a settlement, or wishes to have the dispute decided through an award which is not made public. In such an event, the legal aid granted will not result in a leading case. Furthermore, the question arises of which authority is to decide when a test case situation exists, and how one should collect information about similar cases in any other authority. This authority possibly considers most of the cases as being similar in an effort to limit the government's legal aid costs. These legal aid issues are very complicated. They belong in part to the broader issue of class actions. This is not regulated in Sweden, and has not been carefully examined.

PART III

EMPLOYMENT AND SOCIAL SECURITY LAW

THE CURRENT LAW OF LABOUR RELATIONS IN BRITAIN

by

Steve Anderman

The existing framework of law for trade unions and collective bargaining in Britain has a dialectical quality to it. On the one hand historically the system of labour relations has operated under a legal framework with a relatively limited role for law in regulating trade unions, collective bargaining and industrial action. Commentators have described the traditional legal framework which extended into the 1960's as "voluntarist" or "non-interventionist" or even "abstentionist" because by comparison with other countries there has been a relative absence of close legal regulation in those spheres of activity. As Otto Kahn Freund once put it, "there is no major country in the world in which the law has played a less significant role in the shaping of industrial relations"[1]. And as the Donovan Commission commented, ". . . it has been the traditional policy of the law not to intervene in the system of industrial relations"[2].

On the other hand, certain legislative developments in the past decade appear to be antithetical to a voluntaristic or non-interventionistic system. One inroad into voluntary collective bargaining has come somewhat subtly and indirectly from laws which provide extensive positive legal rights, both in the form of rights for individual employees as well as rights for trade unions against employers. A second and more direct intrusion comes from the growth of legislation which seeks to place wider legal restrictions upon the use of industrial action and upon the operation of the closed shop in Britain. A major task in understanding the British system today is to obtain a perspective to evaluate just what effect these more recent legislative interventions have had upon the system of autonomous collective bargaining, as that system has evolved over the decades. The paper is divided into three parts (I) The Traditional System; (II) The Growth of Positive Rights; and (III) The Growth of Legal Restrictions.

I. The Traditional System
A good starting point is to look at the scope of the so-called voluntarist or

[1] "Labour Law" in M. Ginsberg (ed.) *Law and Opinion in England in the 20th Century* Stevens 1959 p. 244.
[2] Royal Commission on Trade Unions and Employer Associations 1965-68 1968 Cmnd 3623 para. 25.

non-interventionist tradition in British industrial relations[3].

This tradition stretches back to the formative period of British labour relations, roughly from 1850 to 1909. During this period trade unions and industrial action were first "decriminalised" by the Trade Union Act of 1871 and the Conspiracy and Protection of Property Act 1875 and then given immunities against civil action by the Trade Disputes Act of 1906. In Britain, rather uniquely, trade unions obtained legitimacy for their objects and their methods in a relatively hostile social order by a series of immunities from civil and criminal action rather than by a positive right to strike or a positive right of association. Faced with common law liabilities created and applied by a judiciary antagonistic to the growth of collective action, trade unions asked for protective legislation which did no more than negate these liabilities and provide specific immunities first against "restraint of trade"[4] and criminal conspiracy[5], and then against "civil conspiracy" and "inducement to breach of employment contracts", and "interference with trade" all of which made the organisation and leadership of strikes unlawful[6]. In the 1906 Act trade unions also obtained an immunity against the possibility of being sued in tort, an immunity which ensured that their organisations, and hence their funds, would not be vicariously liable for the industrial action of the members and officials[7].

The fact that they obtained a freedom to strike in the form of negative immunities rather than a positive right to strike has entailed certain disadvantages for British trade unions. Over the years the legal immunities have been relatively easily outflanked by the judiciary creating new forms of liabilities[8]. Moreover, legal immunities have appeared to the untutored eye as legal privileges, the form concealing the substance that a liberty or right to strike had been won[9]. Yet the negative immunities have also had a functional advantage to British trade unions. They were obtained without the burden of any corresponding legal responsibilities. This was true in 1871 and 1875 and again in 1906 when an alternative form of legal framework providing positive rights could be obtained only at the cost of a statutory definition of trade union responsibility for industrial action which was not limited to industrial action expressly authorised by the Union executive. The tendency

---

[3] See e.g. O. Kahn-Freund *Labour and the Law* (2nd ed. 1977) London Stevens; Flanders The Tradition of Voluntarism 1974 *Brit. Jnl. Ind. Rels.* 352
[4] Trade Union Act 1871 s. 2
[5] Conspiracy and Protection of Property Act 1875.
[6] Trade Disputes Act 1906 ss 1 and 3
[7] Trade Disputes Act 1906 s. 4.
[8] See e.g. Taff Vale Ry. Co. v A.S.R.S. (1901) and other cases discussed in Wedderburn, *The Worker and the Law* (1971) Penguin; see also Griffiths *The Politics of the Judiciary* (1970) London: Fontana.
[9] K.W. Wedderburn, *New Structure of Labour Law in Britain* 13 Israel Law Review Oct. 1978 at p. 70.

of British trade unions to reject positive rights and settle for negative immunities was based on their concern to avoid the embrace of an extensive legal framework of regulation which would inevitably be interpreted by unsympathetic judges[10].

During the formative period British trade unions also rejected positive legal assistance with recognition in the form of compulsory arbitration. Whilst some of the weaker TUC trade unions favoured compulsory arbitration because of its potential for forcing recognition from recalcitrant employers, the majority clearly rejected this alternative. In this they were joined by employers and their associations who were also wary of government intervention. The Conciliation Act of 1896 set the pattern for voluntary conciliation and arbitration which has persisted, with two wartime exceptions, to the present day[11]. Unlike other systems, third party dispute settlement was grafted onto the British collective bargaining system without any legal strings.

The rejection of legal intervention in this form was part of a more positive commitment to autonomous collective bargaining – a positive endorsement of "voluntarism" rather than merely a negative rejection of legal intervention. Certainly, the reforms that were introduced in the wake of the militancy of the shop stewards movement of the First World War confirmed this picture of a voluntaristic inclination to the British system. Instead of recommending a modification of the wartime legal constraints into a form of restrictive legislation applicable to industrial action in the post war period, the Whitley Committee suggested the creation of joint councils for industry to resolve conflict through formal consultation and negotiating machinery to reform collective bargaining by voluntary means into a more effective system of dispute resolution[12]. At the same time the Industrial Courts Act of 1919 confirmed the voluntary character of the conciliation and arbitration system and added a permanent arbital body, the Industrial Court. The Whitley Committee recommendations struck a responsive chord in industry and led to the growth of a form of industry-wide machinery for negotiating collective agreements and disputes procedures. These collective arrangements developed without direct legal support to cover more than sixteen million of the twenty three million workforce by the early 1960's[13].

The non-interventionist element in the British system in its formative years then was partly a product of trade union suspicion of legal regulation because of their experience with judicial hostility. Of course, British trade

---

[10] See e.g. S. and B. Webb *The History of Trade Unionism* 1920; Clegg, Fox and Thompson *A History of British Trade Unions since 1889* (1964) Vol. 1.
[11] See O. Kahn Freund *op. cit. supra*
[12] See First Report (1917) Cmnd 8606; Fourth Report (1918) Cmnd 9099
[13] Ministry of Labour Evidence to Royal Commission on Trade Unions and Employers Association 1965.

unions were placed in a position where they could afford to take this line because of their relative success in obtaining recognition and collective bargaining directly from employers long before they were in a position to obtain positive legal support on acceptable terms. In the late 19th century, British employer organisations considered that they could take on the trade unions by themselves. They also wanted autonomy from government intervention in industrial relations as well as in commercial dealings, and it was to these views as well as trade union demands that those succeeding governments acquiesced.

Kahn-Freund's description of the British system as one of "collective laissez-faire" quite nicely captures both its debts to 19th century laissez-faire attitudes and its adjustment to the growth of industrial power by trade union organisations[14]. Yet collective laissez-faire has had its consequences. The absence of legal regulation has meant that the institutions of collective bargaining have developed according to their own logic rather than being shaped by any significant legal influence. And the absence of any significant legal support meant that British trade unions could legitimately argue, as could few other trade union movements, as late as the 1960's that they were not dependent upon the state for their existence:

> "The fact that trade unions in Britain have succeeded through their own efforts in strengthening their organisation and in obtaining recognition, not relying on the assistance of Government through legislation, is one of the most important factors sustaining their strength and independence. Trade unions have not been given privileges. They have fought for what they have achieved. If they had been granted privileges, if their organisation had been strengthened and sustained by Government action, it might well be logical to argue that trade union function would also be the responsibility of Government; the right to bargain had been granted by Government and Government could take it away. Trade union strength has been developed without the help of any external agency[15]."

The continuation of the narrow scope of legal regulation until the early 1960's could also be attributed to the relative satisfaction of upper and middle class opinion with the consequences of collective bargaining as regulated by the prevailing economic conditions. The decline of strikes in the 1930's the collaborative policies of the trade union leadership after the 1926 General Strike and pressures of war time all combined to produce an acceptance of trade unionism and non-regulated collective bargaining. Non-interventionism rested upon a social balance of power in which the role of the trade unions was regarded as essentially defensive.

By the early 1960's, however, the social acceptance of non-interventionism began to break down as the shift in the market power of

---

[14] Labour Law in Ginsberg, *Law and Opinion in England in the 20th Century* (1959 London).
[15] TUC Evidence to the RCTUEA, London HMSO.

labour manifested itself in strong workshop bargaining accompanied by unofficial strikes (that is, strikes unauthorised by the trade-union organisation) and "unconstitutional" strikes (that is, strikes in breach of industrial disputes procedures), "wage drift" marked by leapfrogging wage claims and competitive wage bidding by workshop groups, and a growing awareness of restrictive work practices in many sectors[16].

To Labour and Conservative governments, concerned with the management of Britain's economic performance, the pattern of industrial relations appeared to create not only inflationary tendencies at a macroeconomic level but also inefficiencies caused by workshop power at a microeconomic or enterprise level. The possibility of using legal mechanisms to produce an improvement in the economic performance of collective bargaining was put on the agenda for the first time since the war. The first option considered was a legal basis to incomes policy[17]. Within the Conservative party at an early stage, moreover, there was early evidence of a strong desire to introduce legal restraints on trade union activities such as industrial action and closed shops. This was prompted by a concern that the "giant's strength" of the trade unions should be brought with the rule of law. It was also caused by a concern for individuals who were dismissed for non-membership in the closed shop[18].

During this period the judges, anticipating later statutory responses, reacted to these developments by creating new torts and resurrecting long-unused tort liabilities to justify the use of labour injunctions against the leaders of industrial action[19]. The Labour government partially neutralised this judicial initiative by enacting the Trade Disputes Act 1965. At the same time however, it responded to the growing concern with industrial conditions by appointing in 1965 a royal commission to examine the development of trade unions and collective bargaining.

The report of the Royal Commission on Trade Unions and Employers Associations, known as the Donovan Commission, in 1968 provided both a diagnosis of the cause of the growth of industrial conflict and a prescription for its cure. It diagnosed the causes of industrial conflict as the decline of the effectiveness of collective bargaining institutions at the national, or industry-wide level, to provide regulation at workshop level, and the demonstrable inadequacies of the institutional machinery of workshop collective bargaining that had emerged in the post-war period. Workshop bargaining, with its autonomy, informality and fragmentation, the report

[16] W. McCarthy and N. Ellis, *Management by Agreement* (1973 London).
[17] See e.g. C. Crouch, *Class Conflict and the Industrial Relations Crisis Part IV* (1977 London).
[18] See e.g. *A Giant's Strength* (1959 London): Inns of Court Conservative and Unionists' Society; *Fair Deal at Work*, Conservative Political Centre, 1968 London.
[19] See, for example, *Rookes* v *Barnard* [1964] A.C. 1129; *Stratford and Lindley* [1963] A.C. 269.

argued, could be reformed into a more orderly institution only by an extension of official trade-union activity and formal collective agreements and procedures to the workshop level. The Donovan Report recommended an increase in formal written agreements at plant and company level and the revision of the rule books or constitutions of trade unions to include a description of the powers and functions of shop stewards[20].

The Donovan Report had stressed that the necessary reforms ought to be effectuated by voluntary means rather than compelled by law. But at this time neither the Conservative opposition nor the Labour Government were prepared to rely on a voluntaristic approach to the reform of industrial relations.

In the 1968-70 period the Labour Government attempted to introduce legal regulation selectively to certain "sore points" of collective bargaining and then in 1971-1974 the Conservative Government attempted to introduce a comprehensive system of legal regulation of collective bargaining. Both were ineffective in achieving their aims. The proposals for legislation contained in the Labour Government's White Paper ("In Place of Strife" 1969 were withdrawn in return for a solemn and binding undertaking by the TUC that it would take certain steps to help resolve certain unconstitutional and unofficial strikes. The Conservative Government's legislation, The Industrial Relations Act 1971, was ultimately repealed by the Labour Government when it returned to office in 1974, but long before its repeal it had demonstrated its inability to achieve its objective of applying a viable new legal framework of law to British collective bargaining, and "had virtually been placed in suspended animation because the potential repercussions of bringing actions were too risky for most possible litigants[21]." During this period British trade unions and work groups (with the acquiescence and in some cases the support of employers) quite dramatically demonstrated their capacity to resist by industrial means Parliamentary efforts to bring collective bargaining within the web of legislative regulation[21a].

What was particularly noticeable about the 1971-4 experience was the support given by employers to the pattern of resistance to the legislation. In the first place, during that period it was quite obvious that many employers did not generally see it as in their immediate interests to make use of its provisions. Yet it was also clear that employers actively cooperated in preventing the legal restrictions from reaching the workplace. For example, the 1971 Acts' attempt to make collective agreements legally enforceable by creating a statutory prescription in favour of legal enforceability of collective

---

[20] RCTUEA paras. 38–53.
[21] A.W.J. Thomson and S.R. Engleman, *The Industrial Relations Act: A Review and Analysis* (London 1975) p. 126.
[21a] *Ibid.*; also see Weeks et al. *Industrial Relations and the Limits of the Law* (Oxford 1975).

agreements was met by the response that virtually every agreement concluded after the Act became law included a provision that agreement was
not to be legally enforceable[22]. And although closed shops and closed shop
dismissals had been made unlawful, employers helped to reduce the impact
of that unlawfulness by various means. During that period the number of
workers in closed shops actually increased as employers maintained existing
closed shops because of their usefulness in ensuring the stability of existing
bargaining structures and collective bargaining arrangements. The net effect
of the legislation was only to cause managers to hold back plans to create new
formal closed shop agreements, a process which was only postponed until
1974 when the Act was repealed[23].

With the return to office of a Labour Government in 1974, the traditional
system of immunities was swiftly restored. The Trade Unions and Labour
Relations Act 1974, later amended by the Trade Unions and Labour Relations Act 1976, (TULRA) repealed the Industrial Relations Act 1971 and
re-established a legislative framework which contained relatively few restrictions upon industrial action, collective bargaining and trade unions.

First the 1974 Act provided a wide degree of autonomy for trade union
organisations under the legal framework. For example, under TULRA,
trade unions were given a number of specific attributes of corporate status
but otherwise were not regarded as corporate bodies. Trade Unions once
again received a wide legislative immunity from common law doctrines of
restraint of trade which might otherwise have limited their aims and their
actions under their rulebooks[24]. They were also once again made immune
from actions in tort which technically gave them immunity from any vicarious liability for the acts of their officials or members in connection with
industrial actions[25].

There were statutory limitations on the expenditure of funds on certain
political objects and trade unions could not be "listed" as independent trade
unions qualifying for certain tax advantages and legal rights unless they were
regarded as "independent" by the Certification Officer[25a]. In order to be
"listed" however it was not necessary for a trade union to submit to any
comprehensive regulation of the contents of its rule book or constitution[26].

Moreover, apart from specific statutes placing limits on trade union
discrimination on grounds of race, sex, EEC nationality or non-contribution

---

[22] Trade Union Immunities 1981 Cmnd 8128 (para. 13)
[23] See e.g. J. Gennard *The Extent of Closed Shop Arrangements in British Industry* (1980) 88
D.E. Gazette 16.
[24] TULRA s. 2(5) See e.g. *Cheall* v *APEX* [1982] IRLR 91 (C.A.).
[25] TULRA s. 14
[25a] TULRA s. 30(1) see e.g. *Certification Officer* v *Squibb U.K. Staff Assn.* [1979] IRLR 75
(CA)
[26] TULRA s. 8 (4) see also Trade Union Act 1913.

to political funds, the legal control over trade union activities was left essentially to the common law which gave a right of action to members against union organisations. Although the statute conferred a right upon trade union members to terminate their membership on giving reasonable notice and complying with reasonable conditions[26a], there was no other legislative regulation of internal union affairs. Furthermore, TULRA tacitly permitted the existence of closed shop or union membership shop arrangements. A residual legal protection in the form of a claim for unfair dismissal was given to an employee against an employer where the employer dismissed an employee who either refused to join, or resigned from, a closed shop trade union on religious grounds. Individuals who were refused entry into, or expelled from, a trade union had the possibility of lodging a complaint against such a trade union to an Independent Review Committee, a committee appointed by Government upon the recommendation of the T.U.C. They also had a limited claim against the trade union at common law[27].

Secondly, the 1974 Act, as amended by the 1976 Act, restored the wide immunities given by the Trade Disputes Act 1906 to the leaders and organisers of strikes and other industrial action. The immunities were designed not only to cancel out the existing common law liabilities created in the 1960s for inducing breach of commercial contract[28] and interfering with commercial relations[29] but also to pre-empt the creation of new torts[30]. It was argued that the idea behind the statute was to restore the legal framework that had been intended in 1906 taking into account intervening developments[31]. The new immunities now clearly applied to many forms of "secondary" pressure as well as "primary" strikes. They also continued the tradition of giving immunities to unofficial strikes as well as union authorised strikes as long as the organisation of the industrial action was taken by an individual "in contemplation or furtherance of a trade dispute"[32]. The intention of the 1974-76 Act was to take the injunction out of the realm of labour disputes and allow for such secondary action as was subjectively thought necessary by workers to support their primary dispute.

The width of the 1974-6 statutory immunities made the judiciary distinctly uneasy. It was not long before the Court of Appeal had drastically narrowed the immunities for secondary action "in contemplation or furtherance of a trade dispute" by creating limitations on the meaning of "in furtherance" of a trade dispute. In a trilogy of cases however the House of

[26a] TULRA s. 5.
[27] See Hepple, "A Right to Work", June 1981 Vol. 10 Ind. L.J. No. 2 at pp. 78-81
[28] *Stratford* v *Lindley* 1965 A.C. 269.
[29] *Torquay Hotel* v *Cousins* [1969] 2 ch. 106.
[30] See e.g. TULRA 13(3) repealed by s. 17 (8) EPA 1980.
[31] Wedderburn Parliamentary Debates (Hansard) House of Lords, Thursday 12 June 1980.
[32] TULRA ss 13 and 29(1).

Lords put an end to this development in judicial legislation[33]. Arguing that the language of the Labour Government's statute was not susceptible to the Court of Appeal's restrictive interpretation, the House of Lords restored the full width of the immunities for secondary action. There was even some evidence of judicial sensitivity to the policy behind the 1974-76 Act. Lord Scarman indicated that he was relieved that the judges would not have to sit like "some backseat driver in trade disputes" and that the policy of the 1974-6 Act was to put "the law . . . back to what Parliament had intended when it enacted the Act of 1906 – but stronger and clearer than it was then"[34].

Yet the other Law Lords were careful to indicate quite explicitly to the Conservative Government, now once again in power and preparing new labour legislation, that they were disquieted by the scope of the immunities contained in the 1974-6 Acts[35]. Lord Diplock said that he regarded the much extended immunities as "intrinsically repugnant". Lord Keith saw trade unionists as "privileged persons" able to bring about disastrous consequences with legal impunity"[35a]. As we shall see, the Conservative Government did not fail to respond to these views.

Finally, although the policy of the 1974-6 Act was to create a wide immunity for the leaders and organisers of industrial action, curiously enough it stopped short of extending such immunities to their followers, those employees who participated in strikes and other industrial action. The structure of immunities in the 1974-6 Act, as indeed the 1906 Act, failed to provide any positive protection for such workers against the disciplinary powers of the employer or the consequences of their precarious contractual position when taking industrial action[36]. Indeed paradoxically TULRA provided that where an employer dismissed all employees either participating in a strike or whilst being locked-out by him and the employer re-employs none he can escape any claims for unfair dismissal. Under that Act, industrial tribunals were denied jurisdiction in such situations to consider whether the dismissals were unfair or not[37]. It has been argued that this provision was necessary to avoid industrial tribunals pronouncing upon the merits of collective industrial disputes[38]. But it may equally be observed that such a rule tends to undermine those parts of the legal framework committed

---

[33] *NWL Ltd.* v *Woods* [1979] ICR 867; *Express Newspapers Ltd* v *McShane* [1980] ICR 56; *Duport Steels Ltd* v *Sirs* [1980] 1 All E.R. 541.

[34] *NWL Ltd* v *Woods* [1979] at 886.

[35] *Duport Steels Ltd* v *Sirs* [1980] ICR 161 at 177.

[35a] *Ibid*. at p. 188.

[36] At common law, participation in a strike or other industrial action is often regarded as conduct repudiating the employee's contract of employment. See e.g. *Simmons* v *Hoover* [1976] IRLR 266 (EAT); *Sec. of State for Employment* v *A.S.L.E.F.* [1972] ICR 19.

[37] See now EPCA 1978 s. 62; *McCormick* v *Horsepower Ltd* [1980] IRLR 217 (C.A.)

[38] See e.g. Wedderburn 13 "Israel Law Rev." at 450.

to legal immunities for industrial action as well as to the legal protection of trade union activity. Thus, in cases where all employees are dismissed for industrial action, it has been held under EPCA s. 62 that the tribunal has no jurisdiction to consider a legal claim for protection against dismissal for trade union activities under EPCA s. 58(3)[39].

The legal framework created by the 1974-6 Acts not only restored the tradition of non-interference in internal trade union affairs and the immunities for industrial action. It also reasserted the related virtues of autonomy for collective bargaining. The 1974 Act restored collective agreements to their status prior to 1971 of being presumed not to be legally enforceable between employer or employee associations and trade unions[40]. This did not preclude the contents of collective agreements achieving legal weight as employees' rights against employers by being incorporated into individual contracts of employment, although certain conditions were imposed upon the incorporation of the "peace obligations" contained in collective agreements into individual contracts of employment[41]. Moreover, the legislative framework once again emphasised that negotiation between the parties should be the principal method of resolving collective industrial disputes and negotiation should be backed up by voluntary, i.e. non-legally binding, and independent third party assistance consisting of conciliation, mediation, arbitration and inquiry provided by the Advisory Conciliation and Arbitration Service (ACAS).

The rejection of legally enforceable collective agreements and legally binding arbitration marked a return to a policy of relative non-intervention – one which embodied a general preference for voluntary collective bargaining and a specific concern to avoid any form of legal accountability for trade unions which might result from legally enforceable peace obligations.

Positive Rights Under the 1970s Legal Framework
The close consultation between the trade unions and the Labour Government in the 1974-6 "social contract" however did not stop at simply restoring the negative immunities; it also produced quite extensive protective legislation embodying positive rights. The Employment Protection Act 1975 expanded the statutory floor of individual employment rights applicable to all employees regardless of trade union membership. It also provided a series of new positive legal rights for trade unions against employers[42].

[40] TULRA s. 18
[41] TULRA s. 18(4)
[42] The Labour Government – TUC consultations also included a commitment to produce legislation on industrial democracy which resulted in the Bullock Committee of Inquiry on Industrial Democracy (Cmnd 6706 1977) and a White Paper, "Industrial Democracy (Cmnd 7231 1978) but no legislation.

A. The New Trade Union Rights

The enactment of the new trade union rights, predominantly in the Employment Protection Act 1975 (EPA) constituted a major change in approach by British trade unions. After decades of rejecting legal support because of the strings attached, the trade unions were able to obtain help from a labour government which they regarded as "ours"[43]. The *quid pro quo* for this acquisition of legal rights was participation in a programme of voluntary pay restraint as part of a social contract. It did not include acceptance of restrictions on the right to strike whilst making use of the new legal rights[44]. Nevertheless the positive legal rights that were obtained were carefully curtailed. There was an ambivalence about the use of the law to promote voluntary collective bargaining and in particular an overriding concern to ensure that the impact of the legislation upon collective bargaining along the lines of the American experience with the duty to bargain in good faith would be kept to a minimum[45]. In addition, it was hoped to avoid creating a precedent for coercive legislation for future conservative legislators. The net effect of this concern was to produce legislation which provided only minimal support to trade unionists in a weak bargaining positioning whilst at the same time failing to prevent a significant degree of legal interference with voluntary collective bargaining.

The 1975 Act included provisions that enabled an independent trade union which was refused recognition for the purpose of collective bargaining to obtain legal support[46]. Under these provisions, which were repealed by the Conservative Government's Employment Act 1980, a union could make a complaint to ACAS about the refusal and ACAS was required first to conciliate and then investigate the extent of employee support for recognition. Following the investigation it was, if it saw fit, to make a recommendation that the employer bargain with the union[47]. The employer's duty to bargain under British law was essentially a procedural test requiring the employer to engage in discussions with the trade union over the relevant subject but not requiring any substantial concession[48]. More importantly, a

---

[39] See e.g. *Drew* v *St. Edmundsbury B.C.* [1980] ICR 513.

[43] See Wedderburn, 13 Israel Law Rev. at 450

[44] This was a feature of certain legal rights created by Industrial Relations Act 1971 in particular s. 36 which made it an unfair industrial practice to strike whilst a recognition dispute was pending a decision by the Commission for Industrial Relations or the National Industrial Relations Court.

[45] See e.g. H. Wellington *Labor and the Legal Process* New Haven 1968; *M. Hart* Union Recognition in America – the Legislative Snare (1978) 7 *ILJ* 201.

[46] EPA ss 11–16

[47] The recommendation could consist of a general recommendation to bargain or a recommendation to bargain over "further issues" where the union was already recognised. In the event, claims for further recognition were more.

[48] Anderman, *Employment Protection: A New Legal Framework* Butterworths, London 1976 p. 3–4.

failure to bargain was not penalised by a court order backed up by contempt powers. The ultimate remedy in the enforcement procedure against an employer who refused to comply with an order to recognise, was an arbitration award by the Central Arbitration Committee to give an improvement in pay or other terms of employment to individual employees who were the subject of the recognition claim.

The Act also provided and continues to provide a legal right for recognised independent trade unions to obtain information relevant to collective bargaining from employers[49]. Yet this right is hedged with numerous exceptions e.g. "confidentiality", "substantial injury to the undertaking" and again is backed up by a rather weak and inappropriate remedy. To enforce a legitimate claim for disclosure of information against a recalcitrant employer, a trade union has only the legal sanction of submitting a claim to the Central Arbitration Committee (CAC) for a punitive arbitration award against the employer taking the form of an improvement in the terms and conditions of the contract of individual employees. There is no possibility of a court order compelling the employer actually to disclose the relevant information. These provisions are complemented by a Code of Practice issued by ACAS which operates as a guide to interpretation and suggests quite a wide range of information which might be disclosed[50]. The disclosure provisions however have rarely been used and where used have concentrated on fairly traditional information[51].

Part IV of the 1975 Act also contains provisions that require employers to disclose information and consult with recognised independent trade unions before taking a decision to discuss workers for redundancy. These provisions have been complemented by a more recent Statutory Instrument – the Transfer of Undertakings (Protection of Employment) Regulation 1981 which requires disclosure of relevant information to and consideration with recognised unions over mergers and other transfers of businesses invloving a change of employer. This latter regulation however does not apply to share transfers which is the basis of most mergers and takeovers in the U.K. Further, the Health and Safety at Work Act 1974 s. 2(4) gives trade unions the right to appoint safety representatives who have a legal right to be consulted by the employers on health and safety issues. Moreover, the Social Security Pensions Act 1975 [52] gives trade unions a right to be consulted before employers can contract out of the state occupational Pension Scheme.

[49] EPA ss 17-21
[50] Disclosure of Information to Trade Unions for Collective Bargaining Purposes ACAS Code of Practice (1977)
[51] See e.g. H. Gospel, 'Disclosure of Information to Trade Unions' (1976) 5 ILJ 223; H. Gospel and P. Willman "Disclosure of Information the C.A.C. Approach" (1981) 10 ILJ 10.
[52] S. 30(a).

Finally, the 1978 Act provided three separate types of individual rights which give protection to trade union membership and activity.

First, the dismissal of an employee for reasons of trade union membership or participation in the activities of an independent trade union is automatically unfair[53], and an employee so dismissed has a right to a remedy of interim relief (similar to the Swedish remedy), to continue his contract until the case is finally determined, as well as compensation or reinstatement[54]. Secondly, an employee has the right not to be penalised for or deterred from trade union membership in trade union activities by action short of dismissal taken up against him by his employer[55]. Thirdly, officials including shop stewards, and members of recognised independent trade unions are given a right to reasonable time off to engage in trade union activities[56].

These legal rights have their distinct shortcomings. For example, they do not provide protection from discrimination against trade unions in the hiring process[57] or to protection for trade union activities during working hours without the consent of the employer[58]. Nevertheless they do mark the beginnings of a positive collective right to associate contructed out of the bricks of individual rights[59].

On the whole, however, the experiment with positive trade union rights in Britain has not been conspicuously successful from the trade union point of view. On the one hand, the legislative enactments have brought no real support. Their remedial weakness has meant that they have had little impact upon recalcitrant employers[60]. The deepening recession has meant that the consultation provisions have provided no real base for effective negotiations over redundancies even where formal consultations have taken place. Furthermore, with only a few exceptions[61] the judiciary have not been particularly sympathetic in their interpretation of trade union rights.

Moreover, owing to the approach of the judiciary the provisions for legal support have generated a form of legal regulation which has impinged upon the voluntary system in several different ways. Judges deciding whether an organisation was an "independent trade union"[62] or was "recognised"[63] by the employers have produced results which did not accord with trade union

---

[53] EPCA s. 58
[54] EPCA ss 77-79 and 68-72
[55] EPCA s. 23(1)
[56] EPCA ss 27-32
[57] *City of Birmingham D.C.* v *Beyer* [1977] IRLR 211
[58] *Marley Tile Ltd* v *Shaw* [1980] ICR 72 (C.A.)
[59] Wedderburn, (1976) 39 M.L.R. 169
[60] See e.g. *Grunwick Processing* v *ACAS* [1978] 1 All E.R. 338 in which it was established that ACAS has no sanction against an employer who refused to divulge information about the employees to be balloted on the question of union recognition.
[61] See e.g. *Sood* v *G.E.C. Elliott Process Automation Ltd* [1980] ICR 1
[62] See e.g. *Squibb* v *Vic Staff Assn.* v *Certification Officer* [1977] IRLR 355 EAT
[63] See e.g. *NUGSAT* v *Albury Bros Ltd* [1978] IRLR 504 (C.A.)

views. The judicial review of the criteria to be applied to recognition questions, particularly those involving inter-union disputes, has created trade union concern about the compatability of legal machinery with their own Disputes Procedure for resolving inter-union jurisdictional disputes, the so-called Bridlington Procedure[64]. As Wedderburn put it:

> "Already the movement has been disillusioned by the operation of some of 'its' laws and has realised afresh the limitations that inevitably fall upon trade unions who trust in the regulation of industrial relations by the law[65]"

Moreover, ACAS itself wondered about the compatability of the legal recognition provisions with its system of voluntary conciliation.

In its 1978 Annual Report it said

> "This essential voluntary role (of collective conciliation) does not sit easily with the statutory duties of sections 11-16 of EPA" (p. 30)

The disadvantages of the new trade union legal rights from the trade union point of view went beyond their intrusions into the traditionally voluntary system. The new positive rights also created certain hostages to fortune. The law after 1974-6 gave a one-sided appearance to the uninformed public. It was not easy to convince public opinion that even though the laws were all directed against the employer they still failed to provide an effective counterweight because of the concentrated economic power of employers. The legislation created a vulnerability to the argument that in view of their new rights, "trade unions have too few obligations . . ."[66] The irony of the positive trade union rights achieved in the 1975 legislation is that they may have created the symbols of legal support for trade unions without the substance.

B. Positive Individual Employment Rights

The so called voluntary system was never entirely without certain forms of protective legislation. Although the early Factory Acts were introduced largely upon the initiative of liberal social reformers, trade union support for the later Factory Acts[67], and related safety legislation[68] as well as the Truck Acts of the 19th century and the minimum wage legislation for the sweated

---

[64] *UKAPE* v *ACAS* [1980] 1 All E.R. 612; *EMA* v *ACAS* [980] 1 All E.R. 896; see also *R. Simpson*, "Judicial Control of A.C.A.S." (1979) 8 I.L.J. 69 and (1980) 9 I.L.J. 160

[65] 13 Israel Law Rev. p. 457

[66] *Trade Union Immunities* para. 12

[67] E.g. Factory Act 1874, 1901, 1937, 1961; Coal Mines Regulation Act 1887; the Mines and Quarries Act 1954; the Office Shops and Premises Act 1963 and the Health and Safety at Work Act 1974.

[68] Statutes on compensation for industrial accidents such as the e.g. Employers Liability Act 1880, Workmans Compensation Acts of 1847-1945. Law Reform (Personal Injuries) Act 1945; Law Reform (Contributory Negligence) Act 1945 etc.

trades introduced in the Trade Boards Act of 1909 indicated that British trade unions were not adverse to what the Webbs called "the method of legal enactment" as an alternative to the method of collective bargaining. Yet apart from further developments in safety legislation and selective minimum wages legislation[69], the statutory individual employment rights were not greatly extended until the 1960s. Roy Lewis has suggested that the likely reason for this is that "the unions themselves ultimately ceased to press for the wider statutory protections. Instead they came to rely increasingly on collective bargaining as the single most important method for regulating the terms of their members' employment"[70]. Yet this does not do full justice to the extent to which the trade unions contributed to the creation of the welfare state in the early post-war years.

The recent wave of individual employment rights legislation was initiated by a Conservative government with its Contracts of Employment Act 1963. This was followed by a Labour government's enactment of the Redundancy Payments Act 1965 and its attempt to draft a bill to provide legal protection against unfair dismissal in the Industrial Relations Bill 1970. That Bill was never enacted by Labour but it formed the basis of the unfair dismissals provisions of the Industrial Relations Act 1971.

When Labour repealed the 1971 Act in 1974 the unfair dismissal provisions were largely retained and in 1975 reinforced by the omnibus Employment Protection Act which also created maternity rights, rights on insolvency, rights on medical suspension, rights to a guarantee payment if laid off, and rights to time off work, all later consolidated into the 1978 Employment Protection (Consolidation) Act 1978 (EPCA). To these were added a comprehensive Health and Safety at Work Act enacted in 1974, Equal Pay Act 1970, and Race Relations Act 1975 and Sex Discrimination Act 1975.

The more recent history of individual employment rights legislation in Britain indicates that in contrast with collective labour law, there has been a modicum of joint ground between the two political parties and indeed the CBI and TUC. This may at first sight seem odd but on closer investigation it can be seen that "protective" employment legislation has not had the sole aim of protecting employees against unfair employers; it has also sought to introduce reforms to management practice and procedure. In particular it has attempted to ensure that standards of enlightened managers – particularly reasonable procedural standards – are adopted more widely in industry. Moreover, the judicial interpretation of much of the legislation has entailed that the interests of protecting the employee have been balanced against the interests of the business, often to the detriment of the emp-

[69] E.g. Wages Councils Act 1946.
[70] See *The Historical Development of Labour Law* (1976) XIV Brit. Jnl. of Ind. Rels. p. 8.

loyee[70a]. There is little evidence of the judiciary taking the view that the legislation should be construed in a "purposive" fashion to ensure that the legal protections for employees are given a generous interpretation.

What is particularly interesting from the comparative viewpoint is the way trade unions limited their aims in obtaining protective legislation. Much of the individual rights legislation was drawn up in response to specific demands by trade unions and yet in contrast with the Swedish system, individual employment rights in Britain have not been regarded as a means of providing trade union members in a weak bargaining position with a platform of legal rights which are comparable to and integrated with collective bargaining. Instead, the British rights have been regarded more as a "floor of rights" or "safety net" applicable to employees – whether unionised or not – who could not be reached by effective collective bargaining. The relatively low levels of statutory benefit have had the effect of demonstrating the superiority of collective bargaining by providing a platform upon which collective bargaining can easily improve. Yet another consequence of this approach is that the British individual legal rights have been weaker in remedy, more tenuous in their links with trade union consultation and generally less of a threat to managerial prerogative than the Swedish[71].

Nevertheless, the creation of extensive positive individual rights in Britain has led to certain adverse reactions from employers. Small employers in particular have protested that the edifice of legal rights has made the costs of employment disproportionately high and discouraged the hiring of new employees, although this has been called into question by subsequent empirical research[72]. Academic commentators moreover have raised the spectre that the individual legal rights may not be compatible with the voluntary system.

As Roy Lewis put it

"Perhaps the trade union movement has underestimated the degree of legal intervention in the new laws and has accidentally jeopardised the abstentionist tradition in a sudden eagerness to win statutory victories."[73]

Wedderburn concedes that the new laws have had some "effect on the objects and mechanism of autonomous collective bargaining" but he argues

[70a] See e.g. Anderman *The Law of Unfair Dismissal* (London 1978); Bowers and Clarke "Unfair Dismissal and Managerial Prerogative" (1981) 10 I.L.J. 34; H. Forrest "Political Values in Individual Employment Law" (1980) 43 M.L.R. 361.

[71] See Anderman, "Labour Law in Sweden: A Response" in A. Neal (ed.) *Law and the Weaker Party* Vol. 1

[72] See N. Daniel and E. Stilgoe, *The Impact of Employment Protection Laws* P.S.I. 1978; R. Clifton and C. Tatton Brown *The Impact of Employment Legislation on Small Firms* (D.E. Research Papers No. 6 1979)

[73] Lewis, "The Historical Development of Labour Law" (1976) XIV *British Jnl of Industrial Relations* at p. 15

that the "new individual employment legislation acknowledges in its structure the primacy of voluntary collective bargaining" and that it is premature to conclude (as Roy Lewis did), that there is a 'fundamental trend' in the ever increasing extent of legal regulation of the British *system* of industrial relations"[74].

As was mentioned, from the comparative point of view, one effect of this concern of the designers of the statute law to defer to the autonomy of collective bargaining has been a lower level of statutory protection than would have been the case had the law been regarded to a greater extent as codifying and spreading the best results of collective bargaining to trade union members along the lines of the Swedish employment protection legislation[75]. Paradoxically, trade unionists who were concerned to have legislation with a minimum of interference with collective bargaining have also been disappointed at the resultant weakness of the new individual legal rights.

A second effect of the expansion of individual employee rights is that it may have contributed to a view amongst the electorate that the unions have had the benefits of legislation without concomitant responsibilities. As the Green Paper of *Trade Union Immunities* put it:

> "The effect of this has been to create a dual framework in industrial relations. The role of the law remains non-interventionist as it affects trade unions, but it has clearly become more interventionist as it affects employers" (para. 12).

A third effect of the individual rights legislation worth noting is that it demonstrates how law can work positively to produce changes in collective bargaining and management practice. There is empirical evidence showing that the law of redundancy payments has led to the development of redundancy procedures and the practice of voluntary redundancy in industry. Similarly, the unfair dismissals legislation has stimulated the growth of voluntary disciplinary procedures in industry[75a].

III. The Growth of Restrictive Legislation

The most direct and immediate form of legal intervention however has been the restrictive labour legislation enacted by the Conservative Government since 1979. From its election manifesto to the enactment of the 1980 Employment Act, the Conservatives argued that labour legislation should

---

[74] Wedderburn, *Industrial Relations and the Courts* (1981) I.L.J. at p. 84; In an earlier work he suggested, "I wish to establish there is no inconsistency or paradox in British labour law merely because of the increase of regulatory legislation upon the *individual* employment relationship. Such legislation does affect collective bargaining. But it does not regulate it." 13 Israeli Law Review at 445.

[75] Wedderburn, "Industrial Relations and the Courts" (1981) ILJ at p. 83.

[75a] See e.g. W. Daniel and E. Stilgoe, *The Impact of Employment Protection Laws* (PSI 1978) London.

be used to redress the balance of power between trade unions and employers and between the rights of the individual and the power of trade unions.

The legislative method chosen in the 1980 Act was quite different from that attempted in the 1971 Act. The changes to the legal framework were selective rather than comprehensive. Unlike the 1971 Act, the Employment Act 1980 avoided any attempt to create a package deal of rights and duties. Indeed it even abandoned the rudiments of such a strategy by repealing certain existing collective rights[76] and curtailing certain individual rights[77]. Nor did it attempt to confer upon the Employment Appeal Tribunal jurisdiction to hear applications for labour injunctions, as was the case with the NIRC under the 1971 Act. It left that jursidiction with the ordinary courts. It also avoided the creation of an elaborate registration process for trade unions which could be frustrated by trade union hostility to the legislation. And, apart from the attempt to introduce secret strike ballots for trade unions on a voluntary basis, it was less concerned with the reform of institutions than with the restriction of selected types of collective activity[78].

The 1980 Act placed new legal restrictions upon certain forms of picketing and industrial action in three respects. The immunity for peaceful picketing was limited in most cases to the "place of work" of the individual worker taking part in the picket line[79]. This considerably narrowed the right to picket peacefully as it had been established in the lawful picketing by employees of one plant at another plant of their own employer.

There was also a removal of an immunity for the organisation of industrial action by workers to compel the employees of another employer to be members of a trade union[80]. Finally there was a removal of the immunity in s. 13 for the organisation of secondary industrial action unless that action is directed against the first supplier or customer of the employer in a primary dispute or against an employer "associated" with the primary employer who attempts to substitute supplies for the primary employer[81]. Moreover included in the tests of acceptable secondary action was a return to the so-called "objective" test which had been devised by the Court of Appeal prior to the House of Lords trilogy, namely, that the action taken must be reasonably likely to achieve its purpose[82]. The disquiet of the Law Lords had acted as a spur to a swift amendment at the Report Stage of the 1980 Act.

The 1980 Act also attempted to restrict the growth of the closed shop institution in Britain. It did this by creating a series of legal hurdles for any

[76] The recognition provisions in ss 11 – 16 EPA 1975 and Schedule 11 EPA 1975
[77] Unfair dismissal, maternity rights and guaranteed pay.
[78] R. Lewis and R. Simpson, *Striking a Balance*, M. Robinson, 1981.
[79] Employment Act 1980 s. 16
[80] Ibid s. 18
[81] *Ibid* s. 17
[82] Employment Act s. 17

group of workers attempting to establish a new closed shop. Any new closed shop had to be approved in a secret ballot by 80% of those eligible to vote[83]. Moreover in existing closed shop agreements or arrangements as well as new closed shop agreements, it was automatically unfair to dismiss an employee for non-membership where the employee was a non-member before the closed shop was established and never joined afterwards[84]. Further a dismissal of an employee who resigned from or refused to join a trade union because he objected on grounds of conscience or other deeply held personal conviction to being a member of any trade union or to a particular trade union was also deemed to automatically unfair[85]. Finally, action taken by an employer short of dismissal against a non-member was also protected[86].

In creating these new legal restrictions, the Act also introduced certain inroads into the immunity for vicarious liability enjoyed by trade union organisations. Under the 1980 Act where an employer was brought before an industrial tribunal for dismissing an employee under a closed shop agreement, that employer could join a trade union as well as any other person responsible for organising the pressure upon the employer to dismiss. The joined defendant could then be required by the tribunal to indemnify the employer up to 100% of the unfair dismissal compensation[87].

Further, where an employee has been unreasonably refused admission to a trade union[88] or is unreasonably excluded from a trade union[89] he may now under the 1980 Act bring a claim against the trade union in an industrial tribunal for declaration.

These new statutory rights did not extinguish the traditional common law rights of employees against trade unions. There is at common law a clear legal basis for damages and injunctive relief for employees expelled or about to be expelled from trade unions[90]. There is also a rather more dubious foundation for actions for unlawful refusals to admit individuals to trade unions[91]. Moreover, the new statutory rights overlap with existing rights that emploees have to appeal to the Independent Review Committee set up by

---

[83] *Ibid.*, s. 3(c)
[84] *Ibid.* s. 7(1) amending EPCA s. 58(1)
[85] *Ibid.*
[86] EPCA 1978 s. 23(1) amended by EA s. 15(1)
[87] *Ibid.* s. 10
[88] *Ibid.* s. 4
[89] *Ibid.* s. 5
[90] *Edwards* v *SOGAT* [1971] Ch. 354 (C.A.); *Esterman* v *NALGO* [1974] I.C.R. 625.
[91] See e.g. *Nagle* v *Feilden* [1966] 2 Q.B. 633; and remarks by Denning in *Edwards* v *SOGAT* [1971] Ch. 354; also *Faramus* v *Film Artistes Assn.* [1964] A.C. 925 TULRA ss 2 (5) and 3(5); see Wedderburn, "Discrimination in the Right to Organise and the Right to be a Non-unionist" in *Discrimination in Employment* (ed. F. Schmidt) Stockholm 1978 pp. 410-422 for a good summary of the legal position; see also *B. Hepple,* Right to Work? (1981) 10 ILJ at pp. 78-79

the T.U.C. in 1976 to provide an alternative to legal regulation of trade union internal affairs[92].

To date the 1980 Act has resulted in relatively few cases. Few employers have applied for injunctions against secondary action[93] and picketing away from the individual's place of work[94]. Few employees have applied to industrial tribunals in respect of dismissals[95] or expulsions[96] in closed shop situations.

It has been suggested that the fact that the 1980 Act has been invoked so rarely is an indication of its success in setting legal restrictions on industrial action. Yet it is difficult to conclude that the reasons for the non-use of the Act has been a widespread acceptance of its norms as such. An equally plausible interpretation of the recent experience is that the actual incidence of dismissals or expulsions in closed shops has not been very great. Certainly the number of strikes has declined owing to the low level of economic activity. Moreover, the non-use of the 1980 Act may also be explained by the reluctance of some employees to take their employment disputes to the courts and a pragmatic acceptance by employers of the limited usefulness of legal sanctions in well established collective bargaining relationships.

From the 1980 Act to the 1982 Bill

The strategy of the 1980 Act was one of gradually changing the legal framework and thereby effecting a long term change in industrial relations in Britain. The Act was clearly aimed at reducing trade union power by making industrial action and closed shop dismissals unlawful. Yet it also attempted to avoid provoking an outright confrontation which might have created a united front of opposition by the official trade unions, the shop stewards and "rank and file" of work groups such as occurred in the 1971-4 period. Sir James Prior, the Employment Secretary stated quite openly to the Conservative Party Conference in 1979 that he was attempting to win the consent of the workforce to changes in the law because the lesson had been learnt that whilst it was relatively easy to enact a law it was far less easy to ensure that it was implemented. Hence it concentrated upon changes such as limits on secondary action which would not in themselves be viewed as an outright attack on the very existence of trade unions and workshop power and it was cautious about providing direct legal sanctions against existing closed shop arrangements.

Moreover, during Prior's period of office, a Green Paper on Trade Union

---

[92] See *K. Ewing* and *W. Rees*, the TUC Independent Review Committee and the Closed Shop [1981] ILJ 84

[93] See e.g. *Hadmor Ltd* v *ACTT* [1982] IRLR 102 (H.L.)

[94] See e.g. *The Mersey Dock & Harbour Company* v *Verrinder et al.* [1981] IRLR 152.

[95] See e.g. *Baidwin* v *Laporte Industries Ltd* [1982] (I.T.)

[96] See e.g. *Kirkham* v *NATSOPA* [1981] IRLR 244 (I.T.)

Immunities was published[97] which indicated that there was a limited role for law in reforming industrial relations[98] and that there were important limits to the effectiveness of legal sanctions against workplace bargaining[99].

Nevertheless, the desire of the Conservative Government to use legislation as an instrument to redress the balance of powers between trade unions and employers and create "responsible trade unionism" was not satisfied by the 1980 Act. The reluctance of employers and individuals to make use of the 1980 Act was duly noted. However, rather than accepting the diagnosis of the limits to the effectiveness of legal sanctions to regulate workplace bargaining that had been put quite forcibly in the Green Paper on Trade Union immunities the Conservative Government under a new Secretary of State for Employment, Norman Tebbit, decided upon a further round of restrictive labour legislation.

The Tebbit Bill is a continuation of the step by step approach originated by Prior in the sense that it does not attempt to create a comprehensive legal framework for labour relations along the lines of the 1971 Act[100]. Thus it concentrates this second stage of restrictive legislation upon two selected areas: the law of strikes and the law of the closed shop. Yet it contains a qualitatively different element in its attempts to curb the power of trade union organisations and the institutions of workshop bargaining. Its response to the warnings of the Green Paper on the limits to the effectiveness or restrictive legislation is to ensure that in addition to narrowing still further the limits to lawful action, it provides new financial incentives to managers and individual employees to make use of their legal remedies.

Thus the Act narrows the boundaries of unlawful industrial action by redefining lawful trade disputes to exclude inter-union jurisdictional and demarcation disputes. It did this by excluding disputes between "workers and workers"[101]. It also excludes from legal immunity disputes relating to matters outside the United Kingdom unless those taking part in the sympathetic action are likely to be affected by the outcome of the dispute[102]. Furthermore, it removed immunities for industrial action designed to enforce certain closed shop and recognition arrangements[193]. Finally, it makes it far easier in cases of strikes organised for a mixture of collective bargaining and political moves to conclude that a strike is predominantly political and hence not within the definition of a trade dispute.

Thus under the 1976 Act's definition of a trade dispute which was left

[97] 1981 Cmnd 8128
[98] Paras 13 and 19;
[99] Paras 128 and 327;
[100] See discussion p. 104 *supra*
[101] Employment Bill 1982 cl. 15(1)
[102] *Ibid*. cl. 15(4)
[103] *Ibid*. cl. qq

unmodified by the 1980 Act, it was possible for industrial action taken for a mixture of motives to be regarded as taken in contemplation or furtherance of a trade dispute because all that was necessary was that the motive for the dispute be "connected with" a collective bargaining question. This was held to mean that there was no requirement that the collective bargaining issue be the sole or even the predominant motive[104]. Under the 1982 Bill, the motive for the strike must now be "wholly or mainly" related to a collective bargaining issue. This test will leave to judicial discretion the determination whether the collective bargaining motive was at least the predominant motive[105].

Having narrowed the legal immunities for industrial action, the Bill then proceeds to make trade unions accountable vicariously for the industrial action of its members where such action is "authorised" or "endorsed" by an official or "an official body" or by "any other responsible person" i.e. any other person who is empowered by the rule to authorise or endorse industrial action. A union can avoid such vicarious liability only if its executive committee or other "responsible person" takes steps which the judge (or jury) considers "adequate" to repudiate the industrial action[106].

Where a trade union is sued in tort the Bill provides an upper limit to the damages they may be awarded "in any proceeding" against it, that varies with the size of the trade union[107]. Moreover an award of damages, costs or expenses is not recoverable against the trade union's political fund or provident benefit fund[107]a. The introduction of a right of action directly against trade union funds is partly designed to answer the longstanding ideological cry by Conservatives to bring the unions within the rule of law; it also has the rather more pragmatic aim of encouraging employers to make the greater use of their legal rights.

Finally, the requirements of s. 62 of the EPCA, which deprives industrial tribunals of any jurisdiction to consider the fairness of dismissals of employees participating in a strike as long as all employees who took part in the strike were dismissed and none were re-employed at a later date have been relaxed by the 1984 Bill. As a result it will be easier for employers to dismiss employees selectively for taking part in a strike and nevertheless prevent tribunals from having jurisdiction over any resulting unfair dismissal claims[108].

---

[104] *NWL Ltd* v *Woods* [1979] ICR 867 (H.L.)
[105] But see comments by the House of Lords in *Hadmor Productions Ltd* v *ACTT* [1982] IRLR at p. 108 upon the decision in *G.A.S.* v *T.G.W.U.* [1974] IRLR (C.A.) for an example of how a strike could still be lawful under the more restrictive formula of the 1982 Act.
[106] A repudiation will not be adequate to avoid liability if any steps are taken which are "inconsistent with the purported repudiation" cl. 14
[107] I.e. from £10,000 for a union with less than 5,000 members to £250,000 for a union with more than 100,000 members. cl. 15
[107]a cl. 16
[108] Employment Bill. cl. 8

and individual employees taking part in industrial action will be even more vulnerable to dismissal.

The second major element of the 1982 Bill consists of its provisions designed to create legal disincentives for closed shop arrangements and agreements. First although the Bill continues to avoid the step of directly outlawing closed shops it creates a presumption that all dismissals in existing closed shop situations are unfair, unless there is evidence that a secret ballot has been conducted, within five years of the dismissal, which resulted in an affirmative vote of 80% of those voting or 85% of those eligible to vote[109].

Secondly, to encourage enforcement of these legal rights the minimum compensation for unfair dismissals in a closed shop situation is increased substantially i.e. to £12,000 or £17,000[110] and a remedy of interim relief made available to the dismissed non-unionist to apply to continue the contract in existence until the tribunal hearing[111]. Moreover, an employee who was dismissed in a "closed shop situation" could insist upon joining the trade union as a party to the dismissal even where the employer might prefer not to join the trade union, as long as it could be shown that the trade union or trade unionist exerted pressure on the employee for his dismissal[112].

Conclusions

The 1982 Employment Bill represents yet another throw of the legislative dice by the Conservative Government in its attempts to make use of legal restrictions to limit industrial relations practices. Unlike the 1971 Act, its enactment conincides with a period when the trade unions are weakened by the deep recession. Nevertheless there are grounds for doubting that the legislation will be effective in ending the practices it has attempted to restrict. Where restrictive legislation is unaccompanied by the provision of alternative machinery to resolve the underlying dispute of which the restricted industrial action is a symptom, the question immediately raised is how effective will the "naked" legal sanctions be given that there is unlikely to be a widespread acquiesence in the legal norms. The 1982 Bill appears to act upon the premise that the difficulty was simply to find more plaintiffs; it perhaps underestimates the further hurdle of finding an effective mechanism to enforce the legal norms even if a willing plaintiff should be identified. The legal process by itself can provide either injunctive relief or damages to an interested plaintiff as well as the threat of resorting to either remedy. The narrowing of the immunities for industrial action will in practice mean a

[109] Employment Bill 1982 cl. 2
[110] Employment Bill 1982 cls 3-4
[111] *Ibid*. cl. 7
[112] *Ibid*. cl. 6

wider availability of the legal remedy of the injunction for employers. Yet as the experience of the 1971 Act showed, this was not always an effective remedy. When some employers attempted to make use of a court order in a trade dispute and the trade unionists who were the target of the injunction were not daunted by the legal process, the court order did not end the industrial action. Insofar as the industrial action was "unofficial" and taken by a "spontaneous collectivity" rather than officially initiated action, the injunction against the named leaders might have restricted the active participation of the leaders but it did not end the industrial action.

As the Green Paper itself acknowledged, the effects of court orders directed against the leaders of industrial action are limited when the followers continue to strike, because there are "no powers to force individuals to go back to work . . ." and "while it is possible to penalise a person for breaking his employment contract, it is very difficult to force him to perform the contract if he is determined not to do so"[113].

The Green Paper stopped short however of exploring the wider implications of this limitation on the legal process notably that in such situations "all forms of restrictive labour law – short of police-state measures – directed at forcing large groups of men to return to work, were reduced to a form of persuasion and did not rest upon a foundation of physical compulsion as did many other areas of law"[114].

Nevertheless even at the most immediate level of implication it cannot be ignored that in Britain today an overwhelming proportion of all strikes including secondary action are unofficial.

To a large extent the 1982 Bill attempted to circumvent this difficulty by making trade unions liable for the industrial action of its members where a court decided that a union had "endorsed" or "authorised" such action and that endorsement or authorisation had not been "repudiated". Yet this effort too is not likely to be entirely effective given the internal structure of authority within the British trade unions.

As the Green Paper itself acknowledged:

"opponents of change in the immunity for trade union funds argue that it is fallacious to assume that the trade unions could or would turn themselve into more authoritarian structures under the threat of having to pay out large sums in damages. In their view, the shift in the balance of power within the trade unions to the shop floor has gone too far to be reversed by a change in the law. It is said that some of those who organise unofficial action at plant or shop floor level have come to have little or no regard for their union leaders at national level and would be unmoved by any threat to the central funds of their unions not least because while a strike is unofficial, a union's financial support is withheld. Thus the more

---

[113] Trade Union Immunities para. 327; TULRA s. 17(1)
[114] See discussion in Anderman, "Legal Restrictions on Trade Unions" in Burman and Harrell-Bond, *The Imposition of Law* (Academic Press, 1979) p. 243.

likely effect of putting union funds at risk would be a further weakening of the authority of national leaders and even the breakdown or splintering of some unions under the threat, or as a result, of large scale expulsions. Far from reducing the incidence of unofficial action, they argue, the ultimate result might be to increase it. The existing system of industrial relations, whatever its many damaging imperfections could be imperilled[115]."

Yet the Green Paper did not spell out the full extent of the structural difficulties in the way of change: notably, the relative shortage of full time officials (5-6,000) in relation to shop stewards (about 30,000) the difficulties of increasing dues, and hence raising trade union funds to build up a bigger full time staff; and the recent wave of reforms of trade union constitutions which have decentralised authority within trade unions and have placed shop stewards in key policy-making and disciplinary committees.

Thus whilst the 1982 Bill may create a defendant with the resources to meet a damages action, that defendant would not necessarily have the organisational resources to end the industrial action.

The array of proposals for curbing the closed shop represents a victory of ideology over rational law-making that is reminiscent of the 1971 Act. Insofar as the government is interested in using legal reform to produce trade union responsibility and industrial efficiency it is counterproductive to attempt to use other legal provisions to break down the closed shop institution in large organisations. Despite the greater bargaining power it provides against employers, the closed shop has been recognised by employers as providing greater stability in collective bargaining structures and a higher degree of adherence to collective agreements, partly because of the representativeness of the trade union making the agreements and partly because of the greater disciplines of the closed shop arrangement[116].

It was their perception of the advantages of maintaining closed shop arrangements that led employers to resist the legal restrictions imposed by the 1971 Industrial Relations Act [117] and presumably is likely to lead to a similar resistance to the legal interference with closed shop arrangements that would be created by the 1982 Employment Bill should it become law. The proposals as they now stand attempt to create a wedge through the joint resistance of employer and trade union by allowing the *employee* to decide whether or not to join the trade union as defendant in the unfair dismissal claim. They thus make it far more difficult for the employer to isolate the closed shop arrangement from the legal process by deciding to defend the

---

[115] Trade Union Immunities para. 128.
[116] See W. McCarthy and N. Ellis, *Management by Agreement* p. 65-72; see also B. Weekes, "Law and the Practice of the Closed Shop" 1976 5 *I.L.J.* 211; M. Hart "Why Bosses Love the CLosed Shop" *New Society* February 15, 1979; W. Brown (ed.) *The Changing Contours of British Industrial Relations* (Blackwell 1981) ch. 4.
[117] See n. 23 *supra*

unfair dismissal claim by himself. The proposals for legislation however go further than this. The high minimum compensation awards for dismissals in closed shops create a positive incentive for dismissed non-unionists to bring claims – and therefore an incentive for individuals to decide to resign from a trade union in a closed shop situation. Ironically, as mentioned, were these provisions to be successful they would bring about a degree of disruption to existing collective bargaining that would produce industrial inefficiencies and place even greater limits on trade union responsibility because of their effect on union discipline. Although the disruption that may be caused by isolated individuals using their new rights to non-unionism may be increased by the Bill, if enacted, it is not likely to provide an incentive to large scale defections from trade unions.

These considerations tend to suggest that the stimulus of voluntary reform is a more effective route to reform than restrictive legislation. This was recognised by the Green Paper in two paragraphs which echoed the Donovan Commission's earlier approach:

"... in Britain ... attempts to secure reform by means of legal restraint on trade union power have had to contend with obstructive and uncooperative attitudes. If the law is to be respected and to play a useful role in changing behaviour these attitudes have to be overcome. The law by itself cannot change such attitudes overnight. ... The contribution which changes in the law can make must be seen in the context of our still predominantly voluntary system and of the far reaching changes in the nature of trade union power of industrial action and of the labour market over the last two decades and more. In particular proposals for changing the law which are designed to influence the behaviour of trade unions as formally organised institutions, but which ignore the reality of shop floor power and the current propensity for unofficial action are likely to be effective at either level ...[118]

"Changes in the law can influence attitudes and behaviour over time ... But good industrial relations cannot be legislated into existence. Reform must come from within: from trade unions and employers adapting their institutions and practices to the social and economic pressures for change.[119]"

It appears that the Conservative Government has underestimated this particular lesson of the British experience. There are some historical examples of voluntary reforms of the industrial relations system – e.g. the Bridlington Procedure for resolving inter-union disputes and more recently the Independent Review Committee,[120] the Joint Statement by the TUC and the Government on the economic situation[121]. There are also examples of voluntary arrangements for placing limits on industrial action – e.g. the

[118] Trade Union Immunities para. 13
[119] *Ibid*. para. 19.
[120] See reports of the IRC's work in TUC's General Council's Annual Reports
[121] Apendix 2 TUC Geneal Council's Annual Report 1979

"Concordat" under the last labour government in 1979[122]‡ and the TUC's "solemn and binding" undertaking in 1969[123]. They may not be entirely satisfactory but they may provide the least unsatisfactory alternative.

Yet the final irony of the recent bout of legislation is that it has not only chosen to ignore the lessons of the early 1970s in respect of restrictive legislation. It has also ignored the more recent experience of the late 1970s with positive rights legislation, in particular the fact that such legislation aimed at management in the form of employee protection produced significant reforms of management practices and procedures in areas such as employee discipline, redundancies, shop steward training and facilities, maternity leave, etc[124]. The Green Paper on Trade Union Immunities had acknowledged that employers shared "the responsibility for the present state of our industrial relations".[125] It also gave specific examples of their complicity.[126] Yet it chose to identify trade union activity and industrial action as the sole target of legislation.

Even its proposals for the conversion of the existing system of immunities into a system of positive rights similar to those operating in a number of other countries was limited to a consideration of the law as it related to strikes and other industrial action[127]. As a consequence it never gave adequate consideration to the possibility that the most promising avenue of reform of industrial relations might lie with the regulation of employers rather than the direct restriction of trade unions and employee groups.

The British experience offers forceful evidence of the limits to the use of legal sanctions in collective industrial relations in the sense that a given pattern of legal regulation or restriction cannot succeed if the sanctions are required to bear too heavy a burden of enforcing the legal rules. It reminds us that the legal regulation of collective industrial relations requires some

---

[122] TUC guides – Negotiation Procedure, Conduct of Disputes, Union Organisation Appendix 3 TUC General Council's Annual Report 1979

[123] See P. Jenkins, The Battle of Downing Street (Charles Knight 1970) p. 160

[124] See e.g. W. Daniels and E. Stilgoe, The Impact of Employment Protection Law (P S I 1978); W.W. Daniel, The Effects of Employment Protection Law in Manufacturing Industry, 1978, 86 *D.E. Gazette*, 658

[125] Thus it mentioned "that the tendency of employers, particularly in terms of full employment, to look for the short term solutions in relations with their employees and trade union officials without regard to the long-term consequences and restrictive practices from which we are now suffering" (para. 21). It also stated that employers preferences for "general imprecise arrangements" make "legally binding agreements very difficult" (para. 22), and that employers have contributed to the growth in authority of shop floor representatives at the expense of the "authority of more senior officials" (para. 23). Moreover it made out a powerful case for the need for employees to adopt coherent and consistent policies to involve and communicate with employees (para. 24) and show "a readiness to extend the range of matters on which they are prepared to consult and to take their employees into their confidence." (para. 26)

[126] Trade Union Immunities, para. 21

[127] *Ibid*. para. 340

social agency such as a trade union or employing organisation to adopt them and to incorporate the legal norms into the practices and procedures of that organisation. It follows that it is far more likely that legal sanctions will work upon employers' organisations than upon trade union organisations given the history of British trade unions. In order to make a trade union movement more receptive to the legal embrace, it appears necessary to have either a long period of sharing power with a sympathetic government such as the Swedish trade union movement experienced with the Social Democratic Government, or a dependence upon legislation for its initial acquisition of organisational power such as the U.S. trade union movement experienced with the Wagner Act. Both factors have been conspicuously absent in the development of British trade unions thus far.*

All references to the Employment Bill 1982 are taken from the version printed on July 13, 1982 after the Committee Stage of the House of Lords."

COLLECTIVE LABOUR LAW IN BRITAIN:
A COMMENT

by

Tore Sigeman

Introduction

In comparisons of the legal position in two countries, one frequently starts out with the observation that the basic rules for the subject under consideration are different, but that, on closer study, it is found that there are so many exceptions to the basic rules in both countries that the end result, after all, turns out to be fairly similar. However, nothing or nearly nothing of the kind can be said of a comparison of labour disputes and collective agreements in British and Swedish collective labour law. The differences are, and remain, very great, if not fundamental.

The Regulation of Industrial Action

When one looks at the right to organise strikes and other collective offensive measures in what in Sweden would be called disputes of interest (e.g. in disputes about future terms when the parties are not bound by a collective agreement)[1], the legal points of departure in Sweden and Britain are diametrically opposed. In *Britain*, all such offensive measures are, in principle, unlawful under the general rules on damages contained in the common law. As appears from Steven Anderman's paper, in cases concerning industrial action the general Courts have created a long list of rules for different torts: e.g. the tort of inducing breaches of contracts and the tort of conspiracy to injure. Taken together, these rules mean that, in effect, almost every offensive action on the labour market would be unlawful if the rules were applied strictly. The sanctions would be tough: in the first place, there is a potential liability to compensate for all economic damage caused, including e.g. loss of profit. Furthermore, the Courts could issue injunctions against any persons who fail to desist from taking injurious action: something which most closely approximates in Swedish law to an interim decision under Chap. 15 § 3 of the Code of Procedure (Rättegångsbalken) 1942. In contrast to Swedish law, however, any person who does not observe the terms of an injunction may be committed to prison.

[1] On the distinction between disputes of interest and disputes of rights, see Schmidt, *Law and Industrial Relations in Sweden* (Stockholm 1977) pp. 23 f. Compare Hepple, *International Encyclopaedia for Labour Law and Industrial Relations: Great Britain* (Deventer 1980) paragraphs 44-45.

It is precisely against these torts and their draconian sanctions that the British legislation gives immunity to trade unions and those acting on their behalf who organise offensive industrial action. The rules on immunity are now to be found in the amended Trade Union and Labour Relations Act (TULRA) 1974. In principle, these rules give complete protection for trade union funds against legal actions brought in tort[2]. Furthermore, they give immunity against liability in tort for any person who organises industrial action, so long as the action has been taken "in contemplation or furtherance of a trade dispute".

The extent to which there exists a freedom to take industrial action must be deduced from these rules on immunity, seen against a background of the common law tort rules. The British debate on "trade union immunities" can only be understood against this background, which appears strange to Swedish lawyers.

Certain limitations to the immunity under British law, and thus to the right to organise industrial action, have recently been introduced through the Employment Act 1980[3]. These concern secondary picketing and some other forms of secondary action.

In *Sweden* the legal starting point is completely reversed[4]. During the whole of the time that trade unions in their modern form have been active in Sweden, there has been a basic freedom to withdraw labour in combination without legal consequences. No case has held it to be unlawful for anybody to organise collective offensive action in disputes of interest. Swedish law knows of nothing which corresponds to the tort of inducing breach of contract. Nor are there any equivalents to the other torts which the British Courts have created in order to restrain industrial action. If an individual act is legal under Swedish law, in the labour market it is also permitted for several to carry out such acts in combination[5].

The basic principle under Swedish law appears very clearly from a 1935 decision of the Supreme Court:

> A stevedore had been prevented from carrying on his trade because of a number of different blockade measures adopted by a trade union. *Inter alia* his customers had been forced to break their contracts with him. He therefore brought a claim for damages against the trade union, but his case was dismissed with the briefly stated justification that the measures adopted by the trade union were not contrary to law[5a].

[2] But see now the Employment Bill 1982 cl. 12
[3] Ss 16-17
[4] See, for the following, *Schmidt, op. cit. (supra* note 1) chap. 11-12 and Aaron & Wedderburn (eds), *Industrial Conflict* (London 1972) *passim*.
[5] Sweden has a general antitrust statute *(konkurrensbegränsningslagen* 1953) but this statute is not applicable to labour relations.
[5a] Nytt Juridiskt Arkiv 1935 p. 300.

Thus, there has been no need in Sweaish law for any protective legislation with rules on immunity corresponding to those in England.

On the other hand, it should be added that before 1975 there was no positive regulation of the right to take offensive action either. In that year, however, an express rule was inserted into the Constitution. Chap. 2, s. 17 now provide:

> "Any trade union and any employer or association of employers shall have the right to take industrial action ("fackliga stridsåtgärder"), except as otherwise provided by law or ensuing from a contract."

The provision means that no Court may impose any limitation on the right to take industrial action, unless this is provided for in an *enactment* or in a *contract*.

In Swedish law there is a very important limitation to the right to take offensive action by virtue of the rule in the Joint Regulation Act 1976 that collective agreements carry with them a peace obligation. To this rule I shall return below.

Where no collective agreement exists, however, *statute law* provides only a few relatively minor limitations upon the right to take industrial action. One example, is the 1936 Act which limits the right of an employer to evict striking workers from homes which they rent from the employer.

In the 1930s there was a lively debate as to whether there was a need for a more general limitation through statute of the trade union's rights to take industrial action. Several legislative proposals were put forward which contained *inter alia* rules on limiting secondary action and which, in part, were not dissimilar from those which have been introduced in England through the Employment Act 1980. However, these legislative proposals were never enacted. Instead in 1938, SAF and LO undertook, in the Basic Agreement of that year, to observe certain limitations in their use of economic offensive action. It was generally held that this agreement made legislative intervention unnecessary. The Basic Agreement[6] has been adopted as a collective agreement in large areas of the Swedish labour market.

The rules in *the Basic Agreement* dealing with limitations on industrial action[7] are the closest approximation in Swedish law to the general restrictive rules which in Britain arise from the inter-play between common law, torts and statutory trade union immunities. Nevertheless, the differences are of vital significance, even disregarding the fact that the Swedish rules are

---

[6] An English translation of the Basic Agreement is printed in Schmidt, *The Law of Labour Relations in Sweden* (Uppsala 1962) Appendix 5; see further Robbins, *The Government of Labor Relations in Sweden* (New York 1942) pp. 129-143, and *Schmidt, op. cit. (supra* note 1) pp. 187-190.

[7] Chap. IV of the original version; since 1974 (when the original Chap. III was cancelled) often cited as Chap. III.

established by the parties themselves and not as in Britain by the courts and the legislator. Thus, the Basic Agreement contains only a number of specific prohibitions against industrial action commonly regarded as improper. It provides no general regulation. The sanction it provides is damages, the amount of which may be reduced below the level of the actual damage caused. Labour injunctions corresponding to the British legal sanction are not available in this context.

One example of the contents of the rules in the Basic Agreement is the prohibition against industrial action which involved persecution on political or religious grounds. In addition, certain kinds of secondary action were forbidden, e.g. when the primary action was designed to force some person to join a trade union. However, by contrast with the British Employment Act 1980, the Basic Agreement gives broad freedom to the organisations to take *sympathetic action* in support of lawful primary action over disputes about the conclusion of collective agreements. This is in line with the notion that sympathetic action in Sweden is considered an important instrument for achieving an evening-out of unjustified differences in terms of employment for different categories of employees, e.g. for groups in different industries. The right to take sympathetic action is, therefore, a precondition to enable trade unions at the central level to implement an effective "solidarity wage policy".

In accordance with the spirit of the Basic Agreement, the organisations on the labour market have shown restraint in making use of improper industrial action. It remains an open question whether the agreement's rules are legally binding beyond the parties to the agreement direct area of application; it is not clear whether the Labour Court considers that trade unions which are not formally bound by the Basic Agreement should also observe the "good practice" which is laid down in that agreement.

In this context it may be mentioned that the Labour Court has suggested *obiter*[7a] that a blockade may be contrary to law even where no collective agreement is applicable, if the blockade is intended to compel the person against whom it is directed to act in contravention of mandatory law. In this case a question arose as to an employer's obligations towards an employee under the Employment Protection Act 1974 where that employee was not a member of the trade union taking the action. By way of sanction for improper industrial action in such a situation it is – presumably – possible for the Court to order the offending party to stop the action, on pain of a contingent fine.

Collective Agreements

I shall now turn to the question of the legal consequences of collective

---

[7a] *Decision 1977 nr. 38*

agreements. It is here we encounter the most important differences between British and Swedish law.

In Sweden the collective agreement is legally binding for both the parties to it and for their members[8]. As a consequence, industrial action may not be taken with a view to amending the collective agreement during its periods of validity[8a]. Collective agreements are normally entered into for a fixed period – often one or two years – and the agreement thus ensures peace for a period of time which is known in advance. The primary sanction for breach of the peace obligation or of other obligations under the agreement is damages. This sanction is flexible. On the one hand, the amount of damages may be reduced below the level of actual economic loss. On the other hand, however, a sum of damages may be awarded even if economic loss cannot be established. There is no immunity here for the funds of the trade unions. The amounts awarded have usually been small. The highest sum awarded against a national union has been 40,000 S.Kr.[9] and the highest sum awarded against a union branch has been 25,000 S.Kr.[10]

In Britain, by contrast, the collective agreement is normally not legally *enforceable*[11]. Under TULRA s. 18, there is a presumption that the parties do not intend such an agreement to be binding between them in a legal sense. Consequently, the fact that a collective agreement has been entered into does not in Britain carry with it any legal obligation to refrain from taking collective offensive action. Industrial action may be taken both in order to exert pressure in disputes over the content of the agreement and with a view to achieving amendments to the terms agreed.

Members of a trade union in Sweden are directly bound by and receive rights under the collective agreement (s. 26 of the Joint Regulation Act). They are also bound in respect of the peace obligation. In Britain, certain terms of collective agreements are incorporated in members' contracts of employment. If the collective agreement contains a term providing for a peace obligation, this may also be read into contracts of employment. However, so many preconditions are laid down in TULRA s. 18(4) before such a clause can be incorporated that, in practice, there are major obstacles in the way of binding a member by a peace obligation.

[8] See, for the following, *Sigeman* in A. Neal (ed.) *Law and the Weaker Party,* Vol. 1, pp. 138–141 and *Schmidt op. cit.* (*supra* n. 1) Chap. 9–11.
[8a] See ss 41-2 of the Joint Regulation Act.
[9] Approx. £4000. Decision of the Labour Court 1963 nr. 12 in a case against the Swedish Pilots' Association.
[10] Approx. £2500. Decision of the Labour Court 1965 nr. 28. In this case (against the Stockholm Bricklayers' Union) the plaintiff had only claimed the sum awarded.
[11] See, for the following, *Hepple, op. cit.* (*supra* n. 1) para. 93–100 and 454–458 with references. See also, e.g., Kahn-Freund, *Labour and the Law* (2nd ed. London 1977) Chap. 6 and Riddall, *The Law of Industrial Relations* (London 1981) Chap. 3.

A Brief Comparison

In terms of a brief comparison, we may say that in both countries there is to be found the basic freedom to invoke stoppages of work which is the hallmark of democratic societies which are built upon a division of power and freedom of opinion.

The freedom to take industrial action is, overall, significantly greater in Britain than in Sweden, since the collective agreement imposes a peace obligation in Sweden which is not to be found in Britain.

However, during the time that a collective agreement is not in force, the legal freedom to take industrial action is somewhat greater in Sweden than in Britain, *inter alia* in so far as it applies to secondary action. A further point is that trade unions in Sweden are normally restrained, and do not fully exercise their legal freedom to take action in periods of renegotiation of agreements.

How one evaluates one or other country's rules on industrial disputes and collective agreements depends upon what values one proceeds from. For example, those who consider that the conflicts between capital and labour are fundamental and irreconcilable may prefer the British system. It gives in Britain 300,000 shop stewards the opportunity to carry on a continuous class struggle out in the workplaces[12]. The capitalist system can thus be weakened through repeated disruptions to production. According to quite another view it is the principal purpose of labour law to establish an equilibrium of power between many different groups in society with divergent interests: between those who argue for more investment (to the welfare of future generations) and those who claim a maintained or improved standard of living now; between producers and consumers; between different groups of employees who seek to gain advantages at the expense of each other[13]. If one accepts such a pluralistic view, the Swedish solution may be preferable. It brings about a centralisation of power and a general pattern of central negotiation of employment terms. A centralised bargaining system seems to facilitate the co-ordination and adjustment of divergent collective interests.

The Complexity of British Legislation

From a legal-technical point of view, however, a weakness may be noted in the British rules on immunities. The rules are extraordinarily complex. The explanation for their complicated linguistic formulation lies in the ordinary courts' principles of interpretation. The legislator feels obliged to use the courts' own, very complex, conceptual approach in order to avoid the rules

---

[12] Compare *Schregle*, "Comparative industrial relations: pitfalls and potential", (1981) *120 International Labour Review* (Geneva) 15, 20-22.
[13] Compare *Kahn-Freund, op. cit. (supra* n. 11) Chap. 1 and 8, and *Roy Lewis*, "Kahn-Freund and Labour Law: an Outline Critique", (1979) 8 *The Industrial Law Journal* 202–221.

being misinterpreted. The complexity of these rules is one example – one of many – of the powerful influence which the ordinary courts exert over collective labour law in Britain. Consequently, the rules are written for the courts and not for those persons who are most immediately affected by them. Perhaps one cannot ask that ordinary people should be able to understand statutory texts, but in this area it would be a reasonable demand that trade union leaders might be given some idea of what the law provides[14], Such a demand is certainly not met by the TULRA and the Employment Act 1980 where they deal with immunities. In contrast to this, it may be said that the Swedish legislator does not have to face the same difficulties when drafting legislation. The Labour Court, in common with other Swedish Courts, makes genuine efforts to implement the intentions of the legislator[15].

European Social Charter

On one issue it may be questioned whether the present British law satisfies the requirement of an important international convention. The European Social Charter, to which the United Kingdom like Sweden, is a party, contains in Article 6 paragraph 4 a regulation of the right to take industrial action:

> "With a view to ensuring the effective exercise of the right to bargain collectively, the Contracting Parties . . . recognise:
> 4. the right of workers and employers to collective action in cases of conflicts of interest, including the right to strike, subject to obligations that might arise out of collective agreements previously entered into."

The United Kingdom as well as Sweden has accepted this article.

As part of a system of control which the Social Charter has installed, the contracting states shall render reports at two-yearly intervals concerning the application of the Charter, and these reports shall be examined by a Committee of Independent Experts whose findings are published.

In its first report, published in 1969-70, the Committee of Experts noted that under British law strikes were regarded as constituting a termination of the contracts of employment. The Committee took the view, in principle, that such a rule was not compatible with the right to strike as envisaged by the Charter, and the Committee considered that, even if the practice in Britain were compatible with the Charter, it would still be desirable that

---

[14] See interventions by Wedderburn and Sigeman, International Society for Labour Law and Social Security, 9th International Congress Munich 1978, Reports and Proceedings I (Heidelberg 1979) pp. 319 f.
[15] See *Sigeman*, "Ascertainment of Law and Doctrine of Precedent in the Swedish Labour Court" (1978) 22 *Scandinavian Studies in Law* pp. 196 ff.

legislation be amended in order to bring it into conformity with Article 6 paragraph 4[16].

In 1971 the Conservative Government then introduced into British statute law – in section 147 of the Industrial Relations Act – the concept of suspension of employment contracts[17], and the Committee of Experts could note in a later report that important changes had ensued from the 1971 Act and "that in case of strike or lock-out maintenance of contracts of employment was now formally guaranteed"[18].

However, when the 1971 Act was repealed in 1974 and replaced by TULRA, the provision concerning the suspensive effect of the strike was not re-enacted[19]. That means, in principle, that the earlier legal situation is restored: "the worker who gives the proper notice terminates the contract and . . . the worker who does not, breaks it"[20]. And according to the Employment Protection (Consolidation) Act 1978 s. 62 the jurisdiction of Industrial Tribunals over unfair dismissals is excluded when an employer dismisses all the employees on strike. Thus, workers who are dismissed while on strike may not complain, unless some or all the other strikers are permitted by the employer to go back to work.

British legislation only provides immunity to trade unions and to those who organise strikes – not to individual participants in a strike. Consequently, at least in a formal sense, British workers break their contracts of employment when they go on strike without giving notice to terminate their contracts, which is what usually happens. In practice, it is true, it is not normal for these breaches of contract to give rise to any legal action, but it would be desirable for British law to be brought into line formally with the requirements of the Social Charter[21].

Effects of the Different Regulations

Conditions in the British and Swedish labour markets differ in many respects. It may be a matter for discussion as to the extent to which the legal rules on industrial disputes and collective agreements may be considered to

[16] Council of Europe, Committee of Independent Experts, Conclusions I (Strasbourg 1969–1970) pp. 38 f. On Sweden, see p. 40.
[17] About this concept, see e.g. *Blanc-Jouvan*, "The effect of industrial action on the status of the individual employee" in Aaron & Wedderburn (eds), *Industrial conflict* (London 1972) pp. 175 ff.
[18] Council of Europe, Committee of Independent Experts, Conclusions III (Strasbourg 1973) p. 38.
[19] A manifestation of the suspension theory still occurs in Employment Protection (Consolidation) Act 1978 Sch. 13 para. 15.
[20] *Kahn-Freund, op. cit. (supra* n. 11) 269-271. See also, e.g. *Hepple, op. cit. (supra* n. 1) para. 465 and Smith & Wood, *Industrial Law* (London 1980) 198-200, 318-319.
[21] The Committee of Experts has, however, in later reports not criticised the British legal situation on this issue, see Conclusions V (1977) p. 52, VI (1979) p. 42 and VII (1981) p. 40.

have influenced the circumstances in various directions. It is, of course, not possible to point to definite links.

In Britain, the central organisations are weak both on the employee and on the employer sides. Within the trade union movement, fragmentation is great. By contrast, the central organisations in Sweden are very strong. One may put forward here the hypothesis that the system of binding collective agreements in conjunction with broad rights to take sympathy action has contributed to bringing about this centralisation. By virtue of a concentration and centralisation of power within the Swedish trade union movement, the leadership has had opportunities to carry on a "solidarity wage policy".

Strikes as well as lock-outs are a waste of social resources. According to statistics of industrial stoppages the average number of working days lost per 1,000 employees has for a long time been significantly larger in Britain than in Sweden[22]. The Swedish centralised bargaining system entails, of course, a risk of very large industrial conflicts in the periods of renegotiation of the collective agreements – a risk which was realised in 1980 – but nevertheless it seems to be an advantage that industrial conflicts clearly tend to be concentrated in these periods.

As far as such serious disputes are concerned which endanger national health and safety ("emergency disputes") one can note that since 1945 the armed forces have been used in Britain in at least 23 disputes [23] whereas in Sweden military personnel never have intervened during the same period.

Of course, what is most important is how the respective legal orders can contribute to improving the position of individual employees. We have no instruments for measuring the quality of life. One particularly imperfect instrument is the level of wages, but, given the absence of anything else, we may compare the figures for the costs of labour in some industrial countries for 1979, the latest year for which figures are available. The relative figures for the total labour costs per hour for industrial workers were[24]:

Sweden	100
Federal Republic of Germany	97 (or 99)
Britain	48.

The wage situation in a country is, naturally, influenced by many factors other than the legal character of the collective agreement, but, as can be seen, labour costs were in 1979 much higher in Sweden and Germany, where the collective agreement is binding and carries with it a peace obligation,

---

[22] See, e.g. Hepple, *op. cit. (supra* n. 1) p. 190.

[23] C. Whelan, "Military Intervention in Industrial Disputes", (1979) 8 *The Industrial Law Journal* 222-234.

[24] These figures have been compiled from the Bureau of Labor Statistics, United States Department of Labor, and from the Institut der deutschen Wirtschaft, Cologne. Source: *Märta Finné SAF-tidningen* (Stockholm) 1981 nr. 11 p. 7.

tnan in Britain, where such an agreement lacks legal effect. And it is, of course, open to put the argument that employers are prepared to pay more in countries where the collective agreement is a genuine exchange contract. The major item which the trade union gives in return, is the promise of peace for a given period. One could express this in terms that, in countries where the collective agreement carries with it a peace obligation for the parties and their members, the trade union has something to sell in its negotiations over the collective agreement. The British trade union does not possess such an item of value to its counterpart.

The wage statistics for 1979 are such as to tempt one to put forward, with a view of being provocative, the theory that the British trade union movement, in reality, lacks influence over the general level of wages in the country. This hypothesis means that the level of wages would be almost as high if market forces were left to have their effect free from interference.

In order not to be misunderstood I will repeat that the wage situation in a country is influenced by many factors other than the legal character of the collective agreement. What I have chosen to say is only that there is a possibility that the rules on the collective agreement may have a general impact upon the wages level in a country.

Concluding Remarks

It would, of course, be presumptuous of a foreigner to give advice as to how British labour law should be reformed. Many writers have warned of the difficulties in transplanting foreign legal institutions into collective labour law of a country bound by old tradition. In particular, Otto Kahn-Freund sounded this warning in his article "On Uses and Misuses of Comparative Law" in the 1974 Modern Law Review[25]. We are all also aware that the legal rules cannot do more than play a subordinate role in altering the circumstances of the labour market.

Nevertheless, I shall just mention how the legislator in Sweden got on when introducing legally binding collective agreements. The legislator had provided for some modest experimentation, with a central arbitration board being set up by statute in 1920. This resolved disputes concerning collective agreements between parties who had voluntarily subjected themselves to arbitration. The experience derived from this activity was used to advantage when legislation on binding collective agreements was later introduced in 1928. If a similar experiment were to be tried in Britain, it would have to be facilitated through special rules and measures. There is, of course, already a

[25] Reprinted in Kahn-Freund, *Selected Writings* (London 1978). – See also Colneric, *Der Industrial Relations Act 1971. Ein Beispiel ineffektiver Gesetzgebung aus Bereich des kollektiven Arbeitsrechts.* (Münchener Universitätsschriften. Juristische Fakultät. Vol 36. Ebelsbach am Main 1979).

possibility that the two parties can enter into binding collective agreements in Britain, but it is understandable that the opportunity is used hardly at all, since the legal consequences are both uncertain and inappropriate. For example, the sanctions for breach of contract are far too strict and rigid.

In order for any experiment to make progress, it is, obviously, necessary to influence public opinion. British legal academics have, in the past, generally looked with disfavour on proposals which make incursions into the voluntarist tradition in collective labour law. Otto Kahn-Freund, who was a brilliant scholar of great authority, idealised for a long time the British system of collective bargaining. In a famous article from 1954, he extolled the English system as "dynamic", while the continental system was rather contemptuously characterised as "static"[26]. In another article in the same year he praised the absence of legislation as a reflection of the "state of maturity" which British industrial relations had reached[27]. Yet, in his last writings, he began to evince a somewhat altered attitude towards the British voluntary system. In "Labour Relations: Heritage and Adjustment"[28] he called attention to the fact that the social effect of industrial action had undergone a profound change: the consumers had become the primary target of industrial action, and since 80 or 90 per cent of the consumers are workers, the victim of this change was to an appreciable extent the working class itself. He also pointed out "the need for centralized authority within the union movement (such as exists in Sweden) and the need for curbing by strict organization that spontaneity which in other respects is so positive a feature of labour relations in this country". As I have understood him, in the following lines he indicated the need for legislative intervention concerning the collective agreement and its effects:

> "That which, on previous occasions, I have called 'collective laissez-faire' may be in need of adjustment more than any other part of the British heritage . . . I repeat that conservatism, the cult of tradition, is our worst enemy, and it is completely irrelevant whether this disease affects the Right or the Left."

The achievements of Otto Kahn-Freund during more than four decades were, indeed, of great advantage to British labour law and society. Sometimes, however, I have wondered: maybe he would have provided a still greater service to British society if the reconsideration which he indicated in the cited lines had occurred earlier?

---

[26] "Intergroup Conflicts and their Settlement", (1954) 5 *British Journal of Sociology*. The article is reprinted in "Selected Writings" (1978).

[27] "Legal Framework" in Flanders & Clegg (eds), *The System of Industrial Relations in Great Britain* (Oxford 1954) pp. 42 ff.

[28] (Oxford 1979). Chap. III. – Compare Lord Wedderburn of Charlton, "Current Directions in Labour Law. The British Perspective" in *Arbetsrättsliga uppsatser* (Skrifter utgivna av juridiska fakulteten vid Stockholms Universitet. Vol. 1. (Stockholm 1982) pp. 1, 4ff.

THE FREEDOM AND THE RIGHT TO STRIKE

by

H. Göransson

The late Professor Folke Schmidt described the historical evolution of the right to strike in the following five steps.

> "1) the right of the workers to refuse to perform work in a concerted action without interference from courts, public prosecutors or other authorities, 2) the right to protection against harassments by the employer, a right generally known as the right to organise, 3) the recognition of the principle that the strike does not end the employment relationship but merely suspends it, 4) a claim that during the strike the employer must not try to replace the strikers with other workers, and 5) a right to bargain collectively[1]."

In his opinion one has reason to assume on the basis of comparative studies that the "rights" under 1, 2, and 3 are acknowledged in most democratic societies, while claims under 4 and 5 are more controversial[2].

The "right" according to point 1. in Professor Schmidt's survey refers to the permissibility of strikes under public law, whereas the points 2 – 5 refer to the private law relationship between employers and employees in connection with strikes. A proper right to strike presupposes that the employees in various ways are protected against retaliatory measures from the side of the employer (points 2 – 4). An effective right to strike also presupposes that the trade unions have a legal right to force the employer to bargain collectively in order to reach a collective agreement (point 5).

In writing on labour law a distinction is sometimes made between the "right to strike" and the "freedom to strike"[3]. The notion "freedom to strike" refers to the idea that the employees are free to strike without being made subject to sanctions from the state, i.e. what is referred to as point 1 in Professor Schmidt's evolutionary survey. The notion "right to strike" refers to the protection against countermeasures taken by the employer according to private law. In this paper I shall distinguish between these two notions.

[1] F. Schmidt, "The right to strike in a national context", in *En Hommage à Paul Horion*, Liège 1972, p. 240

[2] *Ibid*.

[3] See e.g. X. Blanc-Jouvan, "The effect of industrial action on the status of the individual employee", in B. Aaron & K.W. Wedderburn (eds), *Industrial Conflict*. A Comparative Legal Survey, London 1972, p 178 f., O. Kahn-Freund, *Labour and the Law*, 2nd ed., London 1977, p. 268 (cf. p. 166 and 233) and H. Seiter, *Streikrecht und Aussperrungsrecht*, Tübingen 1975, p. 61 f. and 207.

The freedom to strike
A characteristic feature of the development of the labour law systems in the industrial world is that the trade unions and workers first obtained certain legal freedoms. During the 19th century it became possible for the workers to associate, to bargain collectively and to strike without risking criminal prosecution. The criminal law rules on concerted actions in labour relations were repealed, rules which were among the criteria of the mercantilist regulation of trade.

In Great Britain the labour movement during the whole 19th century struggled for trade union freedoms. The terminal point of these struggles was the enactment of the Conspiracy and Protection of Property Act, 1875. The Act gave protection against charges of criminal conspiracy, *i.e.* for striking in pursuit of a trade dispute. It was a case of criminal law *immunity* for trade union actions which otherwise would have been unlawful according to the common law rules on criminal conspiracy. The trade unions obtained – as Steve Anderman put it – "a freedom to strike in form of negative immunities rather than a positive right to strike"[4].

To a foreigner this system of immunities rather appears as *special legislation making acts lawful* that would otherwise be actionable according to criminal law.

In Sweden too the freedom to strike has not been granted in a positive way. Even today there is no constitutional provision which grants protection to the citizen against parliament legislation in connection with trade disputes in a way similar to the constitutional protection of basic democratic rights and liberties. This does not mean, however, that the Swedish freedom to strike can be placed on a par with the British system of immunities. Under the criminal law, the point of departure as to the lawfulness of strikes is the very opposite of that in Britain. In Sweden there is a freedom to strike simply because there are no rules making strikes criminal. In consequence of the maxim of the bourgeois state that all acts that are not made unlawful are lawful, *special legislation* is needed in order *to make strikes or certain acts* in connection with strikes *unlawful*. With one exception there has been no such legislation concerning industrial workers since 1864. The exception – the Åkarp Act[5], 1899 – 1938 – was an amendment to the Penal Code making it a crime to induce any person to participate in a strike.

There is an obvious connection between the abolition of the early regulatory society in Sweden and the freedom to strike. According to the old regulation system it was unlawful for the workers to take concerted actions in order to protect their interests. As this system during the first half of the 19th century was gradually dismantled, the possibilities for the workers to

[4] *Supra*, p. 128 Cf. O. Kahn-Freund, *op. cit.*, p. 233.
[5] SFS 1899: 55

combine and to strike increased. The definite break-through of the freedom to strike can be dated to the coming into force of the Royal Ordinance 1864 on the extension of freedom of trade[6]. The Ordinance did not contain any provisions to the effect that it was made lawful for workers to form trade unions, to bargain with the employer or to strike. But, on the other hand, it did not contain any provision to the opposite effect. This meant, in consequence, that the freedom to strike and to negotiate collectively was granted, although no proper trade unions existed at all at that time.

The right to strike

It is characteristic of the right to strike that it has not been enacted as a positive legal right in the same way as have the rights to organise and to bargain collectively. Under Swedish law an employer is liable for damages if he violates the right to organise or if he refuses to bargain collectively[7]. There are no corresponding sanctions in relation to the right to strike. In labour law the right to strike is protected indirectly. Several rights in various enactments have a bearing on the right to strike.

Apart from the four criteria characteristic of the right to strike mentioned by Professor Schmidt (2 – 5 above) one may point to a number of measures which ought to be taken in order to improve the right to strike. One example is statutory protection in Sweden against evictions of the tenant-employee in connection with industrial disputes[8]. Another example is the limitations of the employer's right to lock out that are found in several countries in the Western world. It is a matter of values to what extent such demands ought to be fulfilled before one may speak of a genuine right to strike.

In Great Britain the Trade Disputes Act, 1906, was the first step towards protection of the right to strike. The employer could no longer bring an action for damages against trade union funds at all[9]. For the individual organisers of strikes the employer's claim for damages and possibilities of obtaining an injunction were circumscribed[10]. A further step towards protection of the right to strike was taken as late as during the 1970s with the introduction of a certain amount of protection against violations of the right to organise[11].

Apart from this it is difficult to see that there is a genuine right to strike in Great Britain. So far there is no legal obligation to bargain collectively[12]. An employee who participates in an industrial action in breach of his contract of

---

[6] SFS 1864: 41
[7] Joint Regulation Act (SFS 1976: 580) §§ 8 and 10
[8] SFS 1936: 320
[9] S. 4
[10] Ss 1 and 3
[11] Cf. O. Kahn-Freund, *op. cit.*, p. 171 ff.
[12] *Ibid*, p. 72 ff.

employment faces the risk of lawful dismissal[13]. The employer can use the lockout weapon without any other limitations than giving previous notice to terminate the contracts of employment[14].

The statutory peace obligation makes the factual use of industrial action as well as the possibilities of taking such lawful actions less in Sweden than in Great Britain. However, provided that a strike is lawful, the protection of the right to strike is considerably stronger. I have already mentioned the statutory protection of the right to organise and to bargain collectively and the fact that an employee cannot be evicted from his dwelling by the employer-landlord during a strike. In his paper Sigeman has also pointed to the fact that it has never been possible for employers to bring claims for damages in disputes of interest[15].

Furthermore, for a long time the view has been predominant in Sweden that an individual contract of employment is only suspended and not terminated during an industrial action[16]. It is unlawful to dismiss workers only for the reason that they have participated in a lawful strike[17]. Since 1975 the right to strike has also been provided for in the Constitution. The constitutional protection seems however in this case to be of little value. It is clear from the constitutional provisions that there is a right to take industrial action only so far as statute or contract do not provide otherwise[18]. However, the attitude in Sweden towards the lockout undermines the right to strike. The lockout is the traditional weapon of the employers against lawful strikes. It has the same legal status as the strike in private law and it is also protected in the Constitution alongside with the strike. Such a friendly attitude towards the lockout is unique. There has however been a reaction. After the extensive conflict of May 1980 in the labour market, the Swedish labour movement has put into question whether the lockout ought to be circumscribed along the same lines as in, e.g., France, Italy and Western Germany[19].

It appears that the idea of converting trade union immunities to positive rights holds no attraction to the trade unions in Britain[20]. However, it may be argued that if the right to strike is to give adequate protection to employees it will have to rest upon a foundation of positive rights rather than immunities.

---

[13] Anderman, *supra* p. 135; see also X. Blanc-Jouvan, *op. cit.*, p. 196 ff. and 205
[14] *Ibid*, p. 224 f.
[15] *Supra*, p. 00
[16] See X. Blanc-Jouvan, *op. cit.*, p. 186
[17] This follows from the Employment Protection Act (SFS 1982: 80) § 7. Cf. F. Schmidt, *Law and Industrial Relations in Sweden*, Uppsala 1977, p. 221 f.
[18] Regeringsformen (SFS 1974: 152 reprinted in SFS 1979: 933), chap. 2 § 17.
[19] See e.g. parliamentary motion 1980/81: 218 and 279.
[20] See *Anderman supra*, p. 128

UNEMPLOYMENT COMPENSATION AND WORK INCENTIVES IN BRITAIN
– A TOUR THROUGH THE MAZE

by

Laurence Lustgarten

In this paper I shall attempt a description of the various means by which workers in Britain who lose their employment receive financial compensation. The "system" of compensation – the word suggests a coherence and purposefulness which does not exist – includes multiple public and private sources, and cannot be considered in isolation from tax considerations, which have a major impact on effective income replacement. Description will be interlaced with critical comments, mostly directed to pointing out internal inconsistencies and irrationalities. At the end a set of criteria for a more fundamental evaluation are offered in skeletal form.

A scheme for unemployment compensation could be devoted single-mindedly to relieving the economic and psychological losses involved. No such scheme has ever existed in Britain (nor indeed anywhere else to my knowledge). In Elizabethan times, the Poor Law authorities were haunted by the spectre of the "sturdy beggar" – the man physically capable of working but supposedly preferring poor relief; in contemporary garb, he reappears as the "scrounger". Over the centuries one can clearly see periodic shifts of emphasis on the part of the authorities, in which deterrence of the "unworthy" assumes greater or lesser importance. This paper will not try to document that assertion[1], nor seek to relate these cycles to economic pressures and political conflicts, nor explore the fascinating and important question of how and why suspicion and distrust of the unemployed have come to be shared by a substantial portion of manual and lower white collar workers. Rather it will attempt, within the descriptive framework outlined above, to highlight the ways in which concern to maintain work incentives has shaped and altered provision for the unemployed.

I should at the outset make clear my own general orientation. I accept that, *at a time when jobs are available*, it is socially useful and morally acceptable to set unemployment compensation at a level that makes work financially attractive[2]. I do not believe, however that the economic spur is the primary incentive to work: personal self-esteem, family, peer and other psychological pressure, and the sheer intolerability of the tedium of idleness seem to me as a matter of fact to be much more important. Put another way, what may be called the "incentive calculus" reflects a grossly deficient understanding of human behaviour. Nor does acceptance of a limited role for monetary incentives in a system of unemployment compensation entail that benefit be administered in a manner degrading to the claimant, or that he suffer a severe degree of income loss, let alone descend into absolute poverty. Indeed it seems to me that the political order has a responsibility to offer practical assistance in matters such as training or retraining in occupational skills, and mobility and housing grants to people who have unusual difficulty in finding the type of work they have been accustomed to do in the area where they have done it. It follows that I regard unemployment compensation in Britain as at best a lottery subtly rigged in favour of the organisers and at worst an unmitigated failure.

For those unfamiliar with the terminology of social security in Britain, the key terms are explained in a brief Appendix.

I. Beveridge

The present system of state unemployment compensation owes its basic structure to the Beveridge Report of 1942. One should emphasise, however, that Beveridge did not write on a blank slate. A statutory scheme of unemployment compensation was first created in 1911; indeed Beveridge, in his capacity as a civil servant at the Board of Trade, had considerable influence on its development as well. Unemployment benefit was significantly expanded in coverage in the years after 1911, most dramatically in response to strikes during the First World War. It was also subject to periodic financial pressures, of which the most spectacular occurred in 1931, when the Labour Government split and resigned office over the Treasury demand for cuts. The greatest novelty of the Beveridge Plan in relation to unemployment benefit was its extension to every employed person in the country. The Report also enunciated certain principles which may be taken as points of departure and comparison in studying the subsequent development of the unemployment compensation system.

These principles were (a) flat rate subsistence benefits in return for (b) flat rate contributions, with (c) benefit to be the same in amount regardless of

---

[2] The italicised qualification is important. One of the ironies, demonstrated in Deacon's work, is that preoccupation with "scrounging" usually occurs in hard times, i.e. when for structural reasons jobs are scarce and difficult for any individual to obtain, notwithstanding energetic effort.

cause of interruption of earnings. (Thus sickness, unemployment, retirement, and widowhood would all carry entitlement to identical sums of money)[3]. Moreover, (d) benefit was to last for the duration of the contingency causing the loss of earnings.

Certain assumptions were critical to Beveridge's approach. Foremost was that policies outside the social security system would work in tandem with it. The Report was one of the few attempts in British history – conceivable only in the circumstances of war – to treat every form of deprivation as a facet of a single whole. With imagery that typified the Christian and classical elements in the upbringing and education of the governing elite of his era, he proclaimed an attack on the "Five Giants on the Road to Recovery": Want, Squalor, Ignorance, Disease and Idleness. The chief weapon against the latter would be a public policy of full employment – a central buttress of his Plan, for he saw National Insurance as a relatively short term income replacement for those who would be expected to find another job. (It should be noted, however, that his definition of full employment involved a rate of unemployment of $8\frac{1}{2}\%$, a figure never remotely approached until the mid-1970s and only reached in 1980).

A corollary was that National Assistance, the means-tested "safety net" underpinning the "benefit as of right" (because based upon contribution) that was the essence of National Insurance, was designed as a residual income support for those unable to amass sufficient contributions. Beveridge never imagined many such people would be of working age; he thought they would consist of the inevitably dwindling number who had retired before expiration of the twenty year run-in period required for entitlement to full National Insurance pensions[4]. Hence those unable to contribute whom Beveridge ignored or did not foresee – notably people never able to enter the labour market due to disability, or the hundreds of thousands who now leave school without hope of employment – are compelled to live entirely on Supplementary Benefit. Yet Beveridge had laid great emphasis on the "strength of feeling against the means test". Here he was harking back to the 1930s, when the household means test, reducing the benefit of parents whose children could find work after leaving school at 14, gave rise to an abiding bitterness among the long-term unemployed. The

---

[3] Beveridge did propose slightly higher rates for those suffering serious injuries (about one-tenth of all expected recipients of industrial injury benefit). However, for political reasons the government decided in 1946 to pay the higher rate to everyone receiving this form of compensation.

[4] This 20 year period was based on calculations of the Government Actuary and accepted by Beveridge. However, in the 1950s, again for political reasons, it was decided to pay full pensions to everyone of the appropriate age – a remarkable windfall which made a nonsense of the financing of the entire scheme.

idea that upwards of 4.7 million people, including 1.66 million unemployed and their dependants[5], would be forced onto Supplementary Benefit for a subsistence level of income would have been anathema to him. Though the abandonment of full employment as a central feature of economic policy since 1975 is largely responsible for this development, the contribution requirement has exacerbated matters considerably.

Indeed Beveridge's exaltation of what he called the "duty and pleasure of thrift" has had even more unfortunate though quite unintended consequences. The contribution was initially regressive: everyone paid an identical sum each week. It is now proportional, but has been raised to such a high level – 8¾% of all earnings up to a high cut-off – that it has become a significant contribution to the poverty of low-paid workers. The alternative of financing the National Insurance Scheme by direct taxation was made impossible by the fact that the vast majority of working people paid no income tax at all, because the tax threshold in peacetime was set at a level substantially above average earnings. To pay for the Welfare State – the National Health Service, expanded secondary education, large scale house-building, as well as National Insurance – the tax threshold began to fall radically in the mid-1950s, so that in addition to their contributions, workers on a low wage also lose significant amounts in income tax as well[6]. (It must be remembered that the standard marginal rate of income tax is 30%, probably the highest in the world).

Thus a system designed to alleviate poverty among those unable to work has become a significant contributor to the poverty of hundreds of thousands of those in work. It has also led to the phenomenon known as the "poverty trap"[7]. This phrase describes the predicament both of the low-paid worker seeking a wage rise, and the unemployed worker comparing his financial circumstances in a new job with drawing benefit. For the former, the combination of taxation, contributions, and the withdrawal of various means-tested benefits, produces a loss of the wage rise – effectively a marginal tax rate – much higher than that imposed on someone earning ten times his salary, and which in extreme cases can exceed 100%· It has been argued that this "wage-tax spiral" played a major role in stimulating

[5] These are the latest available detailed Supplementary Benefit figures, and refer to November 1980. Since then unemployment has risen by nearly one million persons, so the corresponding figures are now very much higher.
[6] This well-know phenomenon is most conveniently documented in F. Field et al., *To Him Who Hath* (Penguin 1977) Ch. 2. The tax burden on the low paid has increased since the book appeared.
[7] *Ibid.*, p. 52-56 The first thorough analysis of the problem was that of *Piachaud* "Poverty and Taxation", in B. Crick & W. Robson (eds), *Taxation Policy* (Penguin, 1973), Ch. 5. A subsequent intriguing account by a Conservative M.P. is R. Howell, *Why Work?* (Conservative Political Centre, 1981).

inflationary wage demands and industrial militancy in the early 1970s[8]. For the unemployed man, particularly if he can only expect to receive a relatively low wage on resuming work, a similar type of calculation will show that his circumstances improve only slightly in work.

Both these calculations, however, apply only to people with children, for it is the loss of child-related means-tested benefits – notably free school meals, medical charges exemptions and offset of higher housing costs – that devours the wage gain and reduces the differential between wages and unemployment benefit. Although not envisaging these specific benefits, which did not then exist, Beveridge was quite alert to the problem of incentives. He believed firmly in their necessity, indeed their moral value, but – unlike all social policy since the War – was prepared to maintain them by generosity rather than meanness. One of the three critical preconditions he identified for the success of his Plan was the payment of family allowances at a level sufficient to cover the full cost of supporting all children except the first in each family. For him there was no contradiction between alleviating poverty among the unemployed and maintaining incentives: if children were adequately supported by family allowances whether or not their father worked[9] the gap in income between subsistence-level benefit and wages would provide adequate incentive for the unemployed to return to the labour market. Only recently have newly-available documents revealed that this argument was indispensable in overcoming initial Treasury opposition to his Plan[10]. By failing to enact a programme of family allowances at the level recommended by Beveridge, by allowing their real value to deteriorate more severely than any other major benefit, and by attempting to compensate for this failure by the haphazard creation of separate means-tested benefits, the post-War Labour Government and every one of its successors ensured that the question of incentives would increasingly dominate provision for the unemployed. The Beveridge Plan was still-born; and the way was open for a right-wing government, committed to cuts in public spending and driven by a simplistic notion of incentives, to act upon the logic on which discussion of social policy had increasingly been cast. Virtually all benefits except pensions have been cut in real terms in successive years, with unemployment benefit perhaps most drastically reduced.

II. *Evolution of Unemployment Benefit, 1946–1981*
Every one of the Beveridge principles noted earlier was either never accepted or subsequently abandoned.

[8] Wilkinson, "The Wage-Tax Spiral and Labour Militancy", in D. Jackson et al., *Do Trade Unions Cause Inflation?* (C.U.P., 1972) pp. 63-103.

[9] Beveridge, looking backward to pre-War Britain when some factories dismissed women, on their marriage, simply regarded married women as essentially outside the labour force.

[10] J. MacNicol, *The Movement for Family Allowances, 1918-1945* (Heinemann, 1980) Ch. 7.

A. Those Rejected

1.   The subsistence level of benefit was not instituted in 1946. National Insurance benefits have always been below Supplementary Benefit, which includes an amount for housing costs. Hence anyone whose sole source of income upon loss of employment is Unemployment or Sickness Benefit automatically qualifies for Supplementary Benefit if he submits to a means test.

2.   The post-War government also imposed an exhaustion rule on receipt of unemployment compensation, which ceases after one year. This was not a serious problem until the 1970s, because unemployment never exceeded 3% until then and indeed for most of the time was about half that. Now, however, approximately one-quarter of the unemployed have exhausted their benefits and their number is growing monthly. They are all swelling the Supplementary Benefit rolls.

B. Those Abandoned

1.   The flat rate principle was renounced for pensions in 1959 and for Unemployment and Sickness Benefit in 1966. In its stead, the earnings-related principle – the norm on the Continent – was introduced. The decision on pensions was the result of a mixture of the weakening of the War-time sense of social solidarity and growing dissatisfaction with subsistence level retirement income. But the introduction of the earnings-related principle for Unemployment Benefit flowed from a deliberate policy of encouraging labour mobility by removing some of the hardship of unemployment, i.e. to give greater compensation to those who lost their jobs and would have to seek another. Consequently an earnings-related supplement (ERS) for the unemployed was paid for the period beginning after the first fortnight of unemployment and ending six months afterwards. One can see how this time period fitted nicely with the purpose of encouraging labour mobility: both those unemployed for a very short term and those who remained unemployed for extended periods were excluded.

The twenty-eight week cutoff may also be seen to reflect a concern with incentives: the unemployed must not be permitted to become *too* comfortable when not working. In fact it is precisely those least attractive to employers – the unskilled, older persons, the chronically ill – who find it most difficult to obtain re-employment, even in prosperous times and despite energetic efforts. They are most likely to suffer from this economic carrot-and-stick policy, but the least able to adjust their behaviour accordingly[11]. Empirical studies purporting to measure the impact of ERS suggest that its effect on the incidence of unemployment, though palpable, is slight,

---

[11]   See e.g. the results of the study by W. Daniel, *A National Survey of the Unemployed* (PEP, 1974) pp. 144-45.

perhaps adding 0.5% of the total[12]. In any case the manner of calculation of ERS kept it ludicrously low when inflation accelerated in the mid-1970s. However, like flat-rate Unemployment Benefit, it was not taxable. The result was that a well-paid skilled worker would still suffer a sizeable drop in income, whilst a low paid worker with several children (each of whom attracted a dependant's addition) might suffer very little. Hence one incentive effect was "deskilling" – pressure on the skilled worker to take a job demanding less than his full qualifications, to avoid a severe reduction in his standard of living. This perverse result, causing loss to the individual and the economy alike, is a clear illustration that economic incentives can influence the unemployed. It is hardly, however, what those who stress the importance of incentives desire to bring about; perhaps for this reason, the phenomenon of deskilling, though adequately documented[13], has received little popular attention or understanding.

Indeed the present government, which has both uncritically accepted and energetically propogated the myth of widespread "scrounging", has cut the maximum earnings-related supplement for the present year and abolished it as from 1982. The inevitable consequence of course will be that the number of people dependent on Supplementary Benefit will rise. Indeed anyone who is unemployed and has no other source of income – such as a working wife[14] – is automatically pauperised in that his "benefit as of right" leaves him below the poverty line and forces recourse to a means test. Anyone in this position is also subject to a different administration which can be – it is not always – more intrusive and imbued with a sense of the claimant's moral inferiority than is true of the National Insurance system.

2. In the early 1970s, a differentiation in the amount between categories of benefit was introduced. This at first was a modest 40p, but once the principle of uniformity had been breached, it became easier to make invidious distinctions between the favoured "long-term" benefits – i.e. those paid to people

---

[12] See e.g. Nickell, "Effect of Unemployment and Related Benefits on the Duration of Unemployment", (1979) 89 *Econ. J.* 34. A good review of the problem which remains resolutely agnostic in its conclusions is Atkinson, "Unemployment Benefits and Incentives", in J. Creedy (ed.), *The Economics of Unemployment in Britain* (Butterworths, 1981), Ch. 5.

[13] Well documented in Daniel, *op. cit.*, p. 150

[14] Given his view of married women as workers (*supra* n. 8), Beveridge proposed that those who did work be permitted the option of paying reduced contributions in return for forfeiting the right to unemployment benefit, and indeed virtually all other benefits except retirement pension. The great majority of married women chose this course, with two important consequences. First, when they lose their jobs, they are ineligible for benefit. It is therefore quite common for a man receiving unemployment benefit to have a wife in work, but the reverse is very rare. Secondly, a large number – at least 500,000 and possibly considerably more – of married women do not register as unemployed and hence do not appear in the unemployment statistics. Thus official figures grossly understate the true extent of unemployment in Britain. The reduced rate contribution option was eliminated in 1978, but only for new entrants to the labour market; the effects described above will persist for years.

not expected to be in the labour market, especially pensions, but also widows' and disability benefit – and "short-term" benefit for the sick and unemployed. The distinction between the deserving and the undeserving poor has thus been reintroduced in all but name, and the former now receive about 30% more each week than the latter.

III. Special Compensation Schemes

The earnings-related supplement to unemployment benefit was unusual in that changing economic policy with unemployment implications was handled through existing social security schemes. More common is the establishment of alternate forms of compensation operated outside that scheme. It will be recalled that Beveridge made no distinction between the *causes* of unemployment as a basis of compensation. In the 1960s social security increasingly became a tool of economic as distinct from the social policy[15], and encouragement of labour mobility became one of the key elements in the grandiose plans of the early years of the Wilson government to generate a "white heat of technology" to regenerate British industry. Thus was created the Redundancy Payments Scheme of special compensation on top of unemployment benefit for workers who lost their jobs in the course of the "rationalisation" of their industries or their particular employer's operations. It is in reality partly a state scheme, since although payment is received from the employer the latter is entitled to claim a 40% rebate from a state fund. However, in legal terms, it is claimed by the worker from the employer, and disputes are settled by industrial tribunals and the courts, not through social security adjudicative machinery.

Since the method of calculation favours the elderly, the long serving and the reasonably well paid, and since redundancy even now is a small (but growing) proportion of total unemployment, the result has been that the vast majority of workers (until recently over 90%) receive only Unemployment and/or Supplementary Benefit; most who are made redundant receive at best a few hundred pounds; and a favoured few may receive very large sums indeed[16]. A growing number of redundant workers, particularly in the nationalised industries, have received substantial ex-gratia payments modelled on the so-called "golden handshake" with which companies have long bade farewell to executives who have become an embarrassment. Both statutory and "voluntary" redundancy payments receive favourable tax treatment – the former are completely tax free, the latter tax free up to

---

[15] I follow the distinction made by the economist Kenneth Boulding (quoted in R. Titmuss, *Commitment to Welfare* (Allen & Unwin 1968) p. 21 between economic relationships centred upon exchange, and social policies which seek to foster the existence of community and the value of social integration.

[16] Notwithstanding some well-published exceptions, in 1979 the average redundancy payment was £874. A. Sinfield, *What Unemployment Means* (M. Robertson, 1981) p. 60.

£10,000, with the tax bill further mitigated by a complicated spreading system.

There is a highly complex – indeed impossibly labyrinthine – interaction between redundancy payments and state unemployment benefits. A long-established Regulation disqualifies those in receipt of "payment in lieu of notice or remuneration" from entitlement to unemployment benefit for each day covered by such collateral payment. In 1972 a National Insurance Commissioner, adopting the theory that a statutory redundancy payment represented recognition of past services, held that receipt of it did not come within the aforementioned Regulation, a decision ratified by the Court of Appeal several years later[17]. Non-statutory payments – e.g. those negotiated by trade unions over and above the statutory entitlement – are much trickier, and a sizeable corpus of National Insurance law has developed which, summarised roughly, holds that receipt of a payment will not disentitle the claimant to unemployment benefit if such a payment is not a contractual entitlement and if it is given for past services rather than in place of lost future earnings[18]. The potential for manipulation by trade unions and management – and also bungling by incompetent or ignorant negotiators – is obvious, and very wide.

Ironically, now that the assumption of mobility has been negated by economic policies which ensure that few people have jobs to go to, the result of redundancy payments is often to save the state money on Supplementary Benefit, which is not open to anyone with capital of more than £2,000. Consequently those with large redundancy payments and no source of income once their Unemployment Benefit has expired, will literally have to eat up the capital sum until they fall below the £2,000 cut-off.

(b) Unfair Dismissal

The background and purpose of this legislation is doubtless well-known to participants of this Conference. Of particular relevance here, and much less well-known, is the interaction between unfair dismissal awards and entitlement to unemployment benefit.

The problem first arises because there is invariably a delay between the sacking and the hearing, during which, unless he is very lucky in finding alternative employment, a dismissed employee will be claiming unemployment benefit. Until the mid-1970s unemployment benefit received was simply totted up and deducted from the unfair dismissal award by the industrial tribunal. The result of course was that the public purse was in effect defraying the cost of the employer's wrongdoing, since the award he

---

[17] *R. v N.I. Comm'r., ex. p. Stratton* [1979] 2 All E.R. 278. The earlier Commissioner's decision was R(U) 6/73.
[18] See especially R(U) 1/80.

was ordered to pay was reduced by the amount of unemployment benefit received. In 1976 Recoupment Regulations were promulgated which are supposed to enable the benefit authorities to recover the equivalent sum from the employer. It is now possible however for a claimant to be substantially worse off if he wins an unfair dismissal case than if he loses. A Regulation modelled closely on the payment in lieu provision quoted earlier disqualifies him from unemployment benefit for every day covered by an unfair dismissal award. Unfair dismissal awards are subject to percentage reductions based on the purported contribution the employee has made to his own dismissal. If, as is often the case, this contribution is substantial – e.g. 50% or more – he may find that his award is substantially less than he would have received had he been eligible for unemployment benefit, a loss which may last for a considerable time if the award covers a period extending beyond the date of the hearing. Whether claimants are aware of this risk and whether it affects their willingness to enter unfair dismissal claims is unknown, but very doubtful.

IV. The Problem of Short Time Work

Beveridge gave no attention at all to the problem of short time work – where the employee remains contractually attached to a given employer, but temporarily cannot be given full time employment for economic or other reasons. Because of the historic connection of unemployment benefit with job replacement – labour exchanges and unemployment benefit were adminstered together from the very beginning in 1911 – the National Insurance system has never really been geared up for people in this position. There is a three-day "waiting day" rule designed to exclude those unemployed for a very brief period, and people on short time were always barred from receipt of earnings-related supplement. However, the phenomenon is of increasing importance, particularly in the industrial West Midlands, and implementation of "work sharing" proposals would increase its incidence substantially.

In the 1960s the government attempted to encourage employers to assume the responsibility of guaranteeing a minimum number of hours for their employees each week, but apart from certain industries, notably engineering, adoption of the so-called guaranteed week never became prevalent. Moreover the Regulation barring payments in lieu of remuneration makes impossible the system developed in certain parts of the United States and Canada, particularly by the United Auto Workers and the motor manufacturers, under which the employer is contractually bound to top up state unemployment benefit so that employees on short time receive in all 90% or 95% of their normal take-home pay. The solution adopted in the United Kingdom is that of statutory guarantee payments, first introduced in the Employment Protection Act 1975. However, these are limited to a maximum of £8.55 a day for five days within any quarter; they exclude certain classes of employees such as part-timers; and may, because they pay no dependants' additions, actually make certain workers with large families worse off than they would have been claiming unemployment benefit. Moreover, where a private guarantee agreement has been adopted, employees covered by them are barred both from unemployment benefit and guarantee payments, though private guarantee agreements usually pay more generously than the state scheme. The result is some mitigation of the three waiting days rule but only marginal help for the worker on short time.

V. Evaluation

Particularly from 1982 when earnings related supplement is abolished and unemployment benefit becomes taxable, the U.K. system of unemployment compensation is, along with that of the Republic of Ireland, perhaps the least generous in industrial Europe. Its inadequacy in income replacement terms is complemented by its limited duration, rigidity, and consequent restriction upon privately negotiated compensation. I postulate the following goals for an unemployment compensation system:

(1) Provision of adequate income replacement; which nonetheless

(2) retains sufficient incentive to seek re-employment; and is

(3) administered in a way that respects claimant's dignity; whilst

(4) treating justly, that is to say evenhandedly, all those who have lost their employment regardless of cause[19]; and

(5) gives adequate help and/or retraining to those who cannot find satisfactory re-employment; and

(6) does not interfere with the efforts of those workers whose representative organisations seek to make better provision for them by negotiation (perhaps as a trade-off for higher wages in more prosperous times).

The U.K. system has always been a disaster in terms of (5) and (6). This is now also true of (1). It progressively worsened with respect to (4), especially in the 1960s, and the increased reliance on Supplementary Benefit will almost certainly make achievement of (3) increasingly remote. (2), which perhaps is the most difficult when an economy with a large number of low paid workers seeks to mesh with a social security system that seeks to meet the needs of dependants, is now dealt with simply by a reversion to the 1834

---

[19] I put to one side the question of whether and in what form so-called "self-induced" unemployment should result in reduced compensation. The U.K. system has from the beginning excluded those involved in trade disputes, and imposes disqualification for up to six weeks on those adjudged to have been guilty of misconduct or refused an offer of suitable employment. At least some of these categories exist in Swedish law as well: see Christensen, "Disqualification from Unemployment Benefits: A critical study in Swedish Social Security Law" (1980) *Scand. St. L.* 155.

Poor Law notion of "less eligibility". It may also cause the waste of the talents of workers who are induced to deskill themselves in order to find alternative employment at a level higher than the mere subsistence paid by the state. None of the Opposition parties have done more than criticise specific retrograde measures of the past two years; no-one has put forward a coherent programme for restructuring the system. The best one may realistically expect is a reversion to the *status quo ante*, mitigating the present harshness whilst leaving most of the enumerated inadequacies unaltered. It seems very clear that no fundamental reform will ever occur until the dominance of the incentive calculus is overthrown, and consideration of it relegated to one among many influences shaping a rational and humane system of compensation for unemployment.

Appendix

British Social Security Terms

As noted, the Beveridge Report and subsequent implementing legislation built upon existing structures. Contributory benefit under the new scheme was called *National Insurance*, the title given to previous contributory benefits, whose availability had been much more restricted. Means-tested benefits, which had been administered separately depending upon cause of entitlement (old age, unemployment etc.) were unified as *National Assistance* and run by central government. (Local authorities, many of which were regarded by the Conservatives in power in the 1930s as too generous to the unemployed, were relieved of their powers in this area at that time.) To remove some of the odium that still surrounded memories of the means test and the Unemployment Assistance Board, National Assistance was renamed *Supplementary Benefit* in 1966. In the 1970s, the Continental phrase *social security* began to be used in legislation that governed both the contributory and non-contributory elements of income support, and is now commonly used to describe national income maintenance generally.

Family Allowances were renamed *Child Benefit* and paid for all dependants in 1976. After a transition period ending in 1979, their value was increased to compensate for the simultaneous abolition of child tax allowances.

BIOGRAPHICAL NOTES ON THE AUTHORS

Steve Anderman is Reader in Law at Warwick University.

Håkan Göransson is Lecturer in Law at the University of Stockholm.

Jan Hellner is Professor of Insurance Law at the University of Stockholm.

Carl Hemström is Docent at the University of Uppsala.

Lars Heuman is Docent at the University of Lund.

Laurence Lustgarten is Lecturer in Law at Warwick University.

C.J. Miller is Professor of Law at Warwick University.

Tim Murphy is Lecturer in Law at the London School of Economics.

Francis Reynolds is Reader in Law in the University of Oxford.

Tore Sigeman is Professor of Private Law with special reference to Labour Law, in the University of Stockholm.

Anders Victorin is Professor of Law at the University of Stockholm.

David Yates is Professor of Law at Essex University.